LUCRETIUS

DE RERUM NATURA

LUCRETIUS
DE RERUM NATURA

Translated by

R. C. TREVELYAN

CAMBRIDGE
AT THE UNIVERSITY PRESS
1937

CAMBRIDGE
UNIVERSITY PRESS

University Printing House, Cambridge CB2 8BS, United Kingdom

Cambridge University Press is part of the University of Cambridge.

It furthers the University's mission by disseminating knowledge in the pursuit of education, learning and research at the highest international levels of excellence.

www.cambridge.org
Information on this title: www.cambridge.org/9781107437562

First published 1937
First paperback edition 2014

A catalogue record for this publication is available from the British Library

ISBN 978-1-107-43756-2 Paperback

To

LASCELLES ABERCROMBIE

PREFACE

I wish to thank Mr L. H. G. Greenwood for his great kindness in reading the whole translation with meticulous attention, and giving me the benefit of his ripe scholarship. I also wish to thank Mr Hugh Sykes Davies, who has not only helped me with detailed criticism and advice during the labour of revising the translation, but has given me most valuable assistance in preparing the textual notes, and has written the illuminating essay on Macaulay's *Marginalia* which stands at the end of the book. His sympathetic collaboration has greatly enriched my pleasure in the task, and the value of the work.

R. C. T.

CONTENTS

INTRODUCTION

The embryo of this translation of the *De Rerum Natura* was a version of the last two hundred and fifty lines of the third book, made by me twenty years ago, and published by the Omega Workshops. Afterwards from time to time I tried my hand at several other of the less severe sections of the poem, until at last, when only the more intractable parts remained, I felt that it would be poor-spirited not to complete the task in which I had found myself so pleasantly entangled almost against my will; so I set about it resolutely, and with much labour filled in the gaps.

Now that the work is finished, I can hardly expect a wide audience for it. Those who already know and love Lucretius will prefer to read him in his own magnificent hexameters; while few of those who do not yet know him will discover his full greatness and his austere charm under the disguise of my blank verse. But just as Lucretius, despite his ostensible apostolic fervour, must have written not so much to convert the profligate politician Memmius, nor to entertain the crowd of Rome's intellectual worldlings, but rather to please and express his own poetic soul, so a translator of Lucretius should find a sufficient reward in the labour itself, and in a more complete and intimate understanding of his poetry and thought than would otherwise be possible. His genius has often been enthusiastically praised; yet in general the praise has been confined to the more obviously poetic passages, such as the preludes to the first two books, or the discourses on the nothingness of death and the vanity of love at the end of the third and fourth books, and the history of mankind that forms the last half of the fifth. But this is to do Lucretius an injustice. His artistic mastery is as powerfully, though less attractively, displayed in the more didactic parts of his work. It is a narrow and arbitrary, but too common, conception of poetry, that would judge of it by the nature of its material, and would condemn as unpoetic the expression, however impassioned, of scientific and philosophical ideas. But above all, those more generally admired passages, admirable as they are by themselves, yet lose much of their grandeur if they are isolated from the expositions and discussions which they introduce, or out of which they grow. The poem is an organic unity. Readers who fail to comprehend it as such will have missed more than half its greatness. It matters little that Lucretius left his work in an unfinished state, and that there are various redundancies, loose ends, imperfect transitions, harshly or carelessly written sentences. Had he lived a few years longer, he would no doubt have remedied many of these defects. But at the worst they do not seriously impair the lucid progress of his exposition, or the splendour of his poetry, still less do they damage the imaginative scope and comprehensiveness of his vision of Nature.

The fundamental unity of the *De Rerum Natura* is no doubt to a large degree dependent upon the completeness and consistency of the Epicurean philosophy. It is now the fashion to depreciate the system of Epicurus as a mere eclectic patchwork clumsily pieced together out of the speculations of Democritus and other predecessors. But such views are hardly likely to be shared by those who are acquainted with the writings of Giussani, and with Mr Cyril Bailey's remarkable study of the Greek Atomists.[1] Into whatever absurdities his fearless logical honesty may have sometimes led Epicurus, at least, to quote Mr Santayana, "he sees the world as one great edifice, one great machine, all its parts reacting upon one another, and growing out of one another in obedience to a general pervasive process of life". It is true that Mr Santayana is here speaking of Lucretius, and not of Epicurus;

[1] *The Greek Atomists and Epicurus*, by Cyril Bailey, Clarendon Press, 1928. This book is of first-rate importance for all students of Epicurus and Lucretius.

but in no single matter, either of principle or of detail, does the poet appear to have diverged from his master's teaching. It was accepted by him in its totality, with unquestioning faith, and a well-nigh religious dogmatism, as a truthful description of the nature of things, and consequently of the nature of mind. But though he contributed nothing of his own to the doctrine, he was able to transform its emotional quality, and so to turn the dull leaden prose of Epicurus into gleaming poetic gold. A passionate interest not only in the invisible substance and mechanism of Nature, but in the sensible world of changing appearance and illusion; a tragic sense of the beauty and transitoriness of created things; delighted contemplation of every form and phase of animal and human life; a noble impatience both of the blindness that will not recognize the limitations of mortal happiness, and of the superstitious fears and vicious follies that prevent men from enjoying it—all these qualities, meeting together in his imagination, flowered into a poetic eloquence of incomparable grandeur and intensity. There have been poets of a finer artistry, of a more genial wisdom, and of far more varied emotional experience; but none before or since, except Dante, and Leopardi at certain fortunate moments, have shown themselves masters of a style in which a great philosophical and scientific poem could be written.

If such be his view of the matter, it is evident that the task of a translator of Lucretius will be difficult, and in a sense impossible. None should know better than he that great poetry can never be adequately translated. Those who think that such a miracle has sometimes been performed, must either be ignorant of the original, or else deficient in poetic sensitiveness. Yet the attempt may perhaps be worth making upon a writer like Lucretius, whose material is intellectually and morally of universal interest. Much will depend upon the method. There have been almost as many theories of translation as there are ways of writing poetry. Each generation has had its own prejudices as to the amount of freedom or literalness that is permissible; and in aiming at scrupulous fidelity in word and phrase, I am no doubt instinctively conforming to the literary spirit of my own age. The too frequent failure of literal translators has generally not been caused by over-literalness, but by incapacity to take sufficient pains, or the lack of poetic mastery in their own language. Be that as it may, in the case of so precise a philosophical writer as Lucretius, it appears to me that it would be doing him a serious injustice to adopt any other mode of translation than that of rigorous verbal accuracy. Nor do I think that his poetry should suffer unduly by such a method, so long as a satisfactory metrical medium be chosen.

Ideally no doubt the hexameters of Lucretius should be translated line by line into English hexameters. But though Robert Bridges has shown that it is not impossible to write true English hexameters, yet such a verse form is at present too unfamiliar to be successfully used for a poem of great length. Moreover it is a metre so difficult to write in, and one that involves so many limitations of vocabulary and phrasing, that the result would be paraphrase rather than translation.

On the other hand any kind of rimed verse would be unsuitable. Rime not only makes accuracy of rendering needlessly difficult, but it brings with it all the familiar associations and conventions of English rimed poetry, which, however admirable in themselves, the reader of a translation from the classics should wish to forget. It is this more than anything else that makes the versions of Homer, Virgil and Lucretius by Pope and Dryden, for all their brilliant qualities, appear nothing less than intolerable travesties, devoid of almost everything that gives the original poems their greatness and individual charm.

Ten-syllabled blank verse, being the most familiar and universal of English verse-forms, is also unavoidably infected with poetical anglicisms; but these are far more varied than the mannerisms of rimed stanzas or couplets. Furthermore blank verse allows of the greatest possible freedom and diversity of movement and of phrasing. It has been used by Shakespeare and Milton, by the Georgian and Victorian poets, in so many ways for such different purposes, that it has become, if not "the stateliest measure ever moulded by the lips of men", yet perhaps the subtlest and most plastic measure that ever moulded human speech. For these reasons I have chosen blank verse as the least inadequate instrument I could find for my purpose of presenting Lucretius to English readers with as little damage as possible to his thought and to his poetry.

DE RERUM NATURA

BOOK I

Thou Mother of the Aenead race, delight
Of men and gods, bountiful Venus, thou
Who under the sky's gliding constellations
Fillest ship-carrying ocean with thy presence
And the corn-bearing lands, since through thy power
Each kind of living creature is conceived
Then riseth and beholdeth the sun's light:
Before thee, Goddess, do the winds and clouds
Of heaven take flight, before thee and thy coming:
For thee the daedal earth puts forth sweet flowers:
Beholding thee the smooth deep laughs, the sky
Grows calm and shines with wide-outspreading light.
For soon as the day's vernal countenance
Has been revealed, and fresh from wintry bonds
Blows the birth-giving breeze of the West wind,
First do the birds of air give sign of thee,
Goddess, and thine approach, as through their hearts
Pierces thine influence. Next the herds, grown wild,
Bound over the glad pastures and swim through
The rapid streams, as captured by thy charm
Each one with eager longing follows thee
Whithersoever thou wouldst lure them on.
And thus through seas, mountains and rushing rivers,
Through the birds' leafy homes and the green plains,
Striking bland love into the hearts of all,
Thou art the cause that following his lust
Each should renew his race after his kind.
Therefore since thou alone art Nature's mistress,
And since without thine aid naught can rise forth
Into the glorious regions of the light,
Nor aught grow to be gladsome and delectable,

Thee would I win to help me while I write
These verses, which I labour to compose
About the Nature of Things for my friend's sake,
This scion of the Memmii,[1] whom thou, Goddess,
Hast willed to be found peerless all his days
In every grace. Therefore the more, divine one,
Grant to my words eternal loveliness:
Cause meanwhile that the savage works of warfare
Over all seas and lands sink hushed to rest.
For thou alone hast power to bless mankind
With tranquil peace; since of war's savage works
Mavors mighty in battle hath control,
Who oft flings himself back upon thy lap
Quite vanquished by love's never-healing wound;
And so with upturned face and shapely neck
Thrown backward, feeds with love his hungry looks,
Gazing on thee, Goddess, with open mouth,
Supine, and on thy lips his spirit hangs.
O'er him as thus he lies bend down to enfold him
With thy divine embrace, and from thy lips
Pour tender speech, petitioning calm peace,
O glorious divinity, for thy Romans.
For nor can I in our country's hour of trouble
Toil with a mind untroubled at my task,
Nor yet may the famed child of Memmius
Be spared from public service in such times.

. . . .

For the rest, leisured ears and a keen mind
Withdrawn from cares lend to true reasoning,
Lest my gifts, that with loving diligence
I set out for you, ere they be understood
You should leave disregarded and despised.
For of the most high theory of the heavens
And of the deities I shall undertake

[1] Gaius Memmius, a politician of noble family, to whom Lucretius dedicated his poem.

To tell you in my discourse, and will reveal
What are the primal elements of things,[1]
Out of which nature gives birth and increase
And nourishment to all things; into which
Nature likewise, when they have been destroyed,
Resolves them back in turn. These I am wont
In setting forth my argument, to call
Matter, or bodies that engender things,
Or to name them the seeds of things: again
As first-bodies I sometimes speak of them,
Because from them first everything is formed.

When prostrate upon earth lay human life,
Visibly trampled down and foully crushed
Beneath Religion's cruelty, who meanwhile
Out of the regions of the heavens above
Showed forth her face, lowering on mortal men
With horrible aspect, first did a man of Greece[2]
Dare to lift up his mortal eyes against her;
The first was he to stand up and defy her.
Him neither stories of the gods, nor lightnings,
Nor heaven with muttering menaces could quell,
But all the more did they arouse his soul's
Keen valour, till he longed to be the first
To break through the fast-bolted doors of Nature.
Therefore his fervent energy of mind
Prevailed, and he passed onward, voyaging far
Beyond the flaming ramparts of the world,[3]
Ranging in mind and spirit far and wide
Throughout the unmeasured universe; and thence
A conqueror he returns to us, bringing back
Knowledge both of what can and what cannot
Rise into being, teaching us in fine

[1] The atoms.

[2] Epicurus (342–270 B.C.).

[3] The circling streams of fiery aether, which form the outmost layer of the sphere of our world. See v. 457–470.

Upon what principle each thing has its powers
Limited, and its deep-set boundary stone.
Therefore now has Religion been cast down
Beneath men's feet, and trampled on in turn:
Ourselves heaven-high his victory exalts.

Herein this fear assails me, lest perchance
You should suppose I would initiate you
Into a school of reasoning unholy,
And set your feet upon a path of sin:
Whereas in truth too often has this Religion
Given birth to sinful and unholy deeds.
So once at Aulis did those chosen chiefs,
Those foremost heroes of the Danaan host,
Foully defile the Trivian Virgin's altar
With Iphianassa'a lifeblood.[1] For so soon
As the fillet wreathed around her maiden locks
Had streamed in equal lengths down either cheek,
And soon as she was aware of her sire standing
Sorrowful by the altar, and at his side
The priestly ministers hiding the knife,
And the folk shedding tears at sight of her,
Speechless in terror, dropping on her knees
To the earth she sank down. Nor in that hour
Of anguish might it avail her that she first
Had given the name of father to the king;
For by the hands of men lifted on high
Trembling to the altar she was borne,
Not that, when the due ceremonial rites
Had been accomplished, she might be escorted
By the clear-sounding hymenæal song,
But that a stainless maiden foully stained,
In the very season of marriage she might fall
A sorrowful victim by a father's stroke,
That so there might be granted to the fleet

[1] Iphigeneia, whom her father Agamemnon sacrificed to Artemis.

A happy and hallowed sailing. To such crimes
Religion has had power to persuade men.

There yet may come a time when you yourself,
Surrendering to the terror-breathing tales
Of seers and bards, will seek to abandon us.
Aye verily, how many dreams even now
May they be forging for you, which might well
Overturn your philosophy of life,
And trouble all your happiness with fear!
And with good cause. For if men could perceive
That there was a fixed limit to their sorrows,
By some means they would find strength to withstand
The hallowed lies and threatenings of these seers:
But as it is, men have no means, no power
To make a stand, since everlasting seem
The penalties that they must fear in death.
For none knows what is the nature of the soul,
Whether 'tis born, or on the contrary
Enters into our bodies at their birth:
Whether, when torn from us by death, it perishes
Together with us, or thereafter goes
To visit Orcus' glooms and desolate chasms;
Or penetrates by ordinance divine
Into brutes in man's stead, as sang our own
Ennius,[1] who first from pleasant Helicon
Brought down a garland of unfading leaf,
Destined among Italian tribes of men
To win bright glory. And yet in spite of this
Ennius sets forth in immortal verse
How none the less there does exist a realm
Of Acheron, though neither do our souls
Nor bodies penetrate thither, but a kind
Of phantom images, pale in wondrous wise:

[1] Quintus Ennius (239–170 B.C.), the first of the great Roman poets. He believed in the Pythagorean theory of transmigration of souls, and was the first to use the Greek hexameter as a Latin metre.

And thence it was, so he relates, that once
The ghost of ever-living Homer rose
Before him, shedding salt tears, and began
To unfold in discourse the nature of things.
Therefore not only must we grasp the truth
Concerning things on high, what principle
Controls the courses of the sun and moon,
And by what force all that takes place on earth
Is governed, but above all by keen thought
We must investigate whereof consists
The soul and the mind's nature, and what it is
That comes before us when we wake, if then
We are preyed on by disease, or when we lie
Buried in sleep, and terrifies our minds,
So that we seem face to face to behold
And hear those speaking to us who are dead,
Whose bones the earth now holds in its embrace.

Nor am I unaware how hard my task
In Latin verses to set clearly forth
The obscure truths discovered by the Greeks,
Chiefly because so much will need new terms
To deal with it, owing to the penury
Of our tongue and the novelty of the themes.
Nevertheless your worth and the delight
Of your sweet friendship, which I hope to win,
Prompt me to bear the burden of any toil,
And lead me on to watch the serene nights through,
Seeking by what words and what poetry
I may at length avail to shed so clear
A light upon your spirit, that thereby
Your gaze may search the depths of hidden things.

This terror therefore and darkness of the mind
Must needs be scattered not by the sun's beams
And day's bright arrows, but by contemplation
Of Nature's aspect and her inward law.

And this first principle of her design
Shall be our starting point: nothing is ever
Begotten by divine will out of nothing.
In truth the reason fear so dominates
All mortals, is that they behold on earth
And in the sky many things happening,
Yet of these operations by no means
Can they perceive the causes, and so fancy
That they must come to pass by power divine.
Therefore when we have understood that nothing
Can be born out of nothing, we shall then
Win juster knowledge of the truth we seek,
Both from what elements each thing can be formed,
And in what way all things can come to pass
Without the intervention of the Gods.

For if things came from nothing, every kind
Might be born out of every thing; naught then
Would require seed. Thus men might rise from
ocean,
The scaly race out of the land, while birds
Might suddenly be hatched forth from the sky:
Cattle and other herds and every kind
Of wild beast, bred by no fixed law of birth,
Would inhabit tilth and wilderness alike.
No fruit would remain constant to its tree,
But would change; every tree might bear all kinds.
For if there were not for each kind its own
Begetting bodies, how could there be for things
A fixed unvarying mother? But in fact
Since all are formed from fixed seeds, each is born
And issues into the borders of the light
From that alone wherein resides its substance
And its first-bodies. And for this cause all things
Cannot be generated out of all,
Since in each dwells its own particular power.
Again why do we see in spring the rose,

Corn in the summer's heat, vines bursting forth
When autumn summons them, if not because
When the fixed seeds of things at the right time
Have flowed together, there is then revealed
Whatever is thus made, while the due seasons
Are present, and the quickened earth brings forth
Safely into the borders of the light
Her tender nurslings? But if they were formed
From nothing, they would suddenly spring up
At unfixed periods and unsuitable times,
Since there would then be no first elements
That could be kept from a begetting union
By the unpropitious season. Then again,
For things to increase they would have no need
Of lapse of time that seeds might flock together,
If they could grow from nothing. Suddenly
Small babes would become youths; trees would arise
Shooting up in a moment from the ground.
But nothing of the kind, 'tis plain, takes place,
Seeing that all things grow little by little,
As befits, from determined seed, and growing
Preserve their kind: so that you may perceive
That all things become greater and are nourished
Out of their own substance. Furthermore
Without fixed annual seasons for the rain
Earth could not put her gladdening produce forth,
Nor yet, if kept apart from nourishment,
Could living creatures propagate their kind
Or sustain life: so that with greater reason
You may think many things have many atoms
In common, as we see that different words
Have common letters, than that anything
Can come to being without first elements.
Again, why could not Nature have produced
Men of such mighty bulk, that they could wade
Through the deep places of the sea, or rend
Huge mountains with their hands, or in one life

Overpass many living generations,
If it be not because there has been assigned
A fixed substance for begetting things,
And what can thence arise is thus ordained?
Lastly, since it is evident that tilled grounds
Excel the untilled, and yield to labouring hands
A richer harvest, we may thence infer
That in the earth there must be primal atoms,
Which, when we turn her teeming clods with coulters,
Labouring the soil, we stimulate to rise.
But if none such existed, you would then
See all things without any toil of ours
Spring up far richer of their own accord.
Therefore we must confess this truth, that nothing
Can come from nothing, since seed is required
For each thing, out of which it may be born
And lift itself into the air's soft breezes.

Furthermore Nature dissolves each form back
Into its own first-bodies, nor does she ever
Annihilate things. For if aught could be mortal
In all its parts, then each thing would be snatched
From our eyes to destruction in a moment:
For there would be no need of any force
To cause disruption of its parts, and loosen
Their fastenings. But in fact each is composed
Of everlasting seeds; so till some force
Arrive that with a blow can shatter things
To pieces, or can penetrate within
Through their void spaces and so break them up,
Nature will not permit the dissolution
Of anything to be seen. Again, if time
Utterly destroys, consuming all the substance
Of whatsoever it removes from sight
As the years lapse, out of what then does Venus
Bring back into the light of life the race
Of living creatures each after its kind?

Or, once brought back, whence can the daedal earth
Nourish and increase them, giving food to each
After its kind? Whence do its own fountains
And far-drawn rivers from without keep full
The sea? Whence does the aether feed the stars?
For infinite past time and lapse of days
Surely must long since have consumed all things
Formed of a body that must die. But if
Throughout that period of time long past
Elements have existed out of which
Our world of things is composed and remade,
Assuredly such atoms must be endowed
With an immortal nature: none of them
Therefore can turn to nothing. Then again
The same force and the same cause would destroy
All things without distinction, were it not
That an eternal substance held them fast,
A substance interwoven part with part
By bonds more or less close. For without doubt
A mere touch would be cause enough for death,
Seeing that any least amount of force
Must needs dissolve the texture of such things,
None of which had an everlasting body.
But in fact since the mutual fastenings
Of the atoms are dissimilar, and their substance
Is everlasting, things endure with body
Uninjured, till some force arrive which proves
Strong enough to dissolve the texture of each.
Therefore no single thing ever returns
To nothing, but at their disruption all
Pass back into the particles of matter.
Lastly the rain-showers perish, when the Sky-father
Has flung them into the lap of mother Earth.
But then luxuriant crops spring up, and boughs
Are green upon the trees; the trees themselves
Grow, and with fruits are laden: from this source
Moreover both our own race and the race

Of beasts are nourished; for this cause we see
Glad towns teeming with children, leafy woods
Singing with young birds' voices on all sides;
For this cause cattle about the joyous meadows
Wearied with fatness lay their bodies down,
And from their swollen udders oozing falls
The white milk stream; for this cause a new brood
Gambols and frolics over the tender grass
On weak limbs, their young hearts with pure milk thrilled.
None therefore of those things that seem to perish
Utterly perishes, since Nature forms
One thing out of another, and permits
Nothing to be forgotten, unless first
She has been recruited by another's death.

Now listen: since I have proved to you that things
Cannot be formed from nothing, and likewise
Proved that they cannot be brought back to nothing
When once they have been begotten, lest you yet
Should tend in any way to doubt my words,
Because the primal particles of things
Can never be distinguished by the eyes,
Consider now these further instances
Of bodies which you must yourself admit
Are real things, and yet cannot be seen.
First the wind's violent force scourges the sea,
Whelming huge ships and scattering the clouds;
And sometimes with impetuous hurricane
Scouring the plains, it strews them with great trees,
And ravages with forest-rending blasts
The mountain-tops: with such rude savagery
Does the wind howl and bluster and wreak its rage
With menacing uproar. Thus we may be sure
That winds must be invisible substances
That sweep the seas, the lands, the clouds of heaven,
Ravaging and dishevelling them all
With sudden hurricane gusts. Onward they stream

Multiplying destruction, just as when
The soft nature of water all at once
With overflooding current rushes forward
Swelled after copious rains by a mighty spate
Of water swooping down from the high hills,
Hurtling together broken forest boughs
And entire trees: nor can the sturdy bridges
Sustain the oncoming water's sudden force:
In such wise turbulent with much rain the river
Flings its whole mighty strength against the piles:
With a loud crashing roar it deals havoc,
And rolls the huge stones on beneath its waves,
Sweeping before it all that stems its flood.
In this way then must wind-blasts also move;
And when like a strong stream they have hurled themselves
Towards any quarter, they thrust things before them
And overwhelm them with repeated onslaughts,
Often in writhing eddy seizing them
To bear them away in swiftly circling swirl.
Winds therefore must be invisible substances
Beyond all doubt, since in their works and ways
We find that they resemble mighty rivers
Which are of visible substance. Then again
We can perceive the various scents of things,
Yet never see them coming to our nostrils:
Heats too we see not, nor can we observe
Cold with our eyes, nor ever behold sounds:
Yet must all these be of a bodily nature,
Since they are able to act upon our senses.
For naught can touch or be touched except body.
Clothes also, hung up on a shore where waves
Are breaking, become moist, and then grow dry
If spread out in the sun. Yet in what way
The water's moisture has soaked into them,
Has not been seen, nor again in what way
The heat has driven it out. The moisture therefore
Is dispersed into tiny particles,

Which our eyes have no power to see at all.
Furthermore after many revolutions
Of the sun's year, a finger-ring is thinned
Upon the under side by being worn:
Water falling in drops hollows a stone:
The bent ploughshare of iron insensibly
Grows smaller in the fields; and we behold
The paving-stones of roads worn down at length
By the footsteps of the people. Then again
The brazen statues near the city gates
Show right hands wearing thinner by the touch
Of those who greet them ever as they pass by.
Thus we perceive that all such things grow less,
For they have been worn down: and yet what bodies
Are leaving them each moment, this the grudging
Nature of vision has precluded us
From seeing. Finally whatever time
And Nature add to things little by little,
Obliging them to grow by slow degrees,
No effort of our eyesight can behold.
So too whenever things grow old by age
Or through corruption, and wherever rocks
That overhang the sea are gnawed away
By the corroding brine, you cannot discern
What they are losing at any single moment.
Thus Nature operates by unseen bodies.

And yet all things are not on every side
Held packed together by their bodily nature;
For there is also such a thing as void.
To have learnt this will prove in many ways
Most useful to you; for you need not then
Wander in doubt, for ever questioning
About the universe of things, mistrustful
Of my discourse. Space then, intangible, void,
And emptiness exist. If none existed,
Then things would have no power to move at all;

For that which is matter's function, to resist
And hinder, would be present at all times
To all things. Nothing therefore could advance,
Since no one thing would be the first to yield.
But as it is, we see before our eyes
Through seas and lands and through the heights of heaven
That many things in many ways are moving
In divers fashions, which, were there no void,
Would not so much be utterly deprived
Of restless motion, but could never at all
Have been begotten, since on every side
Matter, packed closely, would have been at rest.
Again, however solid things may seem,
Yet that their substance must in truth be porous,
You may perceive from this. In rocks and caves
The liquid moisture of water oozes through,
And the whole place weeps with abundant drops:
Food is distributed through every part
Of an animal's body: trees grow and put forth
Their fruits in season, because nourishment
Through all their stems and branches is dispersed
All over them, upward from their deepest roots:
Sounds pass through walls, and glide into closed rooms;
Stiffening cold penetrates to the bones.
Yet, if there were no void spaces wherethrough
Each particle may find its way, all this
Never would you find happening at all.
Lastly, why do we see some things surpass
Others in weight, though of no larger bulk?
For if there be within a ball of wool
Just as much substance as in a lump of lead,
'Tis natural that both should weigh the same,
Because the function of substance is to press
Everything down, while on the contrary
Void in its nature is always without weight.
So when the one, though just as large, is found
The lighter, this proves clearly that it holds

More void; whereas the heavier of the two
Shows that there is more substance in itself,
And far less empty space. Thus what we are seeking
With such keen reasoning, certainly exists
Mingled in things, which is what we call void.

And here, lest it divert you from the truth,
I must forestall this error, which by some[1]
Has been imagined. Water, so they assert,
Yields to the scaly shoals as they press forward
And opens liquid paths, because the fish
Leave room behind them whereinto the water
Can stream together as it yields: and thus
Other things too can move by exchanging place
Among themselves, although all things be full.
This theory, you must know, has been believed
For reasons wholly false: since on what side,
I ask you, could the scaly shoals advance,
Unless the waters first have given them space?
Again, on what side can the waters yield,
While yet the fishes have no power to move?
Therefore you either must deprive all bodies
Of motion, or must say that void exists
Mingled in things, from which they all receive
The initial power of movement. Finally
When two broad bodies leap asunder quickly
After colliding, to be sure the air
Must take possession of the whole void formed
Between the bodies. Now however swiftly
Its currents stream together from all sides,
Yet in one single moment the whole space
Cannot be filled; for the air must invade
First one place, then another, till the whole
Be occupied. But if someone perchance
Thinks that, when bodies have recoiled, this happens
At that moment because the air condenses,

[1] The Stoics.

He errs; for at that moment a space becomes
Empty which was not so before, while what
Before was empty is filled up; nor can air
Condense in such a way, nor, I presume,
Even could it do so, might it without void
Shrink into itself and draw its parts together.

Therefore, however long you hesitate
And urge objections, you must nevertheless
Admit that there is such a thing as void.
And many arguments there are besides
Which I might set before you, to heap up
Proof that my words are true. But for a keen
Intelligence these light foot-prints should suffice:
The rest by them you may yourself discover.
For just as dogs often track down by scent
Some mountain-ranging beast's leaf-shrouded lair,
Once they have found sure traces of its trail,
So in such inquiries you will learn to see
One thing after another by yourself,
Finding your way into all hidden nooks,
And thence draw forth the truth. But should you flag,
Or swerve even a little from our search,
This, Memmius, I can promise you downright:
Such large draughts from deep well-springs shall my tongue
Melodiously pour forth out of the wealth
Treasured within my breast, that much I fear
Lest sluggish eld should creep over our limbs
And break open the fastnesses of life
Within us, before yet the whole array
Of arguments on any single theme
Has been sped by my verses through your ears.

But now to resume weaving the design
Of my discourse: the nature of the universe
Consists then in its essence of two things;
For there are atoms, and there is the void

Wherein are placed those atoms, and through which
They move hither and thither. It is indeed
Sensation, common to all, which declares matter
To exist by itself. And if belief
In this sensation be not from the first
Firmly established, there is naught whereto
We can appeal concerning hidden things
To prove any fact by reasoning of the mind.
Next, if no room or space, which we call void,
Existed, atoms could nowhere be placed,
Nor could they wander hither and thither at all
On any side, as I have just now shown you.
Besides these two, there is naught else whereof
You could affirm that it exists distinct
From all matter and different from void,
Nothing of such a kind that we could count it
As it were a third nature. For anything
That may exist, that same thing must be something.
Now if it can be touched, however slight
And small may be the contact, it must needs,
Provided it exist, augment the amount
Of matter, whether by a large or little
Increment, and be added to the sum.
But if it be intangible, and so
Cannot prohibit any moving thing
From passing through it anywhere, why then
This will be that which we call empty void.
Again, whatever of itself exists,
Will either act in some way, or itself
Have to be acted upon by other things,
Or else it will be such that things may exist
And come to pass within it. But no thing
Can act or suffer action without body,
Nor can aught furnish room save void and emptiness.
Therefore, beside atoms and void, no third
Nature, existing independently,
Can be included in the list of things,

Such as might either fall at any time
Under our senses' ken, or might be grasped
By any one through reasoning of the mind.

For all things else to which we give a name
You will find either to be properties
Joined to these two things, or you will perceive
To be their accidents. That is a property,
Which in no case may be disjoined and severed
Without fatal disruption, as is weight
To stones, its heat to fire, moisture to water,
Touch to all bodies, intangibility
To the void. Slavery on the other hand,
Poverty, riches, liberty and war,
Concord, and all else which may come and go
Leaving the nature of the things unchanged,
We are wont rightly to call these accidents.
Time also does not of itself exist;
But from things as they happen our feeling grasps
Both what was done in time past, and what now
Is present, furthermore what is to be
Hereafter. And we must admit that no man
May feel time by itself, conceived apart
From the movement of things or their calm rest.
And therefore when men tell us of the rape
Of Tyndarus' daughter,[1] or the vanquishing
Of the Trojan folk in war, that these *exist*,
Beware lest they persuade us to concede
That such things have existence of themselves,
Since past ages, they argue, have swept away
Beyond recall those human generations
Whereof in truth these were mere accidents.
For everything that happened we might call
Either an accident of the Teucrian folk
Or merely of the regions where they dwelt.
The fact is, if no substance had been there,

[1] Helen.

Nor room nor space for events to happen in,
Then never had love's flame, fanned to a blaze
By Tyndaris' beauty, glowed beneath the breast
Of Phrygian Alexander,[1] and so kindled
The famous conflicts of that savage war;
Nor had the timber horse, while none in Troy
Suspected, casting its nocturnal brood
Of Grecian chiefs, set fire to Pergama.
Thus you may clearly see that all events
From first to last do not, as matter does,
Have being and existence by themselves,
Nor are they spoken of in the same way
As void: they are rather such that you may justly
Describe them as the accidents of matter,
And of the space, wherein all things go on.

Again, material bodies are in part
First elements of things, in part are formed
By union of such primal particles.
But those which are first elements of things
No force can quench; for by their solid body
They are certain to prevail. And yet it seems
Difficult to believe that among things
Aught with a solid body can be found.
For heaven's lightning passes through the walls
Of houses, even as noise and voices do;
Iron grows incandescent in the fire;
Stones often burst asunder in fervent heat;
By heat too the rigidity of gold
Breaks up and is dissolved; and the ice of brass
Is vanquished by the flames and liquefies.
Warmth and penetrating cold can ooze
Through silver, since we feel them both, when water
Is poured down into cups clasped in our hands.
So plausible is it to suppose that naught
In things is solid. None the less, because

[1] Paris.

True reasoning and the nature of the world
Constrains us, listen, till in a few lines
I make clear that there *are* things which consist
Of a body that is solid and eternal;
And these I show to be the seeds of things,
And their first elements, out of which the whole
Sum of things now existing has been formed.

First then, since we have found that there exists
A twofold nature, quite dissimilar,
Of matter, and of space wherein all things
Are going on, it needs must be that each
Exists unmingled, for and by itself.
For wheresoever there is empty space
Which we call void, matter cannot be there.
Also, wherever matter maintains itself,
There in no wise can empty void exist.
First-bodies therefore are solid, without void.
Secondly, since there is void in things begotten,
There must be solid matter round about it;
For no thing by true reasoning can be proved
To conceal in its mass and to hold void
Within itself, unless you will concede
That that which bounds the void is solid substance.
Now it can only be a union
Of matter that can bound the void in things.
Matter then, which consists of solid body,
May well be eternal, though all else dissolve.
Furthermore, if there were no empty void,
The whole world would be solid; and conversely,
Were there not definite bodies, to fill up
Whatever places they may occupy,
The whole of space would be void emptiness.
Therefore assuredly matter is marked off
From void, and void from matter, because space
Is neither wholly full, nor yet quite empty.
And so there must be certain definite bodies,

By which void space can be marked off from full.
These cannot either be dissolved by blows
Struck from without, nor yet be inwardly
Pierced and so decomposed, nor may they be
Assailed and ruined in any other way,
As I have shown you above not long before.
For without void nothing, it seems quite clear,
Can be crushed in, or fractured, or by cutting
Be split in two, nor yet can anything
Take in moisture or permeating cold
Or penetrating fire, whereby all things
Are wont to be destroyed. And the more void
Each thing contains within itself, the more
By such foes is it inwardly assailed
And brought to ruin. Therefore if first-bodies,
As I have shown, are solid and without void,
They must be eternal. Furthermore unless
Matter had been eternal, long ago
All things would altogether have returned
To nothing, and whatever things we see
Would out of nothing have been born anew.
But since I have proved above that out of nothing
Nothing can be created, and that what
Has been begotten cannot be recalled
To nothing, first-beginnings must needs be
Of an immortal body, into which
All things may be dissolved at their last hour,
That so a supply of matter may be there
For making new things. Therefore atoms are
Of solid simpleness: no other way
Age after age from infinite time past
Can they have been preserved to make new things.

Moreover, unless Nature had ordained
Some limit to the breaking up of things,
By now the bodies of matter would have been
So far reduced by the breaking of past ages,

That nothing conceived out of them could reach
Life's mature growth in a fixed period.
For it is clear that anything can more quickly
Be dissolved than remade: and for this cause
That which long ages and the infinite lapse
Of all past time had broken up ere now,
Disordering and dissolving it, could never
In all remaining time be reproduced.
But as it is we know that a fixed limit
Is ordained to their breaking, since we see
That each thing is remade, and that likewise
Definite periods have been appointed
For things according to their kinds, that so
They may attain the flower of their age.

This also we may add, that while the atoms
Of matter are quite solid, we may yet
Account for all the things that are formed soft,
Air, water, earth, and fires, in what way
They are formed, and by what force they each go on,
Once we admit that void is mixed in things.
On the other hand, if the first elements
Of things be soft, it is not possible
To explain out of what hard rocks and iron
Can be created; for the whole of nature
Will utterly be without a principle
Of firm stability. Atoms then are strong
In solid simpleness; and when these are joined
In denser union, all things can become
Close-packed and so reveal enduring strength.

Again, even if no limit has been set
To the breaking up of bodies, none the less
The various bodies of which things are made
Must have continued from eternal time
Till now, nor can they yet have been assailed
By any danger. But if they are endowed

With a fragile nature, it is not consistent
That they could have survived through time eternal
Harassed by countless blows age after age.

Furthermore, since to each creature after its kind
A limit of growing and maintaining life
Has been ordained, and since by Nature's laws
It stands decreed what they each can, and what
They cannot do, and since nothing is changed,
But all things are so far invariable
That all the diverse birds one after another
Show the peculiar markings of their kind
Upon their bodies—they must certainly
Also have bodies of unchangeable matter.
For if the primal elements of things
Could in any way be vanquished and so changed,
It would in that case be uncertain too
What can and what cannot arise, in fine
Upon what principle each thing has its powers
Limited, and its deep-set boundary stone;
Nor yet so often could the tribes of creatures
Recall after their kinds the nature, habits,
Manner of life and motions of the parents.

Then further, since there is always an extreme point
Belonging to each body that is no longer
Perceptible to our senses, such a point
Is without parts assuredly, and consists
Of the least substance possible, nor ever
Has it existed by itself apart,
Nor yet hereafter can it so exist,
Since in its essence it is but a part,
Primary and single, of another thing:
And then other and other similar parts
Successively fill up in close array
The atom's substance: and since by themselves
These cannot exist, they needs must cleave to that

From which they may not in any way be torn.
Atoms then are of solid simpleness:
They consist of least parts that are massed together
And cohere closely: they are not compounded
By the uniting of those parts, but rather
Are strong in everlasting simpleness:
From them Nature allows not anything
Ever to be torn off nor further minished,
Conserving them to be the seeds of things.
Moreover, if there be not a least thing,
All very small bodies will be composed
Of infinite parts, seeing that in that case
The half of a half will always have its half,
And there will be no limit to division.
Therefore what difference will there be between
The sum of all things and the least of things?
There will be no distinction; for however
Completely infinite the whole sum may be,
Nevertheless the very smallest things
Will equally consist of infinite parts.
But since true reason here protests, denying
That the mind can believe this, you must yield
And own there do exist such things as have
No parts, and are of a least possible substance.
And seeing that such exist, the atoms too
You must own to be solid and eternal.
Lastly, if Nature, creatress of things,
Had been wont to force all things to dissolve
Into least parts, she would no more be able
To make out of those parts anything new,
Because, being furnished with no parts, they cannot
Possess those properties which must belong
To begetting matter, all those various
Entanglements, weights, blows, collisions, motions,
By means of which all things are carried on.

Therefore those who have thought the primary substance

Of all things to be fire, and the whole
Universe to be formed of fire alone,
Are seen to have lapsed utterly from true reasoning.
Their leader Heraclītus is the first
To enter the battle, he whose fame is bright
Because of his dark sayings rather among
The frivolous than among the serious Greeks
Who seek the truth. For dolts always admire
And love the more what they detect concealed
Under ambiguous verbiage, and suppose
That to be true which prettily can tickle
Their ears, being farded with fine-sounding phrases.

For how, I ask, could things be so diverse,
If they are formed of unmixed fire alone?
For it would not help that theory to maintain
That hot fire is condensed or rarefied,
If the same nature which the whole fire has
Belonged to its parts as well. Fiercer no doubt
Would be the heat if the parts drew together,
More faint if they were sundered and dispersed.
Further than this you can imagine nothing
That by such causes might be brought to pass;
Far less could the diversity of things
Appear so great, if it came from mere condensing
And rarefying of fires. There is this too:
Should they assume void to be mixed in things,
Fires might then condense or be left rare;
But because they can see that many facts
Arise to contradict them, and yet shrink
From leaving unmixed void in things, they lose
The true way in their fear of the steep track;
Nor on the other hand do they perceive
That if void be removed from things, then all
Must be condensed, and so from many grow
To be one single body, such as could not
Discharge anything swiftly from itself,

As a warmth-giving fire shoots forth light
And heat, so that you see it is not formed
Of close-packed parts. But if perchance they think
That in some other way atoms of fire
In union may be quenched and change their substance,
Then surely, if they insist that this takes place
Invariably, all heat will of course be brought
Utterly to nothing without fail, and all
Created things will be formed out of nothing.
For whatsoever so changes as to quit
Its proper limits, straightway by such change
Is wrought the death of that which was before.
Therefore there must be something that survives
Undestroyed in those fires; else you would find
That all things were returning utterly
To nothing, and that the whole store of things
Was being reborn to fresh life out of nothing.
Since then in fact there do exist certain
Specific atoms which preserve their nature
Always the same, through whose going or coming
And change of order things their nature change
And substances transform themselves, then surely
These first-bodies of things are not of fire.
For it would make no difference that of these
Some should withdraw and go away, while others
Were added, and some had their order changed,
If yet they all retained the nature of heat;
Because in every case it would be fire,
Whatever they might form. But as I think,
The truth is this, that there are certain atoms,
Whose meetings, motions, order, position, shapes
Make fires, and which by a change of order change
The nature of the things they make, nor do they
Resemble fire, nor any thing besides
That is able to send bodies to our senses,
Or can arrive at contact with our touch.

To say moreover that all things are fire,

And that except fire no real thing exists
In the whole count of things, as this man does,
Appears to be sheer lunacy: for against
The senses as the champion of the senses
He fights, and undermines them, though on these
All our beliefs depend, though from them too
This that he calls fire to himself is known.
For he believes the senses can know fire
Truly, and yet believes they cannot know
All other things which are no whit less clear.
To me this seems to be not only untrue
But lunatic. For to what shall we appeal?
By what test surer than these very senses
May we distinguish what is false and true?
Moreover why should anyone prefer
To abolish all things and allow the nature
Of heat alone, rather than to deny
That fire exists, and yet allow the existence
Of something else, no matter what? It seems
An equal madness to affirm either theory.

Therefore those who have thought the primary substance
Of all things to be fire, and that the whole
Universe may be formed of fire; and those
Who have determined that in begetting things
Air is the primary element;[1] and all
Who have held that water by itself alone
Fashions things,[2] or that earth produces all
And changes into things of every nature,[3]
Far indeed from the truth are seen to have strayed;
Those likewise who maintain that there are two
First elements of all things, coupling air
With fire,[4] or earth with water;[5] and those who think
That everything may arise out of all four

[1] Anaximenes.
[2] Thales.
[3] Pherecydes.
[4] Oenipodes.
[5] Xenophanes.

Elements, fire and earth and air and water;
Foremost among whom is Empedocles,
The Acragantine. Him within the bounds
Of its three-cornered coast that island bore,[1]
Around which in wide bays the Ionian main
Surging, splashes up brine from its blue waves;
While the sea racing through the narrow strait
Sunders the coasts of Italy from its shores.
Here waste Charybdis seethes; and here the rumblings
Of Aetna threaten once more to collect
The furies of its flames, so that again
With violence it may vomit forth the fires
Erupted from its throat, and once more dart
Flashes of lightning flame up to the skies.
Now though this mighty land in many ways
Seems worthy of mankind's wonder, and its fame
Allures the traveller, though in good things so fertile,
And guarded by a teeming race of men,
Yet it seems to have held within it nothing
More glorious than this man, nothing more holy,
More marvellous and beloved. Also the poems
Wrought by his godlike genius, with clear voice
Proclaim his glorious discoveries,
So that he scarce seems born of human stock.

Yet he and those I have spoken of above,
Many degrees inferior as they are,
And far beneath him, though divinely inspired
They made many discoveries, and gave answers
As from their heart's shrine in more holy wise
And with far surer reasoning than those oracles
Delivered by the Pythian prophetess
From the tripod and laurel leaves of Phoebus,
Yet over the first elements of things
These men came crashing down: there have they fallen:

[1] Sicily.

Great were they; great and heavy has been their fall:
First because they have banished void from things,
Yet suppose motion, and allow things soft
And porous, air, dew, fire, earth, beasts and crops,
Yet in their substance do not mingle void;
Next because they assume there is no limit
Whatever to the cutting up of bodies,
Nor any stop appointed to their breaking,
In fact that no such thing as a least exists;
Though, as we see, the extreme point of each thing
Is that which, judged by our senses, is perceived
To be the least; so that you may infer
From this that each extreme point in those things
You cannot see, for them too is the least.
Then again, since they believe in first-beginnings
That are soft things, such as we see have birth
And are of an altogether mortal substance,
In that case the whole sum of things must needs
Revert to nothing, and the whole store of things
Must be reborn to fresh life out of nothing;
And how wide of the truth are both these doctrines
You will understand already. Furthermore
These elements are unfriendly in many ways
And poisonous to each other; for which cause
They will either perish when they meet, or else
Fly asunder, as we see lightnings and rains
And winds fly asunder when a storm has gathered.

Again, supposing all things are created
Out of four elements, and all once more
Dissolved into those elements, how then
Can *they* be called the first-beginnings of things
Any more than, reversing the assumption,
Things might be called the first-beginnings of *them*?
For they are begotten turn and turn about,
And interchange their colour and whole nature
Throughout all time. But if perchance you think

That fire's and earth's substance and air's breezes
And water's moisture meet in such a way
That in the union none of them transmutes
Its nature, then I tell you that no thing
Can be created from them, neither alive,
Nor with a lifeless body like a tree:
For in the mingling of the diverse mass
Each element will reveal its own nature:
Air will be seen still mixed with earth, and heat
Still joined with moisture. But primordial atoms
Ought in begetting things to bring with them
A nature secret and concealed, that so
No quality may be prominent, which might else,
Conflicting with whatever is created,
Hinder it from possessing its own being.

Nay some there are[1] who go back and begin
From heaven and its fires, and maintain
That fire first is changed to airy breezes,
Thence is begotten water, and from water
Is formed earth, and that all things are changed back
From earth in reverse order, moisture first,
Next air, last heat, and that these never cease
Their mutual changes, passing from the sky
To earth, and from earth to the stars of heaven.
But first-beginnings ought on no account
To behave thus; for something there must be
That abides unchangeable, that so all things
May not be brought back utterly to nothing.
For whatsoever so changes as to quit
Its proper limits, straightway by such change
Is wrought the death of that which was before.
Since therefore those things we have named just now
Pass into a state of change, they must be formed
Of other things which cannot change at all,
Else you would find that all things were returning

[1] Heraclitus and the Stoics.

Utterly to nothing. Why not rather hold
That there are certain first-bodies endowed
With such a nature, that if they should chance
To have created fire, these same first-bodies,
When a few have been removed and a few added,
And when their order and motion have been changed,
May also make the breezes of the air,
And that all other things in the same way
One with another may be interchanged?

"But", you will say, "the plain facts clearly show
That all things into the breezes of the air
Out of the earth grow up and thence are nourished;
And if the season at the propitious time
Be not profuse in showers, so that the trees
Sway in the soaking rain-storms, and unless
The sun too fosters them, and bestows heat,
Corn, trees and living creatures could not grow."
True; and if solid food and soft moisture
Nurtured us not, our flesh would waste away,
And life would wholly be dissolved from all
Our bones and sinews; for past doubt we are nurtured
And nourished each by definite foods, some creatures
By some, others by other definite foods.
It is of course because so many atoms
Common to many things are mingled in them
In many ways, that therefore different things
Are nourished upon different foods. Indeed
It often makes the greatest difference
Both with what others and in what position
The same primordial particles are held
Together in union, and likewise what motions
They impart to one another and receive;
For the same elements compose sky, sea,
Lands, rivers, sun; the same compose corn, trees
And living creatures; but they are mixed up
With different things, and move in different ways.

Nay in my very verses everywhere
You see many letters[1] common to many words;
Yet you must needs admit that words and verses
Are different both in meaning and in sound.
So much can letters by mere change of order
Accomplish; but those elements which are atoms
Can effect more combinations, out of which
All different kinds of things may be created.

Let us proceed now to investigate
The homœomerīa of Anaxagoras,[2]
As the Greeks term it, though the poverty
Of our native language does not suffer us
To name it in our own tongue; yet to expound
The theory itself in words is easy enough.
First of all you must know that when he speaks
Of this homœomerīa of things, he fancies
That bones are made of other very small
And minute bones, and flesh of very small
And minute bits of flesh, while blood is formed
Of many drops of blood coming together;
And he believes that gold can be composed
Of grains of gold, that earth can grow together
From little particles of earth, that fires
Are made of fires, moisture of specks of moisture,
And all else he imagines and believes
To be formed on a like principle. And yet
He neither allows that such a thing as void
Can anywhere exist, nor that a limit
Can be set to the cutting up of bodies.
Therefore to me he appears in both these matters
To reason no less falsely than do those
I have already spoken of above.
Furthermore he imagines first-beginnings
That are too frail, if indeed first-beginnings

[1] The word *elementa* means both "elements" and "letters".
[2] Homœomerīa is a Greek word meaning "similarity of parts".

They be, which are endowed with a like nature
To the things which they make, suffering harm
And perishing like things; nor from destruction
Does anything rein them back. For which of them
Will hold out, so as to escape from death,
Beneath strong pressure within death's very teeth?
Will fire, or air, or moisture? Which of these?
Will blood, or bones? Not one of them, I presume;
Since everything in its essence will be mortal
Just as much as those things we clearly see
Perishing visibly, vanquished by some force.
But that things cannot fall away to nothing,
Nor yet grow out of nothing, I appeal
To facts already proved. Further, since food
Gives increase to the body and nourishment,
It is clear that our veins and blood and bones
And sinews are composed of particles
Alien to them in kind; or if they say
That all foods must be of a mingled substance,
And must contain within them tiny bodies
Of sinew, and small bones, as well as veins
And particles of blood, it then will follow
That all food, solid and liquid, must itself
Be held to be composed of substances
Alien to it in kind, that is of bones
And sinews, and of mingled matter and blood.
Furthermore, if whatever bodies grow
Out of the earth are in its clods, the earth
Must needs be then composed of things unlike
Itself in kind, which rise out of its clods.
Take any case you will, and you may use
Just the same words. If flame and smoke and ash
Lurk hidden in logs, then logs must be composed
Of things that are unlike themselves in kind,
Things which, though unlike logs, rise out of logs.

Here there is left some slight chance of evasion,

Which Anaxagoras seizes when he affirms
That all things must be lying hid, immingled
In all things, but that that alone is visible
Whereof there are most particles in the mixture,
And these placed more in view, on the outer surface.
Yet from true reasoning this is far removed.
For it would then be natural that corn too,
When ground by the relentless force of stone,
Should often show some trace of blood, or some
Of those things that are nourished in our body;
Likewise from grasses too we should expect
That gore would often ooze, when between stone
And stone we crush them; and that water should yield
Sweet drops of a like savour to the milk
In a sheep's udder; and that oft, when clods
Of earth are crumbled, kinds of grasses, corn
And leaves, distributed among the soil,
Should be seen lurking there in miniature;
Lastly that ash and smoke and minute fires
Should be discovered lying hid in sticks,
When they are broken off. But since plain fact
Shows that of all this nothing comes to pass,
You may be certain that things are not thus
Mixed up in other things; but rather seeds
Common to many things must be concealed
And mingled within things in many ways.

"But often on great mountains", you will say,
"It comes to pass that neighbouring topmost boughs
Of tall trees, when the strong south winds constrain them,
Are rubbed together, till the flower of flame
Has shot forth, and they burst into a blaze."
That is true; and yet fire is not implanted
In wood: but there are many seeds of heat;
And when by rubbing these have streamed together
They create forest fires. But if the flame
Were hidden in the forests ready-made,

The fires could not then remain concealed
For any length of time; they would consume
The forests everywhere and burn down their trees.
Do you now see that, as I have just told you,
It often makes the greatest difference
Both with what others and in what position
The same primordial particles are held
Together in union, and likewise what motions
They impart to one another and receive,
And that the same may, when a little changed
In their relations, create fires and firs?—
In just the same way as those very words
Consist of letters only a little changed
In their relations, though the names by which
We denote firs and fires are quite distinct.
Finally, if you should suppose that nothing
Which you perceive among things visible
Can come to be, unless you first imagine
Bodies of matter endowed with a like nature,
If you should reason thus, you will then find
Your first-beginnings of things are such no more:
'Twill come to this, that they will laugh aloud
Convulsed by fits of quivering merriment,
And with salt tears will bedew face and cheeks.

Now listen, and learn what yet remains, set forth
In words more lucid. Nor am I unaware
How dark the theme: but a great hope of praise
Has pierced my heart with a sharp thyrsus wound,
And therewithal has struck into my breast
The sweet love of the Muses, wherewith now
Inspired, I traverse with untiring thought
The pathless haunts of the Pierides,
Never yet trodden by the foot of man.
Joyfully I approach those virgin springs,
And drink deep: joyfully do I pluck new flowers,
And gather for my head a glorious crown

From lawns whence never have the Muses yet
Enwreathed the brows of any: first because
Lofty is the doctrine I expound, essaying
To liberate the mind from strangling knots
Of superstition: next because I write
Poetry so luminous on a theme so dark,
Colouring all things with the Muses' charm:
For that too, surely, is not without good reason;
But as physicians, when they would make children
Drink nauseous wormwood, first will smear the cup
All round the rim with the sweet yellow juice
Of honey, so that childhood's trustful age
May be deluded so far as the lips,
And meanwhile may drink down the bitter draught
Of wormwood, though beguiled, yet not betrayed,
But rather by such means may be restored
To health and strength; so I too now—since often
To those who have not handled it this doctrine
Seems somewhat bitter, and the multitude
Shrinks from it with repulsion—I have chosen
To set our doctrine forth in musical
Pierian song to please you, seasoning it
As though with the sweet honey of the Muses,
If haply by such means I might avail
To hold your mind attentive to my verses,
Till you shall clearly have perceived the whole
Nature of things, how it is framed and shaped.

But since I have shown how these most solid atoms
Are flying to and fro perpetually
Unvanquished through all time, come, let me now
Unfold whether a limit to their sum
Exists or no. Likewise as to the void
Which has been found to exist, or call it room,
Or space, wherein every event goes on,
Let us see clearly whether the whole of this
Be altogether finite, or spreads out
Limitless to immeasurable depths.

Well then, the universe is limited
In no direction, else it needs must have
An utmost border. Now it is clear that nothing
Can have an utmost border, if there be not
Something beyond to bound it, so that a point
Is seen, further than which our sense must fail
To follow the thing. But since we must admit
That nothing can exist outside the sum,
It has no utmost border, and so lacks
Limit and boundary. And it matters not
In which of its regions you may take your stand;
So surely, whatsoever place a man
May occupy, he leaves the universe
On every side as infinite as before.
Moreover, grant that all existing space
Is indeed finite, if a man should run
The whole way to the utmost boundaries
And fling a flying javelin, would you then
Rather suppose that, hurled with vigorous force,
It travels onward whither it was aimed
And flies afar? or do you think that something
Might interfere and check its flight? For one
Of these two theories you must grant and adopt.
Yet both preclude escape, constraining you
To concede that the universe expands
Without limit. For whether there be something
To check the dart, forbidding it to reach
And occupy the goal that was its aim,
Or whether it speed forward, in either case
The javelin has not started from the limit.
In this way I shall follow you; and wherever
You choose to place the utmost boundaries,
I shall ask, what then happens to the dart.
It will be found that nowhere can a limit
Be fixed; that there will always still be room
Wherein the javelin's flight may be prolonged.

Moreover, were it true that all the space 988

Of the whole universe on every side
Was enclosed by fixed borders and so bounded,
Long ago would the store of matter have streamed
Together from all sides to the lowest place
By reason of its solid weight, and nothing
Could now go on beneath the roof of heaven;
Nor indeed would there be a heaven at all,
Nor sunlight, since all matter, settling down
Through infinite time, would lie piled in one heap.
But as it is, no rest, we may be sure,
Is ever granted the primordial atoms,
Because there is no lowest place at all,
Into which they might all stream down together
And as it were fix their abode therein.
Everything is for ever going on
With ceaseless motion on all sides, and bodies
Of matter from beneath are being supplied
As they rush swiftly out of infinite space.
Lastly our eyes behold how one thing bounds 984
Another thing: air fences in the hills,
And mountains air: the land limits the sea,
The sea again all lands: but the universe,
Nothing exists outside which can bound that. 987
So there exists a space and a deep void
Such that neither could bright thunderbolts
Race through the whole of it, though they should glide
Onward through endless lapse of time, nor yet,
For all their travel, lessen by one jot
The distance that remained for them to go;
So huge the room for things that everywhere
Is spread out with no limits on all sides.

Again Nature prevents the sum of things
From setting any limit to itself,
Because she compels matter to be bounded
By void, and void by matter, so that either
Thus by this alternation of the two

She makes the universe infinite, or else
One of the two, if the other did not bound it,
Would with its single nature then spread out
Illimitably: neither sea, nor earth,
Nor heaven's glittering precincts, nor mankind,
Nor yet the hallowed bodies of the Gods,
Could subsist for the brief space of an hour;
For driven asunder from its union
The store of matter would be dispersed and carried
Through the great void, or rather, let us say,
Never would have combined and given birth
To anything, because, being thus scattered,
It could not have been forced to coalesce.
For without question neither by design
Did the primordial particles of things
Arrange themselves each in its own right place
Intelligently; nor indeed did they bargain
What motions each should follow; but because,
Shifting many in number in many ways
Throughout the universe, they are impelled
And buffeted by blows through infinite time,
At length, after attempting every kind
Of motion and of union, they fall
Into such groupings as those out of which
This world of things has been formed and subsists;
By which moreover having been preserved
Through many great cycles of years, when once
It had been thrown into concordant motions,
It causes now the rivers to replenish
The greedy sea with their abundant streams,
And earth, by the sun's heat fostered, to renew
Her offspring, and the race of living creatures
To arise and flourish, and the gliding fires
Of aether to have life. But all these things
They would in no wise do, if a supply
Of matter could not rise from infinite space,
Out of which in due season they are wont

To repair whatsoever has been lost.
For as living creatures, when deprived of food,
Losing their substance waste away, even so
Must all things be dissolved, so soon as matter
Has ceased to be supplied, being turned aside
Out of its proper course in any way.
Nor can external blows from every side
Preserve from dissolution the whole sum
Of what has come together in union.
For though such blows by frequent batterings
Can keep a part in place, till other atoms
Can arrive to complete the sum; yet sometimes
They are forced to rebound and so grant space
And time for flight to the elements of things,
So that these can escape, set free from union.
Therefore again and yet again I assert
That many atoms must keep swarming up,
Nay, that the blows too may not fail, there is need
Of infinite store of matter from all sides.

And herein, Memmius, you should strenuously
Avoid believing, what some hold, that all things
Press towards the centre of the universe;
That for this cause the fabric of our world
Remains fixed without any external strokes,
And that its uppermost and lowest parts
Cannot in any direction break away,
Because all things are pressing towards the centre
(If indeed you can thus believe that anything
Can rest upon itself); likewise that all
The heavy things beneath the earth press upwards,
And so rest on the earth, turned upside down,
Like the images of things which we may see
Reversed in water. And in the same way
They would maintain that living creatures walk
Head down, yet cannot tumble off the earth
Into the spaces of the sky beneath them,

Any more than our bodies can fly up
Of their own motion into the sky above;
That when those see the sun, we are beholding
The stars of night, and that alternately
They share with us the seasons of the sky,
And pass nights which are equal to our days.
But fatuous error has imposed such fallacies
On fools, because the theory they embrace
Is grounded on false reasoning. For since
The universe is infinite, there can be
No centre; no, nor were there such a centre,
Could anything the more on that account
Find rest thereon, but would be driven elsewhere
For some quite different reason. For all room
And space, which we term void, must, through centre
Or else through no-centre, yield equally
To heavy bodies, whatsoever way
Their motions tend. Nor is there any place
Where bodies, when they have come to it, can lose
Their gravity's force, and so stand still in void.
And again what is void can support nothing,
But, as its nature craves, must at once yield.
Things cannot therefore in such wise be held
In union, mastered by desire for a centre.

Again, those who think thus do not pretend
That all bodies are pressing towards a centre,
But only those of earth and those of water,
The seas and the great rivers from the hills,
And those things that are enclosed in the earth's frame;
On the other hand they teach that both the air's
Thin breezes, and the elements of hot fire
Are dispersed from the centre, for which cause
The whole sky round is quivering with stars,
And throughout the blue tracts of heaven is nourished
The sun's flame, because fleeing from the centre
The heat is all gathered together there;

And they hold that the topmost boughs of trees
Could not grow leafy, unless little by little
Nature supplied food from the earth to each 1093
Upward through stem and branches. But herein
Not only is it plain their reasonings
Are false, but that they contradict each other.

Now I have proved already that void space
Cannot be finite: therefore there needs must be
An infinite store of matter on all sides,
Lest the world's ramparts, after the winged fashion 1102
Of flames, should on a sudden be dissolved
And fly asunder through the mighty void,
And all things else follow them in like manner;
Aye, lest the thundering quarters of the heavens
Should fall in from above, and the earth rapidly
Should be withdrawn from underneath our feet,
And the whole world (amidst the mingled ruins
Of things within it and of the heavens, whereby
Their atoms would be let go free) should vanish
Dispersed throughout the unfathomable void,
So that within one brief moment of time
No remnant would remain, nothing save space
Untenanted and viewless first-beginnings. 1110
For on whatever side first you suppose
A deficiency of atoms, on that side
Will be the gate of death for things, through which
The whole of matter will rush weltering forth.

These things you will thus learn and understand
Led on with little labour; for one truth
After another shall grow clear: blind night
Shall not obscure your path; but you shall see
To the utmost depths of nature. In such wise
Will one thing kindle a light for another thing.

BOOK II

Pleasant it is, when winds on the great sea
Are blustering its waves, to look from land
Upon another labouring in distress:
Not that you take delight in any man's
Ill fortune, but because you are pleased beholding
From what miseries you yourself are free.
A pleasure is it also to survey
Mighty contending hosts ranked o'er the plains,
While in the danger you share not yourself.
But no delight is sweeter than to dwell
Within those temples, lofty and serene,
Fortified by the teachings of the wise,
Whence looking down on others you may see them
Wandering hither and thither far astray
Seeking the way of life; may watch them strive
In rivalry of intelligence or birth,
And struggle with vast effort night and day
Till they emerge upon the heights of power,
And lay hands on the empire of the world.
O miserable minds of men! Blind hearts!
In what darkness of life, in how great dangers
Are you not spending this brief span of time!
Can you not understand that Nature craves
Nothing more for herself but this, that pain
Be absent from the body, and that the mind,
Released from care and terror, should enjoy
The pleasures of the senses? Now we see
That for the body's nature but few things
Are indispensable, such things alone
As dispel pain. Though sometimes luxuries
May to our satisfaction minister
Many delights, yet Nature for her part
Will feel no lack, because about the halls

There stand no golden images of youths
In their right hands lifting fiery torches,
That light may be supplied to nightly banquets;
Nor yet because the chambers of the house
Gleam not with silver, glitter not with gold,
Nor does the gilded fretwork of the roofs
Re-echo to the lyre. But couched together
On the soft grass, beside a water-brook
Beneath a tall tree's boughs, at no great cost
Men may refresh their bodies joyously,
At those times chiefly when the weather smiles
And the year's seasons sprinkle the green herbage
With flowers. Nor will hot fevers quit your body
Any the sooner if you toss your limbs
Beneath figured embroideries and sheets
Of blushing purple, than if you must lie
Under a poor man's coverlet. And so,
Since useless to our body are hoarded wealth,
Noble birth and the glory of regal power,
We must believe moreover that such things
Are of no profit likewise to the mind:
Unless perchance, when you behold your legions
Swarming over the fields of exercise,
Waging a mimic war, with strong reserves
And troops of horse to strengthen rear and flank,
Glittering with arms alike, and alike fired
With the same ardour—unless then you feel
That your religious fancies, by such sights
Scared off, fly panic-stricken from your mind;
Or that your fears of death then leave your heart
Empty and freed from care, when you behold
Your fleet swarming and scattering far and wide.
Now if we can but see that all these things
Deserve mere ridicule and mockery,
And if in truth men's fears and haunting cares
Dread not the clash of arms nor wounding weapons,
But boldly sojourn in the courts of kings

And the world's rulers, unawed by the gleam
Of gold, or by the splendent brilliancy
Of purple robes, how can you doubt that power
To put such cares to flight belongs alone
To reason—since indeed the whole of life
Is a struggle in the dark? For just as children
In the blind darkness tremble and are afraid
Of all things, so we sometimes in the light
Fear things that are no whit more to be dreaded
Than those which children shudder at in the dark,
Imagining that they will come to pass.
This terror therefore and darkness of the mind
Must need be scattered not by the sun's beams
And day's bright arrows, but by contemplation
Of Nature's aspect and her inward law.

Now listen, and I will set forth by what motion
The generating particles of matter
Beget different things, and then in turn
Dissolve what was begotten; by what force
They are compelled to act thus; what velocity
Is given them to traverse the great void:
Do thou fail not to give heed to my words.
For without doubt matter does not cohere
Close-packed together, since we behold each thing
To be decreasing, and perceive that all
Are as it were ebbing through lapse of time,
As age withdraws them from our eyes; and yet
The sum is seen to remain unimpaired,
Because the particles that quit each form
Lessen the things from which they pass away,
Augment those they have come to; cause the first
To grow old, but the second to blossom forth—
Nor yet with these do they abide. And so
The sum of things is evermore renewed,
And mortals live by mutual interchange.
Some breeds wax, others wane, and in short space

The tribes of living creatures are all changed,
And like runners hand on the torch of life.[1]

If you should think that the primordial atoms
Can stay still, and by staying still give birth
To new motions of things, then far astray
You wander from true reasoning. For since
They are roaming through void space, it must needs be
That the primordial atoms all move on
Either by their own weight, or else perchance
By the blow of some other. For whenever,
As often happens in their swift career,
They have met and collided, it results
That at once they recoil in opposite ways:
Nor is this strange; since they are very hard,
Of heavy and solid mass, and from behind
Nothing obstructs them. And that you may see
More clearly that all particles of matter
Are darting to and fro continually,
Remember that for the whole universe
There is no bottom, and that primal atoms
Have no place whereon they may sink to rest,
Since I have shown in many words, and proved
By sure reason, that space is without end
Or limit, but spreads round on every side
Immeasurably. Now since this is the truth,
Assuredly no rest has been allotted
To primal atoms throughout the deep void,
But rather, driven along in unceasing
And varied motion, some when they collide,
Rebound over great intervals, while others
Are hurled but a short distance from the blow.
And all those particles that congregating
In denser union, collide and rebound
Through minute intervals, being entangled
By their own close-locked shapes, these atoms form

[1] Runners in the Greek Torch-race.

The strong substance of rocks, and stubborn lumps
Of iron, and all other things like these.
Then of the rest a smaller number roam
Through the great void, and leaping far apart
Recoil afar over huge intervals.
These give us thin air and the sun's bright splendour.
Many moreover roam through the great void,
Which have been thrown off from the combinations
That form things, and wherever they have entered
Have been unable to adapt their motions.
An image illustrating what I tell you
Is constantly at hand and taking place
Before our very eyes. Do but observe:
Whenever beams make their way in and pour
The sunlight through the dark rooms of a house,
You will see many tiny bodies mingling
In many ways within those beams of light
All through the empty space, and as it were
In never-ending conflict waging war,
Combating and contending troop with troop
Without pause, kept in motion by perpetual
Meetings and separations; so that this
May help you to imagine what it means
That the primordial particles of things
Are always tossing about in the great void.
To this degree a small thing may suggest
A picture of great things, and lead the way
To new conceptions. There is another reason
Why you should give attention to those bodies
Which are seen wavering confusedly
In the sun's rays: such waverings indicate
That underneath appearance there must be
Motions of matter secret and unseen.
For many bodies you will here observe
Changing their course, urged by invisible blows,
Driven backward and returning whence they came,
Now this way and now that, on all sides round.

These wandering motions, you must know, are caused
In all these bodies by primordial atoms.
For first the primal particles of things
Move of themselves; those bodies next, that form
Small combinations, and that, so to speak,
Are nearest to the powers of primal atoms,
Smitten by their invisible blows are stirred
To movement; and thereafter they in turn
Rouse other bodies that are somewhat larger.
And so motion ascends from primal atoms,
And issues to our senses step by step.
Thus it is that those bodies also move
Which we can see in the sun's light, and yet
The blows that drive them are not visible.

Now, Memmius, what velocity belongs
To particles of matter, you may learn
Briefly from this. When dawn first strews the earth
With new light, and the various birds, flitting
Through the soft air about the pathless woods,
Fill the whole neighbourhood with liquid song,
Is it not plain and manifest to all
How suddenly at such times the risen sun
Invests all things and bathes them in his light?
And yet this heat which the sun radiates,
And his calm brightness, are not traversing
Void space; therefore they are compelled to move
More slowly, while, as it were, they cleave their way
Through waves of air. Nor is it one by one
That all the minute particles of heat
Move onward, but entangled each with each
And massed together: wherefore they are dragged back
By one another, and at the same time
Impeded from without, and so are forced
To move more slowly. But primordial atoms,
Being of solid simpleness, when they pass
Through empty void, and nothing from without

Retards them (and they themselves, being single wholes
Composed of their own parts, are each borne headlong
Towards that single point they are aiming at),
We may be sure they must surpass in speed,
And be borne onward far more rapidly
Than the sun's light, racing through many times
The extent of space in the same period
Which the sun's beams need to pervade the sky.[1]

. . . .

Nor follow up the several primal atoms
To see by what law each one goes its way.

Yet some, in ignorance of how matter moves,
Oppose this theory, and believe that Nature
Cannot without the providence of the Gods
Change the year's seasons so conformably
With man's requirements, and bring forth the crops,
Aye, and all else besides which divine Pleasure
Persuades men to enjoy, while she herself,
The guide of life, escorts and lures them on
By the arts of Venus to renew their race,
Lest humankind should perish. Yet when thus
They imagine that the Gods have ordained all
For man's sake, then they seem in every way
To have lapsed utterly from true reasoning.
For even were I ignorant of the truth
Concerning the first elements of things,
Yet this would I still venture to affirm,
And prove both from the system of the heavens,
And from much else besides, that the world's nature
Has by no means been made for our benefit
By divine power; so great are the defects
Which are its bane. This truth hereafter, Memmius,
Will I make clear. But now concerning motions
I must set forth what yet remains to tell.

[1] A number of lines seem to have been lost here.

Here should the place be in my argument
To prove this also, that no bodily thing
By its own force can ever be borne upward
Or travel upward; lest herein your mind
Should be misled by watching how flames move.
For with an upward impulse flames are born
And receive increase; upward also grow
Luxuriant crops and trees; although their weights,
So far as they are able, all sink downwards.
And when fires leap up to the roofs of houses
Licking up beams and rafters with swift flame,
Do not imagine that spontaneously
They do this, but that some force drives them up;
Just as when blood, issuing from our bodies,
Spirts out and leaps up high, scattering gore.
Do you not also see with what force water
Spits back logs and beams? For the more deeply
We push them straight down, and with all our might
Toiling many together press them in
With painful effort, all the more eagerly
The water spews them up and flings them back,
So that they rise and leap forth into the air
By more than half their length. And yet, methinks,
We doubt not that these things by their own nature
Are all borne downwards through the empty void.
In this way therefore flames too must be able,
When squeezed out, to shoot upwards through the air,
Although their weights by their own nature strive
To draw them downwards. Do you not also see
How the nocturnal torches of the heavens,[1]
Flying aloft, draw after them long trails
Of fire towards whatever region Nature
Has given them passage? Do you not perceive
How stars and constellations fall to the earth?
The sun too from the height of heaven sheds heat
On every side, and sows the fields with light:

[1] Meteors.

Thus towards earth the sun's heat also tends.
Lightnings you see too fly athwart the rains.
Now on this side and now on that the fires
Bursting forth from the clouds rush to and fro.
Everywhere earthward falls the force of flame.

Herein this too would I have you understand:
That when atoms by their own weights are borne
Straight downwards through the void, then at a time
Wholly uncertain, and at uncertain places
They push aside a little from their path,
Yet only just so much as you could call
A change of inclination. For if thus
They were not wont to swerve, they would each fall
Downward like drops of rain through the deep void,
And no collision would have been engendered,
Nor blow begotten among the atoms. Thus
Never would Nature have created aught.

But if by chance anyone should believe
That heavier atoms, since they move straight down
More quickly through the void, can overtake
The lighter from above, and so give birth
To blows that can produce begetting motions,
He wanders from true reasoning far astray.
For when things fall through water or thin air,
All, in proportion to their weights, must needs
Accelerate their fall, because the body
Of water, and the subtle nature of air
Cannot retard each thing in equal measure,
But yield more quickly when they are overpowered
By heavier bodies. But on the other hand
Empty void is not able to support
Anything anywhere at any time,
But, as its nature craves, must forthwith yield:
And for this reason all things, as they rush
Through the unresisting void, must move along

At equal speeds, though of unequal weights.
Thus never will the heavier things be able
To overtake the lighter from above,
Nor of themselves to generate the blows
That cause the varied movements by which Nature
Carries things on. Wherefore again and again
I say that first-bodies must swerve a little;
And yet not more than the least possible,
Lest we should seem to imagine slanting motions,
Which the facts would refute. For this, we see,
Is plain and manifest, that by their nature,
When they are falling headlong from above,
Weights cannot travel slantwise, in so far
As we perceive. And yet that nothing ever
Swerves from the straight direction of its course,
Who is there can perceive by sense alone?

Again, if every motion is always linked,
And a new always rises from an old
In a determined order, and if atoms
Do not, by swerving thus, make some beginning
Of motion, to break through the laws of fate,
That cause follow not cause through infinite time,
Whence have all living creatures on the earth,
Whence, I ask, has been wrested from the fates
This free will whereby each of us goes forward
Whither desire leads each, whereby moreover
We alter the direction of our movements
Neither at a determined time nor place,
But when and where the mind itself has prompted?
For beyond doubt in these things his own will
For each makes a beginning, and from this
The motions are sent streaming through the limbs.
See you not also, when the barriers
Have been flung open suddenly, how yet
The horses' eager might cannot burst forth
So instantaneously as the mind itself

Desires to do? For the whole store of matter
Through the whole body must be first stirred up,
That, roused through every limb, it so may follow
The purpose of the mind with strenuous effort.
Thus you may see that from the heart is born
The beginning of each motion, and that first
From the mind's will the movement takes its rise,
Then spreads through the whole body and the limbs.
The case is not the same when we move forward
Impelled by a blow, mastered by the strong might
And violent compulsion of another;
For then it is quite plain that all the mass
Of the whole body moves and is thrust on
Contrary to our wish, until the will
Has reined it in throughout the limbs. So now
Do you not see, though often an outside force
Will push men and compel them to advance
And be thrust headlong forward against their will,
That yet there must be something in our breasts
Able to fight against it and withstand it?
And sometimes at the bidding of this power
The whole amount of matter is compelled
Throughout the limbs and frame to change its course,
And having been forced forward, is reined in
And settles back to rest. So too in atoms
We must admit the same, that besides blows
And weights there is another cause of motion
From which this power has been begotten in us,
Since, as we see, nothing can come from nothing.
For it is weight that prevents everything
Coming to pass by the agency of blows
As by some outside force: but that the mind
Feels no necessity within itself
In all it does, and is not overpowered
And so constrained to suffer and endure,
Is caused by a slight swerving of the atoms
At no fixed part of space and no fixed time.

Nor was the store of matter ever packed
More densely, nor yet was it separated
By larger intervals than now; for nothing
Is either added to or lost from it.
Wherefore in time long past the atoms moved
With the same motions with which now they move,
And always will hereafter be borne on
In the same way. Such things as have been wont
To be begotten, will be still begotten
Under the same law, and will exist, and grow,
And become strong and vigorous, in so far
As the compacts of Nature grant to each.
There is no force can change the sum of things;
For neither is there anything outside
Whither any kind of matter could escape
Out of the universe, not yet from which
Some new supply of energy can arise
And, bursting into the universe, so alter
The whole nature of things and change its motions.

And here you need not wonder why it is
That though the primal particles of things
Are all in motion, yet the whole sum appears
To stand wholly at rest, except where something
Is moving as one individual mass.
For beyond our senses, far below their ken,
Lies the whole nature of first elements.
So since they are themselves invisible,
Their motions too they needs must hide away;
The more so that such things as we *can* see
Will yet often conceal their motions from us,
If they should be some distance away in space.
Thus often on some hill the woolly flocks
Creep onward cropping the glad pasturage
Whichever way the grass pearled with fresh dew
Tempts and invites each, while the full-fed lambs
Gambol and butt playfully; yet they all

Seem to us, blent by distance, to stand still
Like a white patch upon the green hillside.
Again, when mighty legions fill wide plains
With rapid movements, waging mimic war,
A glitter rises therefrom to the skies,
And the whole earth around shimmers with bronze,
And beneath the strong tramp of men a sound
Is roused forth, and the hills, struck by the shouting,
Toss back the echoes to the stars of heaven,
And horsemen, wheeling suddenly about,
Gallop across the middle of the plains
Shaking them with the violence of their charge.
And yet high up among the hills there must be
Some point from which they seem to stand quite still,
Resting a patch of brightness on the plains.

Now listen: you must learn next of what kind
And how widely divergent in their forms
Are the first elements of all things, and how
Manifold their varieties of shape:
Not that there are not many of like form,
But that in most cases they are not all
Similar to all others. Nor is this strange:
For since they exist in such great quantities
That, as I have shown, they have no end nor sum,
Surely it needs must be they are not all
Of equal bulk and like shape with all others.
Moreover humankind and the dumb shoals
Of scaly swimming creatures, the fat herds,
Wild beasts, and all the various birds that flock
Round pleasant watering-places, river-banks,
Fountains and pools, or flitting to and fro
People the pathless forests: of all these
Choose any one you will, yet shall you find
That each will be dissimilar in shape
From all the rest of the same species.
And no way else could the young know their mother,

Or a mother know her young: and yet we see
They can, and to each other they are all
No less well known than human beings are.
Thus often before the gay shrines of the Gods
Slaughtered beside the incense-smoking altars
A calf has fallen, spirting from its breast
A hot blood-stream: but the bereaved mother
Roaming the green glades, tracks out on the ground
The footmarks printed by those cloven hoofs,
Examining each spot with restless eyes,
If so perchance somewhere she may catch sight
Of her lost young: then standing still she fills
The leafy woodland with her lamentations,
Again and again returning to the byre
Her heart pierced through with yearning for her calf;
Nor can the tender willows and the grass
Freshened with dew, nor yonder streams that glide
Brimmed to their banks, give comfort to her mind,
Or turn aside the haunting pangs of care;
Nor may the forms of other calves that graze
About the glad pastures, divert her mind,
Or ease its grief; so strong is her desire
For one thing which she knows to be her own.
Thus too the tender kids with tremulous cries
Acknowledge their horned mothers, butting lambs
Their bleating ewes: so surely, as nature craves,
Each to its own milk-giving udder runs.
Lastly, examine any corn you choose,
You will not find each grain so similar
To others of its kind, but that some difference
May always be discerned between their shapes.
And differing in like manner we behold
The race of shells that paint the lap of earth,
Wherever with soft-falling waves the sea
Beats on the thirsty sand of the curved shore.
Therefore again and yet again I assert
That for like reasons (since they are formed by nature,

Not made by hand after the fixed pattern
Of a single atom) the elements of things
Must some of them be flying to and fro
In shapes dissimilar to one another.

Intelligent reasoning easily can explain
Why it is that the fire of the lightning
Has far more power to penetrate than ours
Which is born from pine-torches here on earth.
For you may say that the celestial fire
Of lightning is more subtle, being formed
Of such small shapes that it can pass through holes
Which our terrestrial fire, sprung from logs
And born of pine-wood, cannot penetrate.
Furthermore light will pass through horn, but rain
Is thrown off. Why? unless those particles
Of light are smaller than are those whereof
Water's fostering liquid is composed.
And swiftly as we see wines flow through a strainer,
Yet sluggish olive-oil will take its time,
Undoubtedly because it is composed
Of elements either larger or more hooked
And mutually entangled: and thus it is
These particles cannot become so quickly
Detached from one another, and percolate
Each singly through their several openings.

Moreover liquids such as honey and milk,
Held in the mouth, cause pleasure to the tongue;
Whereas wormwood and pungent centaury
Have such sour natures that they writhe the mouth
With loathsome flavour; thus you may easily know
That things which touch the senses pleasantly
Are made of smooth round bodies; while all those
Which seem bitter and harsh, are held together
By particles more hooked, and for this cause
Are wont to tear their way into our senses,
And as they enter to break through the body.

All things in short whose contact with our senses
Is pleasant or unpleasant, differ thus
One from the other because they are composed
Of unlike shapes: so you must never think
That the harsh shuddering of the strident saw
Is made of elements just as smooth as those
Of tuneful melodies that musicians waken
And shape with nimble fingers on the strings;
Nor must you think that atoms of like form
Pass through men's nostrils when foul carcases
Are burning, and when the stage is freshly sprinkled
With saffron of Cilicia, while hard by
The altar is breathing forth Panchaean odours;
Nor fancy that the pleasant colours of things
Which can regale the eyes, are formed of seed
Like that of those which make the pupil smart
And force it to weep tears, or those of aspect
So foul as to seem hideous and loathsome.
For no shape whatsoever, that has power
To gratify the senses, has been formed
Without some smoothness in its elements;
Whereas no harsh and painful shape is found
To be without some roughness in its atoms.
Also some elements are rightly thought
To be neither smooth nor altogether hooked
With barbed points, but seem rather to have small
Slightly projecting angles, insomuch
That they can tickle yet not hurt the senses;
And of this kind are wine-lees and the flavour
Of elecampane. Further, that hot fires
And cold frost must have fangs of different kinds
Wherewith to prick the senses of the body,
Is proved to us by the touch of each. For touch,
Touch, by the holy powers of the Gods!
Is the sense of the body; whether it be
When something from without makes its way in,
Or when a thing, which in the body had birth,

Hurts it, or gives it pleasure issuing forth
To perform the generative deeds of Venus,
Or else when, owing to some blow, the seeds
Jostle within the body and disturb
The feeling in their conflict with each other.
Of this you can make trial, if you strike
Any part of your body with your hand.
Therefore the first-beginnings must have shapes
That differ widely from each other, seeing
That they can generate feeling so diverse.

Furthermore things which seem to us hard and dense
Must needs be made of particles more hooked
One to another, and be held in union
Welded throughout by branch-like elements.
First in this class diamond stones, inured
To despise blows, stand in the foremost rank,
And stubborn blocks of basalt, and the strength
Of hard iron, and brass bolts which, as they struggle
Against their staples, utter a loud scream.
But things that are liquid and of fluid substance
Must consist rather of smooth round elements;
For the several globules do not hold together:
And you may scoop up poppy seed as easily
As water, which will also, if you spill it,
Glide away with as ready a downward flow.
Lastly, all things which you may see dispersing
In a moment of time, like smoke and mists
And flames, even if they are not wholly made
Of elements round and smooth, yet cannot be
Impeded by close-tangled elements,
And so, piercing the body, they can reach
The senses, yet not cling to one another.
Thus easily may you know that whatsoever
We see to have reached the senses, is not made
Of tangled but of pointed elements.
And when you see that some things which are fluid

Are likewise bitter, as is the sea's brine,
Count it no wonder; for because 'tis fluid,
The brine consists of atoms smooth and round;
While mixed with these many rough particles
Give birth to pains. Yet these need not be hooked
And held together so: in fact though rough
They are also spherical; and thus it is
They can roll on freely, yet hurt the senses.
And to convince you that with smooth are mixed
Rough atoms, whence is formed the bitter body
Of Neptune, there is a way of sundering these,
And noting how the water becomes sweet
When filtered several times through soil, and flows
By itself into a trench, its saltness gone.
For it leaves the elements of nauseous brine
In the earth above, since the rough particles
Remain behind more readily in the soil.

And now that I have taught this truth, I next
Will link thereto a congruent fact, that draws
Its proof therefrom: though first-beginnings of things
Vary in shape, the number of shapes is finite.
Were this not so, then it would further follow
That certain seeds must be of infinite bulk.
For the shapes cannot vary much within
The small compass of any single atom.
Let us suppose that first-bodies consist
Of three least parts, or, if you will, augment them
By a few more. Now when you shall have tried
All those parts of one atom in every way,
Transporting top and bottom, changing right
With left, and so have found what kind of form
In that whole atom each arrangement gives,
If in addition you should haply wish
To vary the shapes still, then you must needs
Add other parts: and it will follow thence

That this arranging will for similar reasons
Require yet other parts, if you perchance
Should wish to vary the shapes yet again.
And so in the atom an increase of bulk
Will follow upon changes to new forms.
Therefore you cannot possibly believe
That seeds have infinitely differing forms,
Lest you force some to be of a monstrous size,
Which, as I have shown above, must be absurd.
Nay, as you then would find, barbaric robes
And gleaming Melibœan purple cloth
Dipped in the colour of Thessalian shells,
Golden tribes of peacocks with plumage steeped
In laughing beauty, all would be cast aside,
Surpassed by some new colouring in things;
Also the smell of myrrh and honey's flavours
Would be despised; the melodies of the swan,
And tunes with varied art plucked from the strings
Of the Phœbean lyre, would in like sort
Be silenced and suppressed; for always something
Would still arise superior to all else.
Likewise all things might sink back to worse states,
Just as we said they might advance to better;
For one thing would, reversely, be more loathsome
Than all else to nose, ears, and eyes, and taste.
Now since this is not so, but a fixed limit
Has been assigned to things, that bounds their range
On each side, you must grant that matter too
Has but a finite number of differing shapes.
Again, from fiery heat to chilling frosts
There is a finite path, that in like manner
Is again travelled back; for all degrees
Of heat and cold and intermediate warmths
Lie between those extremes, and in succession
Fill up the sum. Therefore when things are born,
They differ within limited degrees,
Because they are marked off at either end

By these twin points, on the one side beset
By flames, on the other by congealing frosts.

And now that I have taught this truth, I next
Will link thereto a congruent fact, that draws
Its proof therefrom: those first-beginnings of things
Which are formed of a like shape one to another,
Are infinite in number. For because
The difference of forms proves to be finite,
Infinite must be those that are alike,
Or else the sum of matter will be finite;
Whereas I proved that this cannot be so,
When I showed in my verses that the minute
Bodies of matter out of infinite space
Continually maintain the sum of things
By means of an unbroken series
Of blows from every side. For though you see
That certain animals are more rare than others,
And discern a less fruitful nature in them,
Yet in another region and somewhere
In lands far distant, there may well exist
Many of the same kind, and the full tale
May be completed so;[1] just as we see
That elsewhere in the class of four-foot beasts
Snake-handed elephants come first of all;

[1] This strange case of the elephants is an instance of the Epicurean *ἰσονομία*, or "equal distribution", a principle deduced from the infinity of matter and space. There being an infinite number of atoms of each shape, any combination of shapes will occur an equal number of times. So in the whole universe there will always be an equal number of shapes of each kind. If in one place or in one world there are few samples of one species of thing, the balance will be redressed in some other place or world. The same principle was also supposed to be true not only of atomic shapes but of atomic motions, so that, for instance, the forces tending to atomic combination and the creation of things must be equally balanced, in the whole universe, with the forces tending to atomic dissolution and the destruction of things. (See lines 269–276 of this book.) Other applications of this principle may be found in v. 526–530 and v. 1344–1346. See Bailey's *Greek Atomists*, pp. 461–463.

For by their many thousands India
Is with an ivory rampart so fenced round
That none can penetrate its inner parts;
So great must be the number of the beasts
Whereof we see very few samples here.
But let me grant this also: let there be
Some one thing, if you will, that is unique,
Born in a body sole of kind; and let
Nothing resemble it in the whole wide world;
Yet, were there not an infinite supply
Of matter, wherefrom it might be conceived
And brought to birth, it could not be created,
And furthermore could not have growth and food.
For indeed, were I to assume this too,
That the birth-giving bodies of some one thing
Were tossed about all through the universe
In finite numbers, whence, where, by what force,
And in what way shall they meet and combine
Within so vast a sea and such an alien
Turmoil of matter? For as I conceive,
They have no plan whereby they can unite;
But even as, after many great shipwrecks
Have come to pass, the mighty sea is wont
To tumble to and fro benches, ribs, yards,
Prow, masts and swimming oars, so that stern-fittings
May be seen floating along every shore,
Bidding mortals take warning and resolve
To shun the snares, the violence and the guile
Of faithless ocean, nor at any time
Trust it, when with alluring blandishments
The tranquil deep smiles treacherously; so too,
Once you suppose that atoms of some kind
Are finite, then divergent tides of matter
Throughout all time must be dispersing these
And tumbling them about; so that they never
Can be forced into union and combine,
Nor yet abide in any union,

Nor grow up and increase. But plain fact shows
That each of these events clearly takes place:
Things can be born, and being born can grow.
Hence it is clear that of any kind you like
Infinite numbers of primordial atoms
Exist, out of which all things are supplied.

Thus neither can the motions of destruction
Prevail for ever, and so eternally
Entomb existence, nor yet can the motions
That give birth and increase to things, for ever
Preserve what has been born. Thus the war waged
By first-beginnings throughout infinite time
Is carried on with balanced strife. Now here,
Now there the forces that give life to things
Prevail and are prevailed against in turn.
Blent with the funeral wailing is the cry
That children utter, when first on the borders
Of light they gaze; and never did night follow
On day, nor dawn on night, that hath not heard
Mingled with sickly infant cries, the wails
That escort death and the black funeral.

And herein it is proper that you keep
The truth well sealed, and guard it safely stored
In your remembering mind: that there exists
Nothing whose nature is perceivable
Which consists only of one kind of atom,
Nothing which is not formed of mingled seed.
And the more energies and potential forces
A thing possesses in itself, so much
The greater number of kinds and varied shapes
Of atoms does it show that it contains.
Firstly the Earth holds in her those first-bodies
From which the springs, welling cool waters forth,
Replenish without fail the measureless sea;
She holds those also wherefrom fires are born.

For the Earth's crust breaks into flame and burns
In many places; while from her lowest depths
The fiery violence of Aetna rages.
She has atoms furthermore whence for mankind
She can raise bright crops and luxuriant trees;
Whence also to the mountain-ranging tribes
Of wild beasts she can furnish rivers, leaves,
And joyous pastures. Wherefore she alone
Has been named the Great Mother of the Gods,[1]
And Mother of beasts, and parent of our body.

Of her the learned poets of ancient Greece
Have sung that from her shrine she issues forth
On lofty car, driving a pair of lions,
Teaching thereby that in the expanse of air
Hangs the great world, nor can earth rest on earth.
Wild beasts they have yoked to her car, because a brood,
How fierce soever it be, must yet be tamed
And softened by the loving care of parents.
Her head they have circled with a mural crown,
Because, fortified on commanding heights,
She sustains towns; and adorned with this emblem
The divine Mother's image is now borne
With awe-inspiring ritual through wide lands.
Her, following antique religious use,
The diverse nations call the Idaean Mother;
And for escort they give her Phrygian troops,
Because they tell that from those lands corn first
Began to be produced throughout the world.
Castrated priests they assign her, because thus
They wish to show that those who have offended
The godhead of the Mother, and been found
Ungrateful to their parents, must be deemed
Unworthy to bring living offspring forth
Into the borders of the light. Taut drums
Struck by their palms resound, and concave cymbals

[1] Cybelē, the Phrygian Earth-goddess.

Clash round about them; horns are threatening
With harsh-voiced music, while the hollow pipe
Maddens their souls with Phrygian melody;
And weapons, emblems of their violent frenzy,
They brandish, meet to fill the thankless minds
And profane bosoms of the multitude
With terror for the Goddess's awful power.
Therefore whenever she is drawn along
Through great cities, mutely enriching mortals
With an unspoken blessing, they bestrew
Her path through every street with bronze and silver,
Enriching her with bounteous alms, and snow
Roses upon her, overshadowing
The Mother and her troops of followers.
Then there comes an armed band, which the Greeks call
The Phrygian Curetes; and because
They play at times together a game of arms
And leap in rhythmic dance, gladdened at sight
Of blood, tossing their terrifying crests
With each nod of their heads—they represent
The Dictaean Curetes, who, 'tis told,
In Crete once drowned those infant wails of Jove,
When, circling in swift dance around the boy,
That boy-troop, arms in hand, beat rhythmically
Brass upon brass, that Saturn might not seize
And swallow him in his jaws, piercing the Mother
Deep through the heart with a never-healing wound.
So for this cause they escort the Mighty Mother
Thus armed; or else because they would show forth
How she exhorts men to resolve with arms
And valour to defend their fatherland,
Bidding them be prepared both to protect
Their parents and to adorn them with fair fame.
All which, though well and nobly it be set forth,
None the less from true reason is far removed.
For by their very nature all Gods must
Enjoy immortal life and perfect calm,

Withdrawn and severed far from our concerns;
Since exempt from all grief, exempt from dangers,
Strong in their own powers, wanting naught of us,
They are neither to be won by services
Nor stirred by wrath. And here should someone wish
To call the sea Neptune, or corn Ceres,
And think good to misuse the name of Bacchus
Rather than utter the true term for wine,
Let us allow him to declare the earth
To be the Mother of the Gods, if only
He will in fact forbear to stain his mind
With foul religion. But indeed the earth 652
Is without conscious feeling at all times;
And 'tis because it has received the atoms
Of many things, that it can bring them forth
Many in manifold ways to the sun's light. 654

Thus it is that ofttimes the fleecy flocks,
And the warrior breed of horses, and horned herds,
Cropping grass from one field, beneath the same
Roof of the sky, and from one stream of water
Slaking their thirst, are yet throughout their lives
Dissimilar in appearance, and, retaining
The nature of their parents, imitate
Their habits each after its kind. So great
Is the diversity of matter in grass
Of any kind, so great in every river.
Hence also any single living creature
Is made of bones, blood, veins, moisture and heat,
Of sinews and of flesh; and these again
Are widely different, since they are composed
Of first-beginnings of dissimilar shape.
Furthermore all things that burst out in flames
And are consumed by fire, store in their body,
If nothing else, at least those particles
By means of which they may shoot fire forth,
And throw out beams of light, and make sparks fly

And scatter embers round them far and wide.
If you will now survey all other things
With a like reasoning, you then will find
That in their body they conceal the seeds
Of many things, and contain varying atoms.
Again you may see many things that possess
At once both colour and taste, and odour too;
Especially most of those offerings
Which are burned on the altars of the Gods.
These then must needs be made of varying atoms,
For savour penetrates within the frame
Where colour cannot pass; even so colour
Finds entrance into our senses in one way,
Taste in another; so that you may know
They differ in the shapes of their first-bodies.
Thus unlike forms unite into one mass,
And things are made up of commingled seed.
Nay, in my very verses everywhere
You see many letters[1] common to many words;
Yet you must needs admit that words and verses
Are different and composed of different letters:
Not that there are not many common letters
Which run through all of them, or that no two
Are made up of entirely the same letters,
But that in most cases they are not all
Similar to all others. So likewise
In other things, though there are many atoms
Common to many things, yet they can form
A whole that is dissimilar; thus mankind
And corn and flourishing trees are rightly said
To be composed of different elements.

And yet you must not imagine that all atoms
Can be conjoined in all ways; for you then
Would see monsters created everywhere,

[1] The word *elementa* means both "elements" and "letters". See I. 824.

Forms springing up half man, half beast, and sometimes
Tall branches sprouting from a living body,
And many limbs of land-creatures conjoined
With those of sea-beasts: you would see Nature too,
Throughout the all-procreant lands, feeding Chimaeras
That from their noisome jaws would breathe out flame.
But that of all this nothing ever happens
Is manifest, because we see that all things,
Being from fixed seeds and a fixed mother born,
Can as they grow preserve their kind. Now this
Surely must happen after a fixed law.
For the atoms proper to each body are drawn
From food of all kinds, and disperse within
Throughout the frame, where they combine and cause
The appropriate motions. But on the other hand
We see how Nature cast forth onto the earth
Those elements that are alien: many too
That are invisible, impelled by blows,
Flee from the body, since they were neither able
To combine with any part, nor, when inside,
To accord with and adopt the vital motions.
But do not think that living creatures only
Are bound by these conditions: the same law
Limits and holds apart all things that are.
For even as things begotten are each one
Unlike the other in their whole nature, so
Each of them must consist of first-beginnings
That are of unlike shapes; not that of these
There are not many endowed with a like form,
But that in most cases they are not all
Similar to all others. Since moreover
The seeds are different, different too must be
Their interspaces, paths, connections, weights,
Their blows, meetings and motions: and all these
Not only disjoin bodies that have life,
But keep apart the lands and the whole sea,
And hold all heaven asunder from the earth.

Now listen, I pray you, to the precepts gathered
By my sweet toil, lest haply you should deem
That those things which your eyes perceive as white
Are formed, because they are white, of white first-bodies,
Or that black things are born of black seed;
Or should believe that things which are imbued
With any other colour, bear that colour
Because their elements of matter are dyed
With a like hue. For elements of matter
Have no colour at all, neither like things
Nor yet unlike. But if you should perchance
Deem that the mind cannot project itself[1]
Into such atoms, you wander far astray.
For seeing that men born blind, who have ne'er beheld
The sun's light, can yet recognize by touch
Bodies not linked for them with any colour
From the outset of their lives, you will understand
How bodies, that are painted with no hue,
For *our* minds also can become clear concepts.[2]
Again, when we ourselves touch anything
In blind darkness, we do not feel it dyed
With any colour. Since I have clearly proved
That this can be so, I will now explain
How bodies that possess no colour exist.

[1] *Animi injectus* is a translation of ἐπιβολὴ τῆς διανοίας, the technical Epicurean term for mental examination or apprehension of a concept. Compare line 1047 of this book. See Bailey's *Greek Atomists*, pp. 265, 559.

[2] *Notitia*, which I translate "clear concept", is itself a translation of the Epicurean term πρόληψις, "anticipation". By this was usually meant a general concept, derived from previous sense-perceptions, which enables the mind to recognize and have knowledge of a new instance of some class of perceptible things. But sometimes, as here, a "clear concept" of an imperceptible thing, such as a colourless atom, was deemed to be formed by the combination of already existing concepts; in this case by combining the concept of an atom with that of touch without sight. Other less difficult instances of this idea of "clear concepts" will be found in II. 124, IV. 476, V. 124, 182, 1047. See Bailey's *Greek Atomists*, pp. 427–431.

Now any colour whatsoever changes
To any other: but atoms by no means
Ought to behave thus; something there must be
That abides unchangeable, that so all things
May not be brought back utterly to nothing.
For whatsoever so changes as to quit
Its proper limits, straightway by such change
Is wrought the death of that which was before.
Therefore you must be careful not to dye
The seeds of things with colour, lest you find
All things returning utterly to nothing.

Moreover, if no quality of colour
Is given to atoms, and they are yet endowed
With varied shapes, out of which they beget
And change about colours of every kind,
Therefore, because it makes the greatest difference
Both with what others and in what position
The seeds are each united, and what motions
They impart to one another and receive,
You can at once quite easily explain
Why those things which a little while before
Were of a black colour, may suddenly
Become of marble brightness. Thus the sea,
When mighty winds have stirred its level waters,
Turns into white waves gleaming bright as marble:
For you might say that what we often see
As black, yet when its matter has been mixed up,
And the order of its first-beginnings changed,
Some being added and some taken away,
Straightway it will appear shining and white.
But if the waters of the sea were made
Of blue atoms, there is no way whereby
They could become white; for however much
You jumble together atoms that are blue,
Never to a marble colour can they change.
Or if the atoms that make up the sea's

Uniform and pure brightness, were some dyed
With this, some with that colour (just as often
Out of different forms and varied figures
Some uniform square figure is composed),
Then it were natural that, as we perceive
Dissimilar forms to be within the square,
So in the sea's waves or in any other
Uniform and pure brightness we should see
Varying colours widely dissimilar.
Moreover not one whit do the unlike figures
Prevent and thwart the whole from being square
On the outside; whereas the various colours
Of the elements would hinder and impede
The whole thing's being of one uniform brightness.
Further, the reason that sometimes lures and tempts us
To assign colours to atoms, falls to the ground,
Since in that case white things would not be made
From white, nor black from black, but out of seeds
Of various colours. And in very truth
White things will much more readily arise
And be born from no colour, than from black,
Or any other that fights against and thwarts it.

Besides, since colours cannot without light
Exist, and since atoms do not emerge
Into the light, we know they are not clothed
With any colour. For in blind darkness
What colour can there be? Nay a colour changes
In the light itself, according as it shines
Struck by a straight or slanting beam of light.
So the plumage of doves, that rings their throats
And crowns their necks, shows itself in the sun:
Sometimes it is ruddy as lustrous garnet,
Then again, viewed some other way, it seems
To mingle cobalt with green emeralds.
And the tail of the peacock, when suffused
With plenteous light, as it moves round will change

Its colours in like manner. And since these hues
Are begotten by a certain stroke of light,
Surely we must suppose that without this
They could not be produced. And since the pupil
Receives one kind of blow when it is said
To perceive whiteness, but another kind
When it perceives black or some other hue,
And since it matters nothing with what colour
The things you touch may chance to be endowed,
But rather with what sort of shape they are furnished,
You may be sure that atoms have no need
Of colours, but produce feelings of touch
That vary according to their various forms.

Moreover if no definite hue belongs
To definite atoms, and all conformations
Of atoms may exist in any hue,
Why are the things of all kinds, which are formed
Out of those shapes, not likewise dyed in colours
Of all kinds? For it would be natural
That often, as they fly, crows should throw off
A white colour from white wings, and that swans
Should from black atoms become black, or else
Of any other colour, pure or mingled.

Again, the more minute the parts may be
Into which anything is rent, the more
May you perceive the colour fade away
Little by little and become extinct;
As happens when a piece of purple is torn
Into small shreds. When it has been unravelled
Threadmeal, the Punic purple, brightest far
Of colours, is all destroyed: whence you may learn
That the small shreds dissipate all their colour
Before they separate into the seeds of things.

Lastly, since you will grant that not all bodies

Emit a voice or smell, it follows thence
That not to all do you attribute sounds
Or smells. Even so, since with our eyes we cannot
Perceive all things, we may be sure that some
Are as much bare of colour, as some others
Are without any smell or void of sound,
Yet the observant mind can apprehend
These, no less well than it can note those things
Which are devoid of other qualities.

But lest by chance you should think that first-bodies
Are bereft only of colour, know they are also
Devoid altogether of warmth and cold
And fiery heat; barren of sound and void
Of taste they move along, nor from themselves
Do they throw off any odour of their own.
Even as when you set about preparing
The balmy juice of marjoram or of myrrh,
Or the fragrance of nectar-breathing spikenard,
First of all, if so be that you may find it,
You must seek odourless oil, such as gives out
No perfume to the nostrils, that it so
As little as may be by its own pungency
Should interfere with and destroy the scents
Mixed in its substance and boiled up with it;
So just for the same reason first-beginnings
Can never bring an odour of their own
To the begetting of things, nor their own sound,
Since they can discharge nothing from themselves,
Likewise no taste at all, nor cold, nor heat
Whether violent or moderate, and the like.
For since by nature these are perishable,
Whether pliant with soft, brittle with crumbling,
Or hollow with porous body, they must all
Be kept distinct from the first elements,
If we desire to establish beneath things
Imperishable foundations, whereupon

The sum of life may rest: else you would find
All things returning utterly to nothing.

Next, whatsoever things we see to have sense,
You must admit to be all none the less
Composed of insensible first elements.
The manifest facts, open for all to know,
Do not refute or contradict this truth,
But rather themselves lead us by the hand
And force us to believe that living things
Are, as I say, born of insensible atoms.
Why, we may see worms coming forth alive
From stinking dung, when after untimely rains
The soaked earth has grown putrid: nay, all else
Changes in the same way: rivers and leaves
And fertile pastures change themselves to cattle,
Cattle change their substance into our bodies;
And from these often are increased the energies
Of wild beasts, and the bodies of strong-winged birds.
Thus Nature changes into living bodies
All foods, and from them generates all the senses
Of living creatures, much in the same way
As she dissolves dry timber into flames,
Converting all of it into fire. So now
Do you not see it must be of great moment
Both in what order first-bodies of things
Are severally placed, and with what others
They are mingled when they impart and receive motions?

Further, what argument can so move your mind,
And urging it to utter various thoughts,
Forbid you to believe that what is sentient
Can be begotten from insensible things?
Doubtless it is that stones and logs and earth,
However mingled, yet cannot produce
The vital sense. Well, here you must remember
That not from all and every kind of thing

That creates what is sentient, do I say
That straightway can be generated sense,
But that it matters greatly, first how small
Are the atoms which make up a sentient thing,
Also what shapes they may possess, what lastly
May be their motions, arrangements and positions.
Of these conditions none do we see in logs
And clods: yet these, when rains have rotted them,
Bring forth small worms, because bodies of matter,
Forced from their old arrangements by a new
Condition, are combined in such a way
That living things are bound to be begotten.
Again, those who suppose that what is sentient
Can be created out of sentient atoms,
Which in their turn have got their own sensations
From other sentient elements, render thus
Their own seeds mortal, when they make them soft.
For all sensation is bound up with flesh,
Sinews and veins, all of which things we see
Are soft, and so built up of mortal substance.
But even suppose that such seeds can abide
Eternally, still they must, I presume,
Either possess the sense of a part, or else
Be deemed to have senses like whole living creatures.
But parts can never be sentient by themselves;
For each mere part is heedless of the senses
Elsewhere within the body; nor can the hand,
Nor any part whatever of the body,
When severed from us, by itself alone
Maintain sensation. There remains the theory
That they resemble entire living creatures.
In that case they must needs feel what we feel
In the same way as we do, and so be able
To share completely in our vital senses.
How then could they be called first elements
And shun the paths of death, since they would be
Live things, and things that live are one and the same

With mortal things? Yet grant they could do this,
Still they will make by meeting and combining
Naught but a mob and throng of living things;
Just as indeed men cattle and wild beasts,
By flocking all together, could not so
Beget any new thing. Yet if perchance
They dismiss from their substance their own sense
And take another, what then did we gain
By assigning to them what must be withdrawn?
Moreover, to revert to a former instance,
Inasmuch as we perceive the eggs of birds
Turn into living chicks, and worms swarm forth
When after untimely rains putridity
Has seized on the earth, we may know that sensation
Can be produced from things without sensation.

But if someone should chance to say that sense
May at least arise from what is without sense
By some change, or because it is brought forth
By a kind of birth, it will suffice to clearly
Prove to him that no birth takes place until
There has been a combination, while except
In a combination there can be no change.

For first of all senses cannot exist
In any body, until the living thing
Itself has been begotten, of course because
Its matter remains dispersed abroad in air,
In streams, in earth, or in things sprung from earth,
And has not come together nor combined
In some appropriate way those vital motions,
By means of which the all-discerning senses
Are kindled and protect each living thing.

Again, a blow more severe than its nature
May endure, will immediately prostrate
Any living creature, and will quickly stun

Its every sense of body and of mind.
For the arrangements of the first-beginnings
Are dissolved, and the vital motions checked
Deep within, till the atomic substance, shaken
Throughout the whole frame, loosen from the body
The vital knots of the soul, and force it out
Scattering it abroad through every pore.
For what else should we think a blow can do
Unless to shake asunder and dissolve
The several elements? Oft too, when a blow
Is struck less forcibly, the vital motions
That remain will prevail, and so prevailing
Quiet the huge disturbance of the blow,
Recalling each part to its proper movements,
And will shake off the motion of death, which now
All but reigns in the body, and once more
Kindle the senses that were well nigh lost.
For in what other way could a living thing
Turn from death's very threshold back to life,
Gathering again its mind, rather than pass
On to that goal whither its course had now
Been almost finished, and so pass away?

Again, since there is pain when bodies of matter,
Disturbed throughout the living flesh and frame
By some force, tremble in their seats within,
And since, when they move back into their place,
Soothing pleasure is born, we may be sure
That first-beginnings cannot be assailed
By any pain, nor from within themselves
Derive any pleasure; since they are not composed
Of any primal particles, through whose
Novelty of movement they may feel distress,
Or enjoy the fruit of fostering delight.
They cannot then be endowed with any sense.

Moreover, if in order that living creatures

May all have feeling, we must assign sensation
To their first-atoms, what of those wherefrom
Mankind derives its own peculiar growth?
Surely they must be shaken with loud fits
Of quivering laughter, and sprinkle face and cheeks
With dewy tears, and have the wit to speak
At length of how things are composed, and further
To enquire what their first-beginnings are;
Since, being similar to whole mortal men,
They themselves in their turn must needs be formed
Of other elements, and those again
Of others, so that you may nowhere venture
To make a stand. Yes, I will press you hard,
And whatsoever you say speaks or laughs
Or is wise, you shall admit to be composed
Of other elements doing these same things.
But if we perceive all this to be mere raving
And lunacy, if one may laugh, although
Not grown from laughing elements, may be wise
And argue in learned terms, although not formed
Of wise and eloquent seeds, why cannot all
We see to be sentient, just as well consist
Of mingled seeds wholly devoid of sense?

Lastly we are all sprung from heavenly seed:
There is for all that same Father,[1] from whom
When bountiful Earth, our Mother, has received
The liquid drops of moisture, then by him
Impregnated she brings forth the bright crops
And glad trees and the race of men, brings forth
Every kind of wild creature, furnishing
Nourishment wherewith all may feed their bodies,
And lead a pleasant life, and propagate
Their offspring. Wherefore justly she has won
The name of mother. Also that which once
Came from the earth, sinks back into the earth,

[1] Heaven or the Aether.

And what was sent down from the coasts of aether, 1000
Returning thither, is received once more
Into the regions of the sky. So death
Does not demolish things in such a way
As to destroy the particles of matter,
But only dissipates their union,
Then recombines one element with another,
And so brings it to pass that all things alter
Their shapes, and change their colours, and receive
Sensations, then in a moment yield them up.
Thus you may learn how important it must be
Both with what others and in what position
The same primordial particles are held
Together in union, and likewise what motions
They impart to one another and receive;
And thus you will not think that what we see 1010
Hovering upon the surfaces of things,
Or now being born, then suddenly perishing,[1]
Can be inherent qualities in atoms
That are eternal. Nay, in my verses even
It is of moment with what other letters
And in what order each one has been placed.
For the same letters signify sky, sea,
Lands, rivers, sun, corn, trees and living creatures.
If not all, yet by far the greater part
Are similar letters: but as their position
Varies, so will the sense be different.
Thus too with actual things, whenever change 1019
Takes place in the collisions, motions, order,
Position and shapes of their material atoms,
Then also must the things themselves be changed.

Now to true reasoning turn your mind, I pray;
For a new theme is struggling urgently
To reach your ears, a new aspect of things

[1] Secondary or phenomenal qualities, such as colour and shape.

Would now reveal itself. But there is naught
So easy, that at first it will not seem
Difficult of belief, and likewise naught
So mighty, naught so wondrous, but that all
Little by little abate their wonder at it.
Consider first the colour of the heavens,
So bright and pure, and all that they contain,
The stars wandering everywhere, the moon
And the surpassing radiance of the sun;
If all these sights were now for the first time
To be revealed to mortals suddenly
And without warning, what could have been described
That would have seemed more marvellous than such things,
Or that humanity could less have dared
Beforehand to believe might come to pass?
Nothing, I think: so wonderful had been
This spectacle. Yet think how no one now,
Wearied to satiety at the sight,
Deigns to look up at the sky's shining regions.
Cease therefore, terrified by mere novelty,
To spurn such reasoning from your mind, but rather
Weigh it with eager judgment; and if then
It appear true, surrender; or should it prove
A falsehood, gird yourself to give it battle.
For since the sum of space outside, beyond
This world's walls, must be infinite, the mind seeks
To reason as to what may else exist
Yonder in regions whither the intellect
Is constantly desiring to prospect,
And whither the projection of our thought
Reaches of its own motion in free flight.

Now first of all we find that everywhere
In all directions, horizontally,
Below and above throughout the universe
There is no limit, as I have demonstrated,
And as the facts themselves proclaim; for so

The nature of the deep clearly reveals.
Since then on all sides vacant space extends
Illimitably, and seeds in number numberless
And sum immeasurable flit to and fro
Eternally driven on in manifold modes
Of motion, we must deem it in no wise
Probable that this single globe of earth
And this one heaven alone have been created,
While outside all those particles of matter
Are doing nothing: the more so that this world
Was itself formed by Nature, as seeds of things,
Casually colliding of their own
Spontaneous motion, flocked in manifold ways
Together, vainly, without aim or result,
Until at last such particles combined
As, suddenly thrown together, could become
At any time the rudiments of great things,
Earth, sea, sky, and the race of living creatures.
Therefore beyond all question we are bound
To admit that elsewhere other aggregates
Of matter must exist, resembling this
Which in its greedy embrace our aether holds.

Moreover, when much matter is at hand,
When space is there, nor any obstacle
Nor cause of hindrance, then you may be sure
Things must be functioning and developing.
Now if there is so vast a store of seeds
That the whole lifetime of all conscious beings
Would fail to count them, and if likewise Nature
Abides the same, and so has power to throw
The seeds of things together everywhere,
In the same manner as they were thrown together
Into our world, then you must needs admit
That in other regions there are other earths,
And diverse stocks of men and kinds of beasts.

Besides in the whole universe there exists

No one thing that is born unique, and grows
Unique and sole; but it must needs belong
To some class, and there must be many others
Of the same kind. Consider first of all
Live creatures: you will find that thus are born
The mountain-ranging tribes of savage beasts,
Thus the human race, thus also the dumb shoals
Of scaly fish and every flying fowl.
Therefore by a like reasoning you must grant
That sky and earth and sun, moon, sea, and all
That else exists, are not unique but rather
Of number innumerable; since life's deep-fixed
Boundary stone as surely awaits these,
And they are of a body that had birth
As much as every species here on earth
Abounding in examples of its kind.

If you learn well these truths and hold them fast,
Nature, forthwith enfranchised and released
From her proud lords, is seen then to be acting
In all things of herself spontaneously
Without the interference of the Gods.
For by the holy breasts of those divinities,
Who in calm peace are passing tranquil days
Of life untroubled, who, I ask, has power
To rule the sum of space immeasurable?
Or who to hold in his controlling hand
The strong reins of the deep? Who can at once
Make all those various firmaments revolve
And with the fires of aether warm each one
Of all those fruitful earths, or at all times
Be present in all places, that by clouds
He may cause gloom, and shake the calms of heaven
With thunder, may hurl lightnings, and ofttimes
Shatter down his own temples, then withdraw
To desert regions, there to spend his fury
And exercise his bolt, which often indeed

Passes the guilty by, and strikes with death
The unoffending who deserve it least?

Now since the birth-time of the world, since land
And sea's first natal day and the sun's origin,
Many atoms have been added from without,
Many seeds from all round, which, shooting them
Hither and thither, the great universe
Has brought together: and by means of these
Sea and land have been able to increase;
Thus too the mansion of the sky has gained
New spaciousness, and lifted its high roof
Far above earth, and the air has risen with it.
For to each thing its own appropriate atoms
Are all distributed by blows from all
Regions of space, so that they separate
Into their proper classes: moisture joins
With moisture; earth from earthy substance grows;
Fires fabricate fire, and aether aether;
Till Nature the creatress, consummating
Her labour, has brought all things to their last
Limit of growth; as happens, when at length
That which is entering the veins of life
Is now no more than what is flowing away
And ebbing thence. In all things at this point
The age of growth must halt: at this point Nature
Curbs increase by her powers. For all such things
As you may see waxing with joyous growth,
And climbing step by step to matured age,
Receive into themselves more particles
Than they discharge, so long as food is passing
Easily into all their veins, and while
They are not so widely spread as to throw off
Too many atoms and to cause more waste
Than what their age takes in as nourishment.
For we must surely grant that many atoms
Are flowing away from things and leaving them:

But still more must be added, till at length
They have attained the highest pitch of growth. 1130
Then age little by little breaks their powers
And their matured strength, as it wastes away
On the worse side of life. And out of doubt
The bulkier and the wider a thing is,
Once growth ceases, it does but shed abroad
And discharge from itself more particles
On all sides: nor is food distributed
Easily into all its veins, nor yet
In quantity sufficient that therefrom
A supply may continually rise up
To compensate the copious emanations
Which it exhales. For there is need of food 1146
To preserve all things by renewing them;
Food must uphold, food sustain everything:
Yet all is to no purpose, if the veins
Cannot receive what should suffice, nor yet
Does Nature furnish all that is required. 1149
With good reason therefore do all forms perish
When they have been rarefied by the flux
Of particles, and succumb to external blows; 1140
Since food must fail advanced age in the end,
And bodies cease not ever from outside
To buffet each thing till they wear it out
And overpower it by beleaguering blows.

Therefore in some such way shall the walls too
Of the great world from all sides round be stormed
And so collapsing crumble away to ruins.
And even now already this world's age 1150
Is broken, and the worn-out Earth can scarce
Create the tiniest animals, she who once
Created every kind, and brought to birth
The huge shapes of wild beasts. For, as I think,
Neither did any golden rope let down
The tribes of mortal creatures from the heights

Of heaven onto the fields,[1] nor did the sea
Nor its waves beating on the rocks create them,
But the same Earth gave birth to them, which now
Feeds them from her own breast. At first moreover
Herself spontaneously did she create
Luxuriant crops and rich vines for mankind,
Herself gave them sweet fruits and joyous pastures;
Which now, though aided by our toil, scarce grow
To any size. Thus we wear out our oxen
And the strength of our peasants: we use up
Our iron tools; yet hardly do we win
A sustenance from the fields, so niggardly
They grudge their produce and increase our toil.
And now shaking his head the aged ploughman
Sighs ever and anon, when he beholds
The labours of his hands all spent in vain;
And when with times past he compares the present,
He praises often the fortune of his sire,
Harping upon that ancient race of men
Who rich in piety supported life
Contentedly upon their narrow plots,
Seeing the land allotted to each man
Was far less in those days than now. So too
The planter of the worn-out shrivelled vine 1168
Disconsolately inveighs against the march
Of time, wearying heaven with complaints, 1169
And understands not how all things are wasting
Little by little, and passing to the grave
Tired out by lengthening age and lapse of days.

[1] Referring to an allegory of the Stoics based upon Homer (*Iliad*, VIII. 19).

BOOK III

Thou, who from out such darkness first could'st lift
A torch so bright, illumining thereby
The benefits of life, thee do I follow,
O thou bright glory of the Grecian race,
And in thy deep-set footprints firmly now
I plant my steps, not so much through desire
To rival thee, rather because I love
And therefore long to imitate thee: for how
Should a mere swallow strive with swans; or what
Might kids with staggering limbs, matched in a race,
Achieve against the stalwart strength of a horse?
Thou, father, art the discoverer of truth;
Thou dost enrich us with a father's precepts;
And from thy pages, glorious sage, as bees
In flowery glades sip from all plants, so we
Feed likewise upon all thy golden words,
Golden words, ever worthy of endless life.
For soon as, issuing from thy godlike intellect,
Thy doctrine has begun to voice abroad
The nature of things, straightway the mind's terrors
Take flight; the world's walls open; I behold
Things happening throughout the whole of space.
Revealed is the divinity of the Gods,
And their serene abodes, which neither winds
Buffet, nor clouds drench them with showers, nor snow
Congealed by sharp frost, falling in white flakes,
Violates, but an ever-cloudless sky
Invests them, smiling with wide-spreading light.
Moreover all their wants Nature provides,
And there is nothing that at any time
Can minish their tranquillity of soul.
But on the other hand nowhere are visible
The Acherusian quarters; and yet earth

In no wise can obstruct our contemplation
Of all those operations that take place
Beneath our feet throughout the nether void.
At such thoughts there comes over me a kind
Of godlike pleasure mixed with thrilling awe,
That Nature by thy power has been thus clearly
Made manifest and unveiled on every side.

Now since I have demonstrated of what kind
Are the first elements of all things, and how
Various are the divers shapes wherein
They are flying onward of their own accord
Driven in eternal motion, and in what way
Out of these can be formed each several thing;
After these themes it would seem best that now
The nature of the mind and of the soul
Should be elucidated in my verses,
And fear of Acheron driven headlong forth,
That dread which troubles from its lowest depths
The life of man, and overshadowing all
With the blackness of death, will not allow
Any pleasure to be unalloyed and pure.
For though men often tell us that diseases
And a life of public shame are to be feared
Far more than Tartarus, the house of death,
And that they know the nature of the soul
To be of blood, or even perhaps of wind
If such should be their fancy, and that so
They have no need at all of our philosophy,
Yet from the following proof you may perceive
That all these boasts are uttered to win praise
Rather than from conviction of the truth.
These same men, exiled from their fatherland
And banished far from human sight, disgraced
By some foul charge, beset by every kind
Of wretchedness, none the less still live on,
And to whatever place they bear their misery,

In spite of all make offerings to the dead,
Slaughter black sheep, and to the nether powers
Do sacrifice, and in their bitter plight
Turn their thoughts to religion far more eagerly.
Thus it is well to observe a man in stress
Of peril, and amidst adversities
Discover what he is; for only then
The language of sincerity and truth
Is wrung forth from the bottom of his heart;
The mask is torn off; what is real remains.
Moreover avarice and blind desire
For honours, which compel unhappy men
To overpass the bounds of right, and sometimes,
As partners and accomplices of crime,
To struggle with vast effort night and day
Till they emerge upon the heights of power—
These sores of life are in no small degree
Fostered by fear of death. For foul contempt
And biting penury are mostly thought
To be quite different from a pleasurable
And secure life: rather they seem to be
Already but a kind of lingering
Before the gates of death. And because men,
Urged by an unreal terror, long to escape
Far from these ills and drive them far away,
They pile up wealth by shedding civil blood,
Doubling their riches greedily, while they heap
Massacre upon massacre, rejoice
Ruthlessly in the sad death of a brother,
And shun their kinsmen's board in hate and dread.
Often likewise owing to this same fear
They pine with envy because some other man
In the world's eyes is powerful, some other
Is gazed at, who walks robed in shining honours,
While they complain that they themselves are wallowing
In darkness and in filth. Some sink their lives
In ruin to win statues and a name;

And often with such force, through dread of death,
Does hatred of life and of the sight of day
Seize upon mortals, that with anguished heart
They will destroy themselves, forgetting quite
How this fear is the well-spring of their cares,
This it is that enfeebles honour, this
That bursts the bonds of friendship, and in fine
Is wont to cast all duty to the ground.
Since often ere now men have betrayed their country
And beloved parents, seeking so to shun
The realms of Acheron. For just as children
In the blind darkness tremble and are afraid
Of all things, so we sometimes in the light
Fear things that are no whit more to be dreaded
Than those which children shudder at in the dark,
Imagining that they will come to pass.
This terror therefore and darkness of the mind
Must needs be scattered not by the sun's beams
And day's bright arrows, but by contemplation
Of Nature's aspect and her inward law.

Now first the mind, which we shall often call
The intellect, wherein resides the reasoning
And guiding power of life, I assert to be
No less a part of man than feet and hands
And eyes are part of the whole living creature.
Yet some would have it that the sense of the mind
Resides in no fixed part, but deem it rather
A kind of vital habit of the body,
Which by the Greeks is called a harmony,
Something that causes us to live and feel,
Though the intellect is not in any part;
Just as good health is often spoken of
As though belonging to the body, and yet
It is not any part of a healthy man.
Thus they refuse to place the sense of the mind
In one fixed part: and here to me they seem

To wander far indeed astray from truth.
Wherefore often the body that is visible
Is sick, while in some other hidden part
We experience pleasure; and ofttimes again
The contrary will happen, when a man
Who is distressed in mind, through his whole body
Feels pleasure: in the same way as the foot
Of a sick man may suffer pain, and yet
His head meanwhile is in no pain at all.
Moreover when the limbs are given up
To soft sleep, and the wearied body lies
Diffused without sensation, there is yet
Something else in us which at that same time
Is stirred in many ways, and into itself
Receives all the emotions of delight,
And all the empty troubles of the heart.
Now, that the soul too dwells within the limbs,
And that no harmony is the means whereby
The body is wont to feel, you may thus learn:
When from the body much has been removed,
Yet life often still lingers in our limbs;
Whereas, when a few particles of heat
Have been dispersed and through the mouth some air
Has been forced out, suddenly that same life
Deserts the arteries and quits the bones:
Whence you may learn that not all particles
Have functions of like moment, nor alike
Support existence; but that rather those
Which are the seeds of wind and warming heat
Are the cause that life stays within the limbs.
Therefore there are within the body itself
Heat and wind, that give life to us and desert
Our frame at death. So now that we have found
The substance of the mind and of the soul
To be a part in some sense of the man,
Let us give up the name of harmony,
Which was brought down from lofty Helicon

To the musicians, or else they themselves,
Taking it from some other source, transferred it
To what was then without a name of its own.
However that may be, why, let them keep it.
Do you give heed to the rest of my discourse.

Now I maintain that mind and soul are bound
In union with each other, forming so
A single substance, but that the lord that rules
Throughout the body is the reasoning power
Which we call mind and intellect. Its seat
Is fixed in the middle region of the breast.
For here it is that fear and panic throb:
Around these parts dwell joys that soothe. Here then
Is the intellect or mind. The rest of the soul,
Dispersed through the whole body, obeys and moves
At the will and propulsion of the mind,
Which for itself and by itself alone
Has reason, and rejoices for itself,
Even when naught moves either soul or body.
And just as, when we are attacked by pain
In head or eye, we do not feel distress
Through our whole body too, so at times the mind
Suffers pain by itself, or is envigoured
By happiness, when all the rest of the soul
Throughout the limbs and frame remains unstirred
By any new feeling. But when the mind
Has been perturbed by some more vehement fear,
We see the whole soul feel in unison with it
Through all the limbs; and so sweating and paleness
Spread over the whole body; the tongue halts,
Speech dies away, the eyes grow dark with mist,
The ears ring and the limbs sink under us.
And indeed often we see men drop down
From terror of mind. Hence easily we may learn
That the soul is united with the mind;
For when it has been struck by the mind's force,
Straightway it pushes and propels the body.

The same reasoning shows us that the nature
Of mind and soul is bodily. For since
It is seen to propel the limbs, rouse up
The body from sleep, alter the countenance,
Govern and turn the whole man round about,
None of which things we see can come to pass
Without touch, nor yet touch without a body,
Must we not then confess that mind and soul
Are of a bodily nature? Furthermore
You perceive that the mind within our body
Is acted upon together with it, and feels
In unison with it. When the shattering force
Of a weapon, thrust within and laying bones
And sinews bare, fails to endamage life,
Yet faintness follows, and a pleasurable
Sinking down to the ground, and on the ground
There comes to pass a tumult of the mind,
And now and then a kind of hesitating
Desire to rise. Therefore the mind's nature
Must be material, since it feels distress
When it is wounded by material weapons.

And now, what is the substance of this mind,
And of what elements it is composed,
I will go on to explain to you. First I say
It is extremely subtle, and is formed
Of particles exceedingly minute.
That this is so, if you consider well,
You may be thus convinced. No visible action
Takes place with such rapidity as the mind
Conceives it happening and itself begins it.
Therefore the mind bestirs itself more quickly
Than any of those things which by their nature
Are clearly visible to our eyes. But that
Which is so very mobile, must consist
Of seeds which are quite round and quite minute,
So that they may be stirred and set in motion
By a small impulse. Thus water is moved

And ripples at the least impulse, being formed
Of particles that are small and quick to roll.
The nature of honey on the other hand
Is more stable; it is a sluggish fluid,
And moves more slowly; for its whole mass of matter
Coheres more closely, since it is not formed
Of such smooth bodies, nor so fine and round.
A light and gentle breath has force enough
To blow down a high heap of poppy seed
From top to bottom, but on a pile of stones
Or corn-ears it has no effect at all.
Therefore the mobility of bodies
Is in proportion to their littleness
And to their smoothness; while the greater weight
And the more roughness bodies may possess,
The stabler will they be. Since then we have found
The mind's nature pre-eminently mobile,
It needs must be composed of particles
Exceedingly minute and smooth and round.
The knowledge of this truth you will find useful
And serviceable in many ways, my friend.
Here likewise is a fact which shows how thin
Must be the texture of which the mind is formed,
And in how small a space it might be enclosed,
Could it be gathered into a single mass:
For soon as the untroubled sleep of death
Has laid hold on a man, and mind and soul
Have passed away, you then can discern nothing,
Which sight or weight can measure, taken away
From the whole body: death leaves all intact,
Except the vital sense and glowing warmth.
It follows that the whole soul must consist
Of very small seeds, and is interwoven
Through sinews, veins and flesh; since, when already
All of it has withdrawn from the whole body,
Yet the external contour of the limbs
Is preserved unimpaired and not one jot

Of weight is lost. Even so, when the flavour
Of wine has vanished, or when the sweet breath
Of unguent has dispersed into the air,
Or its taste has departed from some body,
Nevertheless the thing itself appears
No smaller to the eye, nor does aught seem
Subtracted from its weight; surely because
Many but tiny seeds make up the savours
And scent in the whole body of such things.
Therefore you may be certain of this truth:
The substance of the mind and soul is formed
Of very minute seeds, since, when it flees,
It takes none of the weight away with it.

Let us not think however that this substance
Is simple; for a certain tenuous breath,
Mingled with heat, quits dying men: moreover
The heat draws with it air; since there can be
No heat with which air also is not mixed:
For seeing that the nature of heat is rare,
There needs must be many atoms of air
Moving about within it. Thus we have found
The substance of the mind to be threefold.
Yet all these three combined are not enough
To create sensation, since indeed the mind
Does not admit that any one of these
Is able to create sense-giving motions,
Far less the thoughts it ponders in itself.
So to these must be added some fourth substance.
And this is altogether without name:
Than this nothing more mobile can exist,
Nothing more subtle, nor composed of smaller
And smoother elements. This it is that first
Transmits sense-giving motions through the limbs;
For this, being composed of small atoms,
Is the first to be stirred; next heat receives
The motions, then the unseen power of wind,

And then the air; then all things are set moving;
The blood is stirred; next everywhere the flesh
Thrills with sensation; last to the bones and marrow
The feeling passes, whether it be pleasure
Or an opposite excitement. Yet thus far
It is unlikely that pain can penetrate
Or any sharp distress make its way in;
For everything would then be so disordered,
That no room would be left for life, and so
The fragments of the soul would fly abroad
Through all the body's pores. But for the most part
These motions find their limit and are checked
Not far beneath the surface of the body.
For this cause we are able to go on living.

And now, though I long to set forth in what way
These elements are mixed one with another,
And how united so as to show their powers,
The poverty of my native speech restrains me
Against my will: yet I will touch the theme
As best I can in brief. These atoms then
Are coursing to and fro among each other
With atomic motions, so that no element
Can remain separate, nor could exercise
Its functions if divided from the rest
By any interval; but they are like
The various forces of a single body.
Even as in the flesh of any creature
There is smell always, and a certain heat,
And savour too, and yet out of all these
There is made up one single bulk of body,
So heat and air and the unseen power of wind
Mingling create one substance; and with these
Is joined that mobile force, which from itself
Transmits to them the origin of motion,
And from which first is born throughout the flesh
Sense-giving motion. For this substance lies

Lurking deep-hidden in utter secrecy;
Nor is there anything within our body
Farther beneath our ken than this; and so
This is the very soul of the whole soul.
Just as mingled together within our limbs
And our whole body are latent the mind's force
And the soul's power, because they each are formed
Of small and few particles; so, you see,
This force without a name, being composed
Of minute particles, is lying hidden;
Nay, in a sense, it is the very soul
Of the whole soul, and rules throughout the body.
In the same way the wind and air and heat
Must operate by being mixed together
Throughout the frame, and each of them must always
Be more concealed behind the rest, or else
More prominent, so that a single substance
Appears to be composed out of them all;
Lest heat and wind being separate, and the power
Of air, being separate too, by such disunion
Should dissipate sensation and destroy it.
The mind has that heat too which it displays
When it boils up in anger, and fire gleams
Savagely from the eyes. It has moreover
Abundance of fear's comrade, that cold breath
Which calls forth shuddering in the limbs, and shakes
The whole frame. Then there is that condition too
Of quiet air, which takes place when the breast
Is tranquil and the countenance serene.
But there is more of the hot element
In creatures whose fierce heart and passionate mind
Boils over easily in wrath. Of this
A foremost instance is the violent fierceness
Of lions, who will often break their hearts
With fretful roaring, and within their breasts
Cannot contain the billows of their rage.
But the cold mind of deer has more of wind

And stirs more speedily throughout the flesh
Those chilly breaths, that cause a tremulous movement
To shake the limbs: whereas the nature of oxen
Lives rather by the placid air, nor ever
Does anger's smoky torch, kindled beneath,
Excite it overmuch, spreading around
The shadow of blinding gloom; nor is it pierced
And stiffened by the chilly shafts of fear:
It lies midway between the other two,
Deer and fierce lions. So is it with the race
Of men: however equally refined
Training may render some, yet will it leave
Those earliest vestiges of each mind's nature;
Nor must we imagine that infirmities
Can be in such wise torn out by the roots,
That one man will not fall more readily
Into fierce fits of anger, while another
Will somewhat sooner be assailed by fear,
A third bear wrongs more meekly than he ought.
Also in many other ways the varied
Natures of men, and their resulting habits
Are bound to differ; though I cannot now
Set forth their unseen causes, nor find names
For all the different shapes of first-beginnings,
Whence rises this diversity of things.
This herein I feel able to affirm:
So trivial are those vestiges that are left
Of different natures, which philosophy
Cannot expel from us, that naught should hinder
Our living a life worthy of the Gods.

And so this substance of the soul is sheltered
By the whole body, being in its turn
The body's guardian and its cause of life;
For, as by common roots, the two cohere,
Nor, it is plain, can they be torn apart
Without destruction. Even as its perfume

Can hardly be torn from lumps of frankincense
Without its very nature perishing too,
Just so the nature of the mind and soul
Can hardly be withdrawn from the whole body
Without the dissolution of all alike:
So closely interwoven from their birth
Were the atoms whereof being formed they lead
A life of joint partnership: and 'tis plain
That neither mind nor body has power to feel
Separately, without the other's aid;
But by the joint motions of both, sensation
Is kindled and fanned to flame throughout our flesh.
Moreover by itself the body never
Is born, nor grows, nor is it seen to last
Long after death. For never in the way
That water's liquid often throws off heat
Which has been given it, yet is not itself
For that cause riven in pieces, but remains
Uninjured—never thus, I say, when once
The soul has left it, can the frame endure
That separation, but it perishes
Utterly, and riven in pieces, rots away.
Thus body and soul in mutual union
From life's first moment learn the vital motions,
Though hidden yet within the mother's womb,
So that no separation can take place
Without damage and ruin. Thus you may see
That since conjunction causes their existence,
So likewise must their nature be conjoined.

Furthermore he who would argue that the body
Does not feel, and believes it is the soul
Which, mixed through the whole body, takes upon it
This motion we call feeling, he is fighting
Against quite manifest and undoubted facts.
For who will ever find an explanation
Of how the body feels, unless it be

That which experience has made clear and taught us?
"But when the soul has passed away, the body
Lacks feeling in every part": yes, for it loses
What never was its own in life. Much else
Besides it loses, when it is driven from life.

Further, to say that the eyes can behold
Nothing, but that, as though through open doors,
The mind looks through them, is hardly possible:
Their own sensation asserts the contrary;
For by it our mind is drawn and driven on
To the pupils themselves:[1] nay oftentimes
We are unable to perceive bright things
Because our eyes are hindered by the light.
But with doors this is not the case; for doors,
Through which we look, will suffer no distress
When they are opened. Besides, if our eyes
Resemble doors, then, it would seem, the mind
Ought to perceive things better, if the eyes
Were taken out and removed, door-posts and all.

Herein by no means may you accept that doctrine
Which the august opinion of the sage,
Democritus, lays down, that the elements
Of body and of mind, placed each next each,
Come in alternate order, and so weave
The fabric of our limbs. For as the soul's
Elements are far smaller than are those
Of which our body and flesh are formed, so too
They are less numerous, and throughout the frame
Thinly scattered; so thinly at least that this
You may affirm, that the intervals dividing
The soul's atoms are no more than the width
Of the smallest bodies which, if falling on us,

[1] Is forced to conclude that it is the pupils which see.

Can rouse sense-giving motions in our limbs.[1]
For at times, when dust is clinging to our body,
We do not feel it, nor chalk-grains that fall
And settle on our limbs; nor do we feel
A mist at night, nor a spider's delicate threads
Meeting us and emmeshing us as we walk;
Nor do we notice when its flimsy web
Has fallen upon our head; or birds' feathers,
Or flying thistle-down, which oftentimes
For exceeding lightness finds it hard to fall;
Nor do we feel the tread of every kind
Of creeping creature, nor each separate footstep
Which gnats and such-like insects plant upon us.
Such multitudes of atoms must be stirred
Within us first, before the seeds of the soul,
Scattered throughout our frame, feel that those atoms
Have been disturbed, and before, by colliding
Across such wide intervals, they can thus
Clash and unite, then leap apart in turn.

Now the mind is more able than the soul
To ward life's fastnesses, and has a power
More sovereign to preserve life: for without
The intellect or mind, no part of the soul
Can dwell within the frame, not for one brief
Moment of time, but following forthwith
In the mind's train, vanishes into the air,
And leaves the limbs cold in the frost of death.
But he abides in life, within whom still
Abides the mind and intellect. Though the trunk
Be mangled, and its limbs shorn off all round,
Though the soul on all sides should be removed
And severed from the body, yet he still
Lives and draws in heaven's life-giving breath.
Robbed of the larger portion of the soul,

[1] A small body of matter, in order to be perceived, must be wider than the interval between two elements of mind.

Even though not of all, he lingers in
And cleaves to life still; just as, when the eye
Is mangled all around, if but the pupil
Has been left unimpaired, the living power
Of sight remains, if so be you destroy not
The whole ball of the eye, and do not cut
Close round the pupil, leaving only that;
For this cannot be done without destruction
Of both alike. But if that central part
Of the eye, small as it is, be eaten away,
Gone forthwith is the light, and darkness follows,
However much the bright ball otherwise
Remains unharmed. It is upon such terms
That soul and mind are ever bound together.

Now listen: for to the end that you may know
That the minds and light souls of living creatures
Were both born and must die, I will proceed
To set forth verses worthy to guide your life,
Long sought for and discovered with glad toil.
Forget not this, that you must link the mind
And soul under one name; and when for instance
I shall discourse hereafter of the soul
Proving it to be mortal, you must believe
I mean the mind as well, since they are both
A single thing and one united substance.
First then, since I have proved soul to consist
Of a fine substance, formed of minute bodies,
Atoms far smaller than are those whereby
Water's liquid is formed, or mist, or smoke,
It follows that soul far surpasses these
In nimbleness, and that it moves when driven
By a far slighter cause; for it is moved
Even by images of smoke and mist;
Just as, when sunk in slumber, we see altars
Steaming forth heat and sending smoke on high:
For beyond doubt idols are begotten

And reach us from these things.[1] Now therefore, since
When vessels have been shattered you may see
The water flowing away on every side,
And the liquid dispersing, and since mist
And smoke passes away into the air,
You must believe that the soul too is scattered
And perishes far more swiftly, and is dissolved
More quickly into its atoms, when it once
Has been dislodged from a man's limbs, and fled.
For since the body, which was, as it were,
The vessel of the soul, cannot confine it,
If shattered by some chance and rarefied
By loss of blood from the veins, how can you think
The soul might be confined by any air?
Could air do that, being rarer than our body?

Furthermore we perceive that the intellect
Is born at the same moment as the body,
And growing together with it, becomes old
At the same time. For just as children totter
With feeble and tender body, so their minds
Are likewise of but slender understanding.
Then, when their life has ripened, and their strength
Grown sturdy, greater is their judgment too,
And enlarged are the powers of their mind.
Afterwards, when the body has now been shattered
By Time's stern might, and sunk is now the frame
With forces dulled, then halts the intellect,
The tongue dotes, the mind stumbles, all the faculties
Are found wanting and fail at the same time.
Thus it seems natural that the soul's whole substance
Should also be dissolved into the breezes
Of the air above, like smoke, because we see
That it was born together with the body,

[1] The theory of "idols" is explained at the beginning of Book IV. See Bailey's *Greek Atomists*, pp. 407 ff.

And grows together with it, and as I have shown,
Breaks down at the same time worn out with age.

Besides, we see that, even as the body
Suffers dreadful diseases and fierce pain,
So the mind too is subject to sharp cares
And grief and fear; whence it seems natural
That in death also it should have its share.
Nay ofttimes, when the body is diseased,
The mind will stray and ramble; for it grows
Demented, and will utter raving words,
And sometimes in a heavy lethargy,
With drooping eyes and head, falls into deep
Long-lasting slumber, out of which it hears not
The voices, nor can recognize the features
Of those who stand round, and bedewing face
And cheeks with tears summon it back to life.
Therefore you must admit that the mind too
Dissolves, because the infection of disease
Pierces within it; for both pain and sickness
Are fashioners of death; which truth ere now
We have been taught by many a man's destruction.
Again, why is it that, when the eager strength
Of wine, entering within a man, has spread
Its heat abroad throughout his veins, there follows
A heaviness of the limbs; on floundering legs
He reels about; his tongue falters; his mind
Grows sodden; his eyes swim; shouting and sobbing
And quarrelling are rife, and therewith all
Those other usual symptoms of like kind—
Why should all this take place, if not because
The overmastering violence of the wine
Is wont to disturb the soul within the body?
But all such things that so can be disturbed
And disarrayed, testify that if once
A cause somewhat more powerful should find entrance,
They must needs perish, robbed of further life.

Moreover it often happens that some man,
Seized suddenly by the violence of disease,
Falls down before our eyes, as though by a stroke
Of lightning: foaming at the mouth he groans,
Shivers throughout his frame, loses his reason,
Contracts his muscles, writhes, breathes gaspingly,
And tossing to and fro exhausts his limbs.
Doubtless because the violence of disease,
Spreading throughout his frame, disorders him,
He foams, endeavouring to eject his soul,
Just as upon the salt sea the waves boil
Beneath the mastering vehemence of the winds.
Groans also are wrung from him, because the limbs
Are racked with pain, and furthermore because
The particles of voice are driven out
And rush forth in a close crowd from his mouth
Which is their wonted path and well-paved road.
There follows loss of reason, because the powers
Of mind and soul are thrown into disorder
And, as I have shown, are rent and forced apart,
Riven asunder by the same distemper.
Afterwards, when the cause of the disease
Has ebbed, and the sick body's acrid humours
Are now retreating to their hidden lairs,
First to his feet he rises staggering,
And then little by little he returns
Into all his senses and regains his soul.
Since therefore mind and soul even within
The body are tossed by such great maladies
And are rent and distressed so miserably,
Wherefore should you believe that they can still
Continue to exist without the body
In the open air, exposed to violent winds?
And since we see that the mind may be healed
Like the sick body, and can be controlled
By medicine, this too warns us that the mind
Has a life that must die. For it is natural

That he who endeavours to transmute the mind,
Or seeks to change any other organism,
Should add to, or alter the order of its parts,
Or withdraw from the whole some quite small portion.
But that which is immortal neither allows
That its parts be transposed, nor that one tittle
Be added to it, or pass away therefrom.
For whatsoever so changes as to quit
Its proper limits, straightway by such change
Is wrought the death of that which was before.
Therefore the mind shows symptoms of mortality,
As I have shown, whether it be diseased,
Or whether it be controlled by medicine.
So surely do we see true fact make head
Against false reasoning, and cut off retreat
From him who would escape, convicting him
Of falsehood by a twofold refutation.

Furthermore we may often watch a man
Pass gradually away, and limb by limb
Lose vital sense. First on his feet the toes
And nails grow livid; then the feet and legs
Mortify; next over the other members
Creep with slow pace the footprints of cold death.
Now seeing that here the substance of the soul
Is torn asunder, and does not at one time
Come forth entire, it must be reckoned mortal.
But if perchance you think the soul has power
To draw itself inward throughout the frame,
Concentrating its parts into one place,
And so to withdraw sense from all the limbs,
Nevertheless that place, wherein is gathered
So great a mass of soul, ought then to appear
To be possessed of livelier sensation.
But since there is no such place, doubtless the soul
Is torn to pieces and dispersed abroad,
As we have said before, and therefore dies.

Nay, even were I willing to concede
What must be false, and allow that the soul
Might thus be massed together in the body
Of those who leave the light dying piecemeal,
Even then you must admit the soul to be mortal;
For it matters not whether it perishes
Dispersed about the air, or whether drawn
Into one mass out of its various parts
It loses feeling, because everywhere
Ebbing sense fails the whole man more and more,
And everywhere less and less life remains.

Then, since the mind is one part of a man,
Which abides fixed in a determined place
No less than ears and eyes and all those other
Organs of sense that govern the helm of life;
And just as, when the hand or eye or nostrils
Are severed from us, they can neither feel
Nor exist apart, but after a brief while
Waste away in corruption; so the mind
Cannot exist alone without the body,
Which is the man's self, and might well be called
The mind's vessel, or aught else you may imagine
Joined to it yet more closely, since the body
Is linked and bound together with the mind.

Again, it is owing to their union
Each with the other, that the quickened powers
Of mind and body thrive and enjoy life;
For neither without body can the mind
Alone by itself initiate vital motions,
Nor yet can a body, reft of soul, survive
And use its senses. Just as a mere eye,
When torn out by the roots, can discern nothing
Apart from the whole body, so the soul
And mind clearly can do naught by themselves;
Doubtless because, mingled through veins and flesh,

Sinews and bones, their atoms are confined
By the whole body, and cannot freely leap
Asunder, leaving wide spaces between them;
And therefore, being thus pent in, they move
In those sense-giving motions, which outside
The body, forced forth into the winds of air,
They have no power to move in after death,
Since they are not confined in the same way.
For air would be a body and a live thing,
Were the soul able to hold itself together
And keep enclosed within the air those motions
Which it was wont before to carry on
Within the sinews and inside the body.
And therefore I insist that when the whole
Enveloping body has been broken up,
And when the breath of life has been forced forth,
You must admit that both the mind's sensations
And the soul are dissolved, since for both body
And soul the cause of life is their close union.

Furthermore, since the body is unable
To endure the separation of the soul
Without decaying with a noisome stench,
Why doubt that the soul's force, gathering itself
Forth from the inmost depths, has oozed away
And been dispersed like smoke, and that the body
Has suffered change and putrefied and fallen
Into such utter ruin for this cause,
That deep down its foundations have been stirred
And shifted, as the soul is oozing forth
Through the frame and through all the winding paths
And pores of the body? Thus in manifold ways
You may learn that the substance of the soul
Has issued through the frame sundered piecemeal,
And has been torn to shreds within the body
Ere it slipped forth and swam out into the air.
Nay more, the soul, even while it still is dwelling

Within life's confines, yet will often seem,
When shaken from some cause, as though it wished
To escape and be released from the whole body;
And, as in life's last hour, the features seem
To droop and all the limbs to sink down limp
Upon the bloodless trunk. Even so it is
When people say, "it goes ill with his mind",
Or "his soul is quite gone"; when all around
Confusion reigns, and everyone is striving
To keep unbroken the last bond of life.
For then the mind is shaken through and through,
And the whole power of the soul, while both
Collapse in ruin together with the body;
So that a somewhat stronger cause might well
Bring about dissolution. Why then doubt
But that the soul, when driven outside the body,
Frail as it is, without in the open air,
Stript of its covering, must not only then
Be unable to survive throughout all time,
But cannot hold together for one brief moment?
For it is clear that no one, as he dies,
Feels his soul issuing undivided forth
From his whole body, nor first mounting up
To throat and gullet; but all feel it failing
In that particular place where it resides;
Just as they are aware that all the senses
Are each being dissolved in its own place.
But were our mind immortal, then at death
It would not so much mourn its dissolution,
But rather that it needs must issue forth
And leave behind its vesture, like a snake.

Again, why is the mind's intelligence
And reasoning never begotten in the head
Or feet or hands, but for all men is fixed
In one abode and one determined quarter,
Unless determined places are assigned

To each thing for its birth, where each may still
Continue to exist when it is born,
These manifold parts being so organized,
That never can the order of the members
Become perverted? So invariably
Does effect follow cause, nor is flame wont
To be born in rivers, nor yet cold in fire.

Furthermore, if the nature of the soul
Be immortal, and when sundered from our body
Can still feel, then methinks we must suppose it
Endowed with the five senses. Thus alone
Can we imagine souls beneath the earth
Wandering through Acheron. And therefore painters
And writers of old times have represented
Souls thus endowed with senses. Yet apart
From body, neither eyes nor nose nor hand
Can exist for the soul; nor yet can tongue
Nor ears apart. Therefore souls by themselves
Neither have power to feel nor to exist.

And since we feel that vital sense is present
In the whole body, and perceive the whole
To be a living thing, then if some force
Cleave it in twain suddenly with swift blow,
Dissevering the two halves, beyond all doubt
The soul too will be cleft and cut asunder
And riven apart together with the body.
But anything that may be cleft in twain,
Or be divided into parts at all,
Surely disclaims an everlasting nature.
Stories are told of chariots armed with scythes,
Reeking with mingled slaughter, which ofttimes
Have lopped away men's limbs so suddenly
That what has fallen down lopped from the frame
Is seen to quiver on the ground, while yet
The mind and spirit of the man (so swift

Has been the mischief) cannot feel the pain;
And meanwhile, since his mind is given up
Utterly to the fervour of the fight,
He rushes with the body that is left him
Into the slaughterous fray; and oftentimes
Perceives not that the wheels and ravening scythes
Have carried off among the horses' feet
His left arm, shield and all; another feels not,
While he is climbing up and pressing on,
That his right arm has dropped from him; another
Struggles to rise up when his leg is gone,
While, on the ground hard by, his dying foot
Twitches its toes. Then too the head, lopped off
From the warm living trunk, keeps on the ground
The look of life and the wide-open eyes,
Till it yields up the last remnants of soul.
Again, a snake with flickering tongue, long body,
And quivering tail—if you should choose to cut
Its trunk in many pieces with a knife,
You will see all the sections separately
Writhing from the fresh wound and scattering
The earth with gore; the fore part open-mouthed
Making for its own hinder part, to assuage
With burning bite the pain of the wounding blow.
Shall we then say there must be entire souls
In all these pieces? But if we reason so,
It then will follow that one living creature
Must have had many souls within its body.
Well then that soul, which was no more than one,
Together with the body has been divided.
So we must think that both alike are mortal,
Since both alike are cleft into many parts.

Again, if the soul's substance be immortal
And enter into the body at our birth,
Why then are we unable to remember
Our former lives as well? Why do we never

Retain traces of actions past and gone?
For if the powers of the mind are changed
So utterly that lost is all remembrance
Of things once done, that state differs not far,
Methinks, from death. Therefore you must admit
The soul which was before has passed away,
While that which now exists has now been formed.

Furthermore, if the living energy
Of the mind is wont to enter into us
After our body has been fully formed,
At the instant of our birth, when we are crossing
The threshold into life, it ought not then
In such a way to live there as to seem
To have grown with the body and with the limbs
Within the blood itself; but it ought rather
To live alone by itself as in a den,
While yet the entire body must abound
With feeling. But the very contrary
Takes place, as plain fact shows us. For so closely
Is the soul interlaced through veins and flesh,
Sinews and bone, that even the very teeth
Share in sensation; as their aching shows,
And the twinge from cold water, or rough stone
Crunched between them out of a piece of bread.
Therefore undoubtedly we must believe 686
That souls neither exist without a birth,
Nor are exempted from the law of death.
For we ought not to believe they could have been
So closely interwoven with our bodies,
If they had entered into them from without; 689
Nor, since they are so closely interlaced,
Does it seem credible they could have the power
To issue thence entire, and free themselves
Unscathed from all the sinews bones and joints.
But if you haply imagine that the soul
Is wont to enter into us from without,

And ooze through all our limbs, so much the more,
Thus blended with the body, will it perish.
For that which oozes through some other thing,
Dissolves, and therefore dies. For even as food,
When, parcelled out through all the body's pores,
It is distributed about the limbs
And the whole frame, perishes and supplies
Another substance out of its old self,
So the soul and the mind, however pure
And whole they passed into a new-made body,
Yet as they oozed through it would be dissolved,
While throughout every pore into the frame
Were being distributed those particles
Whereof is formed this substance of the mind
Which in our body now is sovereign,
Being born out of that soul which perished then
Dispersed throughout the frame. And for this cause
Clearly the substance of the soul is neither
Without a birthday nor exempt from death.

Furthermore in the lifeless body are seeds
Of the soul left or not? For if they are left
Within it still, then the soul cannot rightly
Be deemed immortal, since it has withdrawn
Diminished by the loss of certain parts.
But if, departing from the untainted limbs,
It fled away, so as to leave no parts
Of itself in the body, whence do corpses
Exude worms out of the now putrid flesh?
And whence does such a swarm of living creatures,
Boneless and bloodless, surge through the swollen
frame?
But if perchance you imagine that the souls
Find their way from without into the worms,
And severally can pass into their bodies,
Even if you do not wonder for what cause
Many thousands of souls should meet together

In a place whence one only has withdrawn,
Yet there is this enquiry that may seem
To need making and bringing to the test,
Whether in fact the souls go hunting out
The various atoms that compose the worms,
And themselves build a home wherein to dwell,
Or enter somehow bodies fully formed.
But why they should themselves take so much trouble
To create bodies, no one can explain:
Since, when they are bodiless, as they flit about
They are plagued by no diseases, cold or hunger;
For 'tis the body that is more prone to suffer
By such infirmities through kinship with them;
While it is through its contact with the body
That the mind is distressed by many ills.
Nevertheless, be it ever so expedient
For souls to make a body wherein to enter,
Yet we can see no way by which they could.
Souls therefore do not fashion for themselves
Bodies and limbs; and yet it cannot be
That they should enter bodies fully formed.
For never with nice precision could the souls
Be inwoven with such bodies, and no contacts
Causing common sensation would take place.

Again, why is fierce violence always found
In the grim breed of lions, cunning in foxes?
And why should stags inherit from their sires
Proneness to flight, so that their fathers' fear
Spurs on their limbs? And why too should it be
That all the other qualities of this sort
Are gendered in the limbs and in the temper
From life's first hour, if it be not because
A power of mind, determined by its own seed
And breed, grows up along with the whole body?
But if the soul were immortal, and were wont
To change its bodies, then the characters

Of living creatures would be interchangeable;
The dog of Hyrcanian seed would often flee
Before the onset of an antlered stag;
The hawk, in flight from the pursuing dove,
Would tremble in mid-air; men would be witless,
The savage tribes of wild beasts would be wise.
For those who assert the soul to be immortal,
But to be altered by a change of body,
Make use of false reasoning. What is changed
Dissolves and therefore dies: for parts of it
Become transposed and quit their former order.
Therefore they must be able in like manner
To dissolve throughout the frame, so that at last
They all perish together with the body.
But if they assert that always souls of men
Pass into human bodies, yet will I ask
How a soul can become foolish that was wise,
Why no child has discretion, why the foal
Is not so clever as the powerful horse.
Doubtless they will take refuge in the theory
That in a young body the mind grows young.
But even were that true, you must admit
The soul is mortal, since it is so changed
Throughout the frame, and loses so completely
Its former life and sense. Then in what way
Will the mind's force be able to grow strong
At a like pace with its allotted body
And reach the coveted flower of age, unless
It be the body's partner at earliest birth?
Or what prompts it to issue forth abroad
From age-worn limbs? Can it be that it fears
To remain shut within a crumbling body—
Fears lest its mansion, worn away by lapse
Of many days, should fall and overwhelm it?
But an immortal being knows no dangers.

Moreover it seems utterly absurd

That souls should stand by at the unions
Of Venus, and the birth throes of wild beasts;
That beings which are immortal should wait there
In number numberless for mortal limbs,
And contend with each other in keen haste
Which shall find entrance first before the rest;
Unless haply there should be bargains made
Between them, that whichever soul arrives
First in its flight should enter first, that so
They make no trial of each other's strength.

Moreover in the sky trees cannot exist
Nor clouds in the deep sea, nor in the fields
Can fishes live, nor blood reside in timber,
Nor sap in stones. Where each one thing may grow
And reside, is determined and ordained.
Thus the mind's nature cannot come to birth
Alone without a body, nor exist
Separated from sinews and from blood.
Nay, were this possible, far more easily
Could the mind's force reside in head or shoulders
Or right down in the heels, and would be born
In any part you choose, and thus at least
Would abide in the same man as its home.
But since even in our body it is seen
To be determined and ordained where soul
And mind can separately dwell and grow,
All the more strongly must it be denied
That mind and soul could have their dwelling-place
Or be begotten wholly outside the body.
So, when the body has died, we must admit
That the soul too has perished, rent asunder
Through the whole body. Nay indeed, to link
The mortal with the eternal, and conceive
That they can feel together, and that one
Can act upon the other, is sheer folly;
For what more incongruous can be conceived,

More discrepant and discordant with itself,
Than that a mortal thing should thus be joined
With that which is immortal and everlasting,
And in such union endure raging storms?
Again, whatever things abide eternally,
Either, since they are of solid body,
Must repel strokes, nor suffer anything
To penetrate them which might disunite
The close-locked parts within, like those material
Atoms whose nature we have described before;
Or they must be able to endure throughout
All time, because they are exempt from blows
(As void is, which abides untouched, nor suffers
One whit from any stroke), or else because
There is around them no supply of space
Into which things might as it were depart
And be dissolved; even as the sum of sums
Is everlasting, nor is there any space
Outside, into which things might fly asunder,
Nor are there bodies which might fall upon them
And so dissolve them with a violent blow.

But if haply the soul is to be deemed
Immortal for the following reason rather,
That it is sheltered by the forces of life,
Either because things hostile to its survival
Do not approach at all, or because those
Which do approach, for some reason retreat
Repulsed, ere we can feel the harm they do,
That this cannot be so, the clear facts prove.
For besides that it grows sick in sympathy
With the ailments of the body, oftentimes
It is assailed by that which tortures it
About what is to be, frets it with fear,
And wears it out with cares; and when its crimes
Are past and done with, yet guilt brings remorse.
Then there is madness and forgetfulness,

Evils peculiar to the mind: then too
It is drowned beneath lethargy's black waves.

Death then is nothing to us, nor one jot
Does it concern us, since the nature of mind
Is known to be mortal. And as in times long past
We felt no unhappiness when from every side
Gathering for conflict came the Punic hosts,
And all that was beneath the heights of heaven,
Shaken by the tumult and dismay of war,
Shuddered and quaked, and mortals were in doubt
To whose empire all human power would fall
By land and sea; so when we shall be no more,
When body and soul, out of which we are formed
Into one being, shall have been torn apart,
'Tis plain nothing whatever shall have power
To befall us, who then shall be no more,
Or stir our feeling, no, not if earth with sea
In ruin shall be mingled, and sea with sky.
[Grant even that the powers of mind and soul,
After they have been severed from the body,
Have feeling still, yet that to us is nothing,
Who by the binding marriage tie between
Body and soul are formed into one being.
Nor if Time should collect our scattered atoms
After our death, and bring them back to where
They now are placed, and if once more the light
Of life were given to us, not even that
Would in the least concern us, once the chain
Of self-awareness had been snapped asunder.
And in fact now we are not concerned at all
About those selves which we have been before,
Nor do they cause us any vexation now.
For when you look back on the whole past course
Of infinite time, and think how manifold
Matter's motions must be, then easily
May you believe this too, that these same atoms

Of which we now are formed, have often before
Been placed in the same order as they are now:
Yet this can no remembrance bring us back;
For a break in life has since been interposed,
And all the atomic motions are dispersed
Wandering far astray from the old sensations.]
For if a man be destined to endure
Misery and suffering, he must first exist
In his own person at that very time,
So that evil may befall him. But since death
Precludes this, and forbids him to exist
To whom these ills might happen, we may be sure
That after death there is nothing we need dread,
That he who exists not cannot become miserable,
And that it makes no difference at all
If he should never have been born before
At any time, when once he has been robbed
By death that dies not of his life that dies.

Therefore when you hear someone crying out
Against his lot, that after death his body
Must either rot away laid in the grave,
Or be consumed by flames or jaws of beasts,
You may be sure that his words ring not true,
That in his heart there lurks some secret sting,
Though he himself deny that he believes
Any sense will remain with him in death.
For he grants not, I think, what he professes
To grant, nor yet the ground of his profession,
Nor by the roots does he expel and thrust
Himself from life, but all unwittingly
Assumes that of self something will survive.
For when a living man forbodes that birds
And beasts will rend his body after death,
He is pitying himself; for he can neither
Distinguish his true self from the dead man,
Nor withdraw wholly from the outcast body,

But while in fancy he is standing there,
He imagines that dead man to be himself
And with his own feelings impregnates him.
So he complains because he was born mortal,
Nor sees that there will be in real death
No other self which living can lament
That he has perished, none that will stand by
And feel pain that he lies mangled or burning.
For in truth, if after death it be an evil
To be mauled by devouring jaws of beasts,
I cannot see why it should be a pain
Less cruel to be laid out on a pyre
And scorched with hot flames, or to be embalmed
In stifling honey and to grow stiff and cold
Couched on the smooth slab of a chilly stone,
Or to be crushed down under a weight of earth.

"Now no more shall thy home nor thy dear wife
Receive thee in gladness, nor shall thy sweet children
Run forth to meet thee and snatch kisses from thee,
And touch thee to the heart with silent joy.
No more canst thou be prosperous in thy doings,
A bulwark to thy friends. Poor wretch!" men cry,
"How wretchedly has one disastrous day
Stript thee of all life's many benefits!"
Yet this thereto they add not: "Nor withal
Does craving for these things beset thee more."
This truth, could men but grasp it once in thought
And follow thought with words, would forthwith set
Their spirits free from a huge ache and dread.
"Thou, as thou art, sunk in the sleep of death,
Shalt so continue through all time to come,
Delivered from all feverish miseries:
But we who watched thee on thy dreadful pyre
Change into ashes, we insatiably
Bewept thee; nor shall any lapse of days
Remove that lifelong sorrow from our hearts."

Of him who spoke thus, well might we inquire,
What grief so exceeding bitter is there here,
If in the end all comes to sleep and rest, 910
That one should therefore pine with lifelong misery.
Why, no one feels the want of self and life 919
When body and mind alike are sunk in slumber.
For all we care, such sleep might be eternal:
No craving for ourselves moves us at all.
And yet, when starting up from sleep a man
Collects himself, the atoms of his soul
Throughout his frame have not been wandering far
From their sense-stirring motions. Therefore death
Must needs be thought far less to us than sleep,
If less can be than what we see is nothing:
For the dispersion of the turmoiled atoms,
That comes with death, is greater; nor has ever
Anyone yet awakened, upon whom
Has once fallen the chill arrest of life. 930

This too is oft men's wont, when they lie feasting 912
Wine-cup in hand with garland-shaded brows:
Thus from the heart they speak: "Brief is life's joy
For poor frail men. Soon will it be no more,
Nor ever afterwards may it be called back."
As though a foremost evil to be feared
After their death were this, that parching thirst
Would burn and scorch them in their misery,
Or craving for aught else would then beset them. 918

Furthermore, if Nature suddenly found voice, 931
And thus in person upbraided one of us:
"What is it, mortal, can afflict thee so,
That thou to such exceeding bitter grief
Shouldst yield? Why thus bemoan and bewail death?
For if the life thou hast lived hitherto
Was pleasant to thee, and not all thy blessings,
As though poured into a perforated jar,

Have flowed through and gone thanklessly to waste,
Why not then, like a guest replete with life,
Take thy departure, and with a tranquil mind
Enter, thou fool, upon repose untroubled?
But if all that thou hast enjoyed has perished
Squandered away, and life is a mere grievance,
Why seek to add thereto what in its turn
Must all come to destruction and be lost
Unprofitably? Why both of life and travail
Dost thou not rather make an end at once?
For there is nothing more I can contrive
Or find to please thee. All things are the same
At all times. Though thy body be not yet
Decayed with years, nor have thy worn-out limbs
Grown feeble, yet all things remain the same;
Though thou shouldst overlive all generations,
Nay, even more if thou shouldst never die"—
What could we answer, save that Nature's claim
Was just, and her indictment a true plea?
But if now someone more advanced in years
Should miserably complain and lament death
Beyond all reason, would she not yet more justly
Lift up her voice and chide him with sharp speech?
"Hence with thy tears, buffoon. Cease thy complaints.
After thou hast enjoyed all life's best gifts
Thou now decayest. But because thou hast yearned
Always for what was absent, and despised
That which was present, life has glided from thee
Incomplete and unprofitable; so now
Ere thou didst look for it, at thy pillow Death
Has taken his stand, before thou canst depart
Satisfied with existence and replete.
Yet now resign all vanities that so ill
Befit thine age: come then, with a good grace
Rise and make room for others; for thou must."
Justly, I think, would she so plead with him,
Justly reproach and chide: for things grown old

Yield place and are supplanted evermore
By new, and each thing out of other things
Must be replenished; and to the black pit
Of Tartarus no man ever is consigned.
Matter is needed, that therefrom may grow
Succeeding generations: which yet all,
When they have lived their life, shall follow thee.
Thus it is all have perished in past times
No less than thou, and shall hereafter perish.
So one thing out of another shall not cease
For ever to arise; and life is given
To none in fee, to all in usufruct.

Consider likewise how eternal Time's
Bygone antiquity before our birth
Was nothing to us. Nature then holds up
This past as a mirror for us of the time
To come after our death. Is aught visible
Therein so appalling? aught that seems like gloom?
Is it not more untroubled than any sleep?

Yes, it is in this life that all those things
Exist for us, which fables tell are found
In Acheron's gulf. No wretched Tantalus,
Numbed by vain terror, quakes, as the tale goes,
Beneath a huge rock hanging in the air;
But in life rather an empty fear of gods
Oppresses mortals; and the fall they dread
Is that fall which Fortune may bring to each.
Nor into Tityos lying in Acheron
Do vultures eat their way, nor verily
Could they find anything for their beaks to grope for
In that vast breast throughout perpetual time.
How vast soever his body's bulk extended,
Though not nine roods merely with outspread limbs
He covered, but the round of the whole earth,
Yet would he not be able to endure

Eternal pain, nor out of his own body
For ever provide food. But here for us
He is a Tityos, whom, while he lies
In bonds of love, torturing anxieties
Devour like rending birds of prey, or cares
Sprung from some other craving lacerate.
A living Sisyphus also we behold
In him who from the people fain would beg
The rods and cruel axes, and each time
Defeated and disconsolate must retire.
For to beg power, that vanity which never
Is truly given, and in pursuit thereof
To endure grievous toil continually,
This is to thrust uphill mightily straining
A stone which from the summit after all
Rolls bounding back down to the level plain.
Then again to be feeding evermore
A mind thankless by nature, and yet never
To fill it full and sate it with good things
(As do the seasons for us, when each year
They return bringing fruits and varied charms,
Yet never are we filled with life's delights),
This surely is what is told of those young brides[1]
Who must pour water into a punctured vessel,
Though they can have no hope to fill it full.
Cerberus and the Furies in like manner
Are fables and that world deprived of day
Where from its throat Tartarus belches forth
Horrible flames: which things in truth are not,
Nor can be anywhere. But there is in life
A dread of punishment for things ill done,
Terrible as the deeds are terrible;
And to expiate men's guilt there is the dungeon,
The awful hurling downward from the rock,
Scourgings, executioners and rackings,
The pitch, the torches and the metal plates.[2]

[1] The Danaids. [2] Instruments of torture.

And even if these be wanting, yet the mind
Conscious of guilt in its foreboding fear
Torments itself with goads and scorching whips,
Nor sees what end of misery there can be,
Nor what limit at length to punishment,
Nay dreads lest these same evils after death
Should prove more grievous. Thus does the life of fools
Become in truth an Acheron here on earth.

This too thou may'st say sometimes to thyself:
"Even the good king Ancus closed his eyes
To the light of day, who was so many times
Worthier than thou, unconscionable man.
Since then many others, kings and potentates
Who had dominion over mighty nations,
Have perished: and he too,[1] even he, who once
Across the great sea paved a path whereby
His legions might pass over, bidding them
Cross dry-shod the salt deeps, and to show scorn
Trampled upon the roaring of the waves
With horses, even he, bereft of light,
Forth from his dying body gasped his soul.
The Scipios' offspring, thunderbolt of war,
Terror of Carthage, gave his bones to the earth
As though he were the meanest household slave.
Consider too the inventors of wise thoughts
And arts that charm; consider the companions
Of the Heliconian sisters, among whom
Homer bears the sceptre without a peer;
Yet he now sleeps the same sleep as they all.
Likewise Democritus, when a ripe old age
Had warned him that the memory-stirring motions
Were waning in his mind, by his own act
Willingly offered himself up to death.
Even Epicurus died, when his life's light
Had run its course, he who in intellect

[1] Xerxes.

Surpassed the race of men, quenching the glory
Of all else, as the sun in heaven arising
Quenches the stars. Then wilt thou hesitate
And feel aggrieved to die? thou for whom life
Is well-nigh dead whilst yet thou art alive
And lookest on the light; thou who dost waste
Most of thy time in sleep, and waking snorest,
Nor ceasest to see dreams; who hast a mind
Troubled with empty terror, and ofttimes
Canst not discover what it is that ails thee,
When, poor besotted wretch, from every side
Cares crowd upon thee, and thou goest astray
Drifting in blind perplexity of soul."

If only men—even as they clearly feel
That weighing down their minds there is a load
Which with its heavy oppression wears them out—
Might learn too what the causes of it are,
And whence comes this great pile of misery
Crushing their breasts, they would not spend their lives,
As now so oft we see, none of them knowing
What it may be he wants, and seeking ever
By change of place to lay his burden down.
Oft he who is weary of home, from his great mansion
Will go forth, and then suddenly return,
Finding himself no happier abroad.
He posts to his villa galloping his ponies,
As though hurrying with help to a house on fire,
Yawns on the very threshold, nay sinks down
Heavily into sleep to seek oblivion,
Or even perhaps starts headlong back to town.
In this way each man flies from his own self;
Yet from that self in fact he has no power
To escape: he clings to it in his own despite,
And loathes it too, because, though he is sick,
He perceives not the cause of his disease:
Which if he could but comprehend aright,

Each would put all things else aside and first
Study to learn the nature of the world,
Since 'tis our state during eternal time,
Not for one hour merely, that is in doubt,
That state wherein mortals will have to pass
The whole time that awaits them after death.

Moreover, what base craving for mere life
Is this, that can so potently compel us
In anxious perils to feel such dismay?
For indeed certain is the end of life
That awaits mortals; nor can death be shunned:
Meet it we must. Furthermore in the same
Pursuits and actions do we pass our days
For ever, nor may we by living on
Forge for ourselves any new form of pleasure;
But what we crave, while it is absent, seems
To excel all things else; then, when 'tis ours,
We crave some other thing, gaping wide-mouthed,
Always possessed by the same thirst of life.
What fortune future time may bring, we know not,
Nor what chance has in store for us, nor yet
What end awaits us. By prolonging life
No least jot may we take from death's duration;
Naught may we steal away therefrom, that so
Haply a less long while we may be dead.
Therefore as many ages as you please
Add to your life's account; yet none the less
Will that eternal death be waiting for you;
And not less long will that man be no more,
Whose life has reached its end today, than he
Who has died many months and years ago.

BOOK IV

Roaming the pathless haunts of the Pierides
Never yet trodden by the foot of man,
Joyfully I approach those virgin springs
And drink deep; joyfully do I pluck new flowers
And gather for my head a glorious crown
From lawns whence never have the Muses yet
Enwreathed the brows of any: first because
Lofty is the doctrine I expound, essaying
To liberate the mind from strangling knots
Of superstition: next because I write
Poetry so luminous on a theme so dark,
Colouring all things with the Muses' charm:
Since that too, surely, is not without good reason.
For as physicians, when they would make children
Drink nauseous wormwood, first will smear the cup
All round the rim with the sweet yellow juice
Of honey, so that the children's trustful age
May be deluded so far as the lips,
And meanwhile may drink down the bitter draught
Of wormwood, though beguiled, yet not betrayed,
But rather by such means may be restored
To health and strength; so I too now—since often
To those who have not handled it this doctrine
Seems somewhat bitter, and the multitude
Shrinks from it with repulsion—I have chosen
To set our doctrine forth in musical
Pierian song to please you, seasoning it
As though with the sweet honey of the Muses,
If haply by such means I might avail
To hold your mind attentive to my verses,
Till you shall clearly apprehend the whole
Nature of things, and feel how it profits you.

Now since I have demonstrated of what kind
Are the beginnings of all things, and how
Varying are the divers shapes wherein
They are flying onward of their own free will
Driven in eternal motion, and in what way
Out of these can be formed each several thing;
And since I have shown what is the mind's nature,
And of what elements it is composed
In vigorous union with the body, and how
It is dissevered thence, and so returns
Into its first-beginnings; I will now
Begin to explain to you, what most urgently
Concerns this theme, that there are what we call
Idols of things.[1] Now these, like films stripped off
From the surface of things, flit through the air
Forward and backward: it is these moreover
That terrify our minds, encountering us
Both when we are awake and in our sleep,
When often we behold strange shapes and idols
Of those now reft of light, which many a time
Have startled us in horror while we lay
Relaxed in slumber. This will I now explain,
Lest by chance we should think that souls break loose
From Acheron, or that ghosts flit abroad
Among the living, or that something of us
Can still be left behind after our death,
When both the body and the mind alike
Have been destroyed, and taken their departure
Into their own several first-beginnings.

I say therefore that semblances of things
And tenuous shapes are thrown off from their surface,
Which may be called a sort of film, or rind,
Because the image bears a look and form
Like to that body, whatsoe'er it be,

[1] To translate the Greek word εἴδωλον, Lucretius uses three words, *simulacrum* (idol), *effigies* (semblance), and *imago* (image).

Whence it is shed and goes its way: which truth
From what follows the dullest wit may learn.
First of all, many among sensible things
Throw off bodies, sometimes loosely diffused,
As oak-logs throw off smoke and fires heat;
Sometimes more close-knit and condensed, as when
The cicadas are wont in summer-time
To shed their sleek coats, or as calves at birth
Cast a caul from the surface of their body,
And likewise when the slippery serpent sloughs
His vesture among thorns; for often we see
The brambles laden with their fluttering spoils.
And since all this takes place, there must likewise
Be thrown off from the surface of each thing
A tenuous image. For why those coarser films
Should drop off and depart from things, rather
Than tenuous films, no reason can be whispered;
Especially since there are multitudes
Of minute bodies on the surface of things,
Which may be cast off in the self-same order
They had before, preserving so the shape's
Outline; and may be cast off far more quickly,
Because they are less liable to be hampered,
Being few and stationed in the foremost rank.
For certainly we may see many things
Throw off, not only from their inmost depths
As we described before, but from their surface,
And lavishly discharge with other things
Not seldom colour itself. And this is done
Ofttimes by awnings, yellow and red and purple,
When stretched over great theatres they flap
And flutter, spread abroad on masts and beams;
For then they tinge in their own colour and cause
The crowd seated below to flutter with them,
And all the stage's bravery and the rich-robed
Assemblage of the Fathers. And the more
The theatre's walls are closed by them all round,

The more does all the scene within them laugh
Bathed in gay beauty, as the light of day
Is straitened thus. And so, since from their surface
Canvasses throw off colour, all things else
Must throw off also tenuous semblances;
For they fling from the surface in each case.
There exist therefore sure traces of forms
That flit about on all sides, and possess
Such delicate thinness that they cannot singly
And separately be seen. Again, all smell,
Smoke, heat and other such-like things stream off
Diffusedly from objects, because, while
Risen from deep within they are coming forth,
They are torn asunder in their winding course,
And there are no straight openings to the paths
Whereby they may issue crowding forth together.
But when a tenuous film of surface-colour
Is thrown off, there is nothing that can rend it,
Since it lies ready in the foremost rank.
Lastly all idols that are seen by us
In mirrors, water, or any shining surface,
Must needs (since they possess a similar
Appearance to the things they represent)
Be formed of cast-off images of things.
Therefore thin shapes and semblances exist
Resembling things: these singly none can see;
Yet, when flung back by constantly renewed
Reflexion, they give back a visible image
From the surface of mirrors: and it seems
That in no other way could they be kept
So entire that figures should be given back
So very similar to each several thing.

Now listen and learn how tenuous must be
The nature of an image. And first of all,
Since atoms are so far beyond our senses,
And so much smaller than those things which first

Begin to be invisible to our eyes,
Now, to confirm this truth, in few words learn
How fine are the beginnings of all things.
First, there are sometimes living things so little
That their third part cannot be seen at all.
What must we think their entrails to be like?
What of the round ball of their heart or eye?
Their limbs, their members? How small must they be?
Further, what of the several first-beginnings
Whereof their soul and mind must be composed?
See you not how fine, how minute they are?
Again, all things which exhale from their body
A pungent smell, panacea, nauseous wormwood,
Rank southernwood and bitter centaury,
Any one of which, if you should chance to press it
Lightly between two fingers, will imbue them
With a strong smell—
. . . .
—but rather you should know
That idols of things are wandering abroad
Many in number and in many ways,
Without force, and exciting no sensation.

But lest perchance you think that only those
Idols, which are like things and come from things,
Are wandering abroad, know there exist
Others which are spontaneously begotten
And are self-formed in this part of the heaven
Which is called air. These shaped in many ways
Are borne along on high, and being fluid
Cease not to change their semblance, turning it
Into the outlines of all kinds of shapes;
Just as we sometimes see clouds quickly gathering
Aloft together, marring heaven's clear face,
While with their motion they caress the air:
For often visages of giants are seen
To float along, trailing a far-spread shadow;

Sometimes mighty mountains, or rocks torn off
From mountains, seem to go before and pass
Across the sun; then some huge beast appears
To lead and drag behind it other clouds.

Now will I show you with what ease and swiftness
Images are begotten, flowing off
And falling away from things perpetually.
For always is the outermost surface streaming
Away from things, that so they may discharge it.
And this, when it meets some things, passes through them,
And most of all through glass. But when it meets
Rough stones or solid wood, there it is straightway
So torn that it can give no idol back.
Yet when objects both bright and dense are placed
Across its path, as above all a mirror,
Neither of these things happens; for it neither
Can pass through, as through glass, nor yet be torn;
For the smoothness is careful to ensure
Its safety. Wherefore idols from such objects
Stream back to us. And however suddenly
At any moment you place any thing
Before a mirror, an image will appear.
Hence you may know that from their surfaces
Thin textures and thin shapes of things are flowing
Perpetually. Therefore many idols
In a brief time are begotten; and so the birth
Of such things is said rightly to be swift.
And as the sun in a brief space of time
Must shoot forth many rays, that the whole world
May ceaselessly be filled with light, even so
From things too in like manner every moment
Many idols of things must be discharged
In many ways, in all directions round;
Since towards whatever side we turn a mirror
To front their surfaces, things answer back
Within the mirror of like shape and colour.

Moreover, though the weather of the sky
Has been but now of limpid purity,
Quite suddenly it becomes so foul and turbid
That you might fancy that from every side
All its darkness had fled from Acheron
And filled full the great caverns of the sky;
So rapidly does the hideous night of clouds
Gather together, and faces of murk horror
Hang over us on high. Yet of these clouds
How small a fraction the image is, no man
Can tell, or give an account of this in words.

Now listen: with how swift a motion idols
Are travelling, and with what velocity
They are endowed as they glide through the air,
So that but a short space of time is spent
Over a long course, towards whatever spot
With diverse impulse they may each be speeding,
In verses few indeed yet sweetly tuned
Will I set forth, even as the swan's brief song
Is better than the clamouring of cranes
Spread through the cloudy sky of the south wind.
First of all we may frequently observe
That light things, made of minute elements,
Move rapidly. Of this kind is the light
And heat of the sun, because these are composed
Of minute first-beginnings, which as it were
Are knocked along, and do not hesitate
As they pass through the intervening air
Driven onward by a blow from those that follow;
For light by light is momently succeeded,
And flash by flash is goaded as in a team.
Therefore it must needs be that in like manner
Idols can course through inexpressible space
In a moment of time; firstly because
Behind them is a tiny cause, to impel
And drive them onward; next because they move

With so rapid a lightness; then again
Because, when thrown off, they possess a texture
So rare that they can penetrate easily
Through things of any kind, and as it were
Percolate through the air that intervenes.
Again, if those small bodies that are thrown forth
From the inmost depths of things, as is the light
And heat of the sun, are seen in a brief moment
To glide and spread themselves throughout the whole
Expanse of heaven, to fly o'er sea and land
And flood the sky, what then of those which stand
Ready in the front rank, when they are flung forth,
And there is naught to hinder their discharge?
Do you not see that they must needs travel
More swiftly and further, racing through many times
The extent of space in the same period
Which the sun's light needs to pervade the sky?
This too above all seems sure evidence
Of the swift motion with which idols of things
Are carried onward, that so soon as ever
A bright surface of water has been spread
In the open air, at once, if heaven be starry,
The serene constellations of the firmament,
Within the water gleaming, answer back.
Do you not then see in how brief a moment
An image from the coasts of aether drops
Down to the coasts of earth? Therefore again
And yet again I say, you must admit
That bodies are sent forth with power to strike
The eyes and provoke vision. Odours too
Perpetually stream off from certain things,
Just as from rivers cold, heat from the sun,
From the sea's waves devouring spray that eats
Into walls near the shore. Then various sounds
Are flying through the air unceasingly.
Moreover a salt-savoured moisture often
Comes into our mouth when we walk by the sea;

And when from close by we are watching wormwood
Being dissolved and mixed, a bitter taste
Assails our sense. In so constant a stream
From all things various effluences are passing
And being dispersed abroad on every side;
And no delay, no respite in this flow
Is ever granted, since continually
We have sensation, and may always see,
Smell, and perceive the sound of all such things.

Again, since a shape handled in the dark
Is known to be the same as what is seen
In the bright light of day, it needs must be
That touch and sight are stirred by the same cause.
If therefore we take hold of something square,
And it excites our feeling in the dark,
What that is square will in the light be able
To reach our vision, except the square thing's image?
Hence, it is plain, images are the cause
Of seeing, and naught can be perceived without them.

Now what I call idols of things are travelling
Everywhere, being flung forth and dispersed
On all sides; but because we can perceive them
With our eyes only, therefore it comes to pass
That to whatever side we turn our sight,
There all things strike it with their shape and colour.
And how far each thing may be distant from us,
It is the image gives us power to see
And the means to distinguish; for so soon
As it is thrown off, straightway it pushes forward
And drives along all the air which intervenes
Between itself and the eyes; thus all that air
Goes streaming through our eyeballs, as it were
Brushing the pupils, and so passes through.
Thus do we come to see how far each thing
Is distant; and the more the amount of air

Driven before the image, and the longer
The breeze whereby our eyes are brushed, the further
Each different thing is seen to be removed.
Now you must know that these events take place
With extreme quickness, so that we perceive
At the same moment both what a thing is like
And how far distant. Herein by no means
Must it be deemed strange, that whereas the idols
That strike the eyes can never one by one
Be seen, the things themselves should be perceived.
For when with gradual force the wind is beating us,
Or sharp cold streams on us, we are not wont
To feel each single particle of that wind,
Or of that cold, but rather the whole at once;
And then we perceive blows are being dealt
Upon our body, just as though some object
Were beating us and giving us the sensation
Of its own body beyond. Again, whenever
We strike a stone with a toe, we merely touch
The outmost surface-colour of the stone;
Yet by our touch we do not feel this colour,
But rather from within its lower depths
We feel the very hardness of the stone.

Now listen, and learn why the image should be seen
Beyond the mirror; for assuredly
We see it there withdrawn to an inner depth.
It is the same as with those real things
Which are viewed through a doorway, when it offers
An open prospect through itself, allowing
Many things to be seen outside the house.
That vision also is brought about by two
Different air-streams. First in such a case
The air inside the door-posts is perceived,
Then follow the folding doors to right and left;
Next the light from without brushes the eyes,
And with it a second air; then those real things

Which are viewed through the doors. Just so, when first
The mirror's image has discharged itself,
While it is coming towards our sight, it pushes
And drives along before it all the air
Which intervenes between itself and the eyes,
Enabling us to perceive all this air
Before we see the mirror. But no sooner
Have we also perceived the mirror itself,
At once the image which goes forth from us
Reaches the mirror, whence it is flung back
And returns to our eyes, driving and rolling
In front of it a second air, and makes us
See this before itself; and for this reason
It seems so far withdrawn beyond the mirror.
Wherefore again and yet again I assert,
There is no cause to wonder why this happens
Both in the case of those things seen through doors,
And of those too which send a vision back
From a mirror's surface, since in either case
It is all brought to pass by the two airs.
Also the right side of our body appears
In mirrors on the left, because the image,
When it has reached and struck the mirror's plane,
Is not turned round unaltered, but is dashed
Straight backward, just as if one were to take
A plaster mask ere it was dry, and fling it
Against a pillar or beam, and it should straightway,
Preserving still its former shape reversed,
Be dashed backward, moulding itself anew.
Thus what was the right eye will now become
Left, and the left in turn will become right.
An image also may be handed on
From mirror to mirror, so that even five
Or six idols may often be produced.
And thus whatever things may chance to lurk
Concealed in the recesses of a house,
However deeply and tortuously secluded,

May yet, by means of several mirrors, all
Be brought out thence through winding passages,
And so be seen to be within the house.
So surely does the image shine across
From mirror to mirror; and what has been presented
As left, is changed to right; then it comes back
And is turned round to what it was before.
Moreover all such mirrors as are flanked,
With a like curvature to our own flanks,
Send back to us idols whose right corresponds
To our own right, either because the image
Is thrown across from one part of the mirror
To another, then, being twice dashed off, flies back to us;
Or else because, when it arrives, the image
Is wheeled round, since the curved shape of the mirror
Teaches it how to turn about and face us.
Again when images step out and put
Their feet down simultaneously with ours,
Mimicking thus our gestures, you must think
The reason to be that from whatever part
Of a mirror you may move away, forthwith
No idols can come back to us from that part;
Since nature compels all things that recoil
Thrown back from things, to return at equal angles.

Bright things moreover the eyes avoid, and shun
To look upon. The sun will even blind them,
Should you persist in turning them towards him,
Because his force is great, and from on high
Through the clear air idols come heavily rushing
And strike the eyes, disordering their structure.
Again, any fierce brightness oftentimes
Scorches the eyes, because it has within it
Many seeds of fire, which penetrate within
And beget pain there. Furthermore, whatever
The jaundiced look at, becomes greenish yellow,
Because out of their bodies many seeds

Of greenish yellow are streaming forth to meet
The images of things; and many too,
Being mingled in their eyes, infect and tinge
All things with sallow hues. Again, we see
Out of a gloom things that are in the light,
Because, when the murky air of darkness first,
Being the nearer, has entered and possessed
Our open eyes, immediately there follows
A bright clear air, that purges them as it were,
And scatters the black shades of the first air.
For this bright air is many times more nimble,
And many times more subtle and powerful.
When this has filled with light and opened up
The passages of the eyes which the black air
Had obstructed before, then instantly
Those idols of things that are within the light
Follow and excite our eyes so that we see.
But we cannot conversely out of the light
See what is in the gloom, because the air
Of darkness, which is grosser, follows behind
Filling up all the openings, and obstructs
The passages of the eyes, prohibiting
The images of anything whatever
To be thrown into and so move the eyes.

Also, when from afar off we descry
The square towers of a town, they often appear
To be round for this cause, that every angle
Is seen by us from a distance to be flattened,
Or rather is not seen at all: its blow
Is lost, and the stroke does not reach our sight,
Because, while the idols travel through much air,
That air by frequent buffetings compels
Their strokes to become blunt. When all the angles
Alike have in this way escaped our sense,
The stone structures seem rounded as by a lathe;
Nevertheless they do not look like things

That stand close to us and are really round,
Though somewhat similar in a shadowy fashion.

Likewise our shadow seems to move in the sun
Following our steps and mimicking our gestures,
If you believe that air deprived of light
Can walk, following men's motions and their gestures;
For that which we are wont to call shadow
Can be naught else but air devoid of light.
Doubtless because the ground in certain places
Successively is deprived of the sun's light
Wherever we obstruct it as we move,
While the part of the ground which we have left
Is filled again with light, therefore what was
The shadow of our body seems to follow us
In a direct line the whole time unchanged.
For the sun's light is ever pouring down
In new rays, and the old are perishing
Like wool drawn into a flame. Therefore the ground
Is easily robbed of light, and again filled,
As from itself it washes the black shadows.

And yet we do not grant that the eyes are cheated
One whit here; for their task is to observe
In what place there is light, in what there is shadow.
But whether or not the lights are still the same;
And whether it may be the same shadow
That first was here and now is passing thither;
Or whether what we said not long before
Be not rather the truth; there is naught else
But the mind's reasoning can determine this:
For the eyes have no power to recognize
The nature of things. Beware then how you fasten
Upon the eyes this frailty of the mind.
The ship on which we are sailing moves along
While it seems to stand still, whereas another
That remains moored is thought to be passing by:

And hills and fields seem to be fleeing astern,
As past them our ship speeds, winged with spread sail.
The stars all seem as though they were at rest,
Fixed in the vaults of ether; yet are they all
In ceaseless motion, since they are ever rising
And ever revisiting their far-off settings
When they have traversed heaven with their bright bodies.
And in like manner sun and moon appear
To remain in one place; yet simple fact
Shows that they move. And mountains rising up
Afar off from the sea's midst, though between them
There opens out a passage wide and free
For fleets to sail through, yet seem to be joined
Into a single island. The hall seems
To whirl about and columns to race round,
When children have ceased from turning round themselves,
So much so that they scarcely may believe
That the whole structure is not threatening
To tumble down upon them. Again, when nature
Begins to raise on high the sun's light, red
With tremulous fires, and lift it above the mountains,
Those hills o'er which the sun seems to you then
To stand, and blazing close at hand to touch them
With his own fire, are yet scarce distant from us
Two thousand arrow-flights, nay often scarce
Five hundred javelin-casts: yet between these
And the sun there are lying vast sea-levels
Spread out below the huge coasts of the sky,
And many thousand lands there are between them
Inhabited by peoples manifold
And tribes of beasts. Moreover a pool of water
No deeper than one finger-breadth, which lies
Between the stones of a paved street, will offer
A view beneath the earth to a depth as vast
As the high gaping mouth of heaven opens
Above the earth; so that you seem to look
Down on the clouds and see the heavenly bodies

Wondrously gulfed in a sky below the earth.
Again, when our swift horse has come to a stand
In the middle of a stream, and we look down
Upon the hurrying waters of the river,
It seems as though some force were carrying
Sideways the body of the standing horse
And rapidly thrusting it up the stream;
And towards whatever point we turn our eyes,
All things appear to move and drift along
In just the same direction as the horse.
Again, though a portico runs in straight lines
And stands throughout its whole extent supported
On equal columns, yet when its whole length
Is viewed from the top end, it gradually
Contracts to the apex of a narrowing cone,
Completely joining roof to floor, and right
To left, until it has drawn all together
Into the point where the cone vanishes.
To sailors on the sea the sun appears
To rise out of the waves, and in the waves
To sink and hide his light; and this is natural,
Since they behold naught else but water and sky.
You must not suppose lightly that the senses
May be discredited on every side.
Then to those unacquainted with the sea
Vessels in harbour appear to be deformed,
And their poops, as they rest upon the water,
Seem to be broken. For all parts of the oars
That are raised up above the sea are straight,
And straight are the rudders in their upper half;
But all that is submerged below the water
Seems to be broken back and twisted round,
Sloping up and returning towards the top,
Bent backward till it almost seems to float
Upon the water's surface. And when winds
Are carrying in the night-time scattered clouds
Across the sky, then the bright constellations

Seem to be gliding against the rack, and travelling
Above it along paths different far
From their true course. Again, if a hand be placed
Beneath our eye and press it from below,
It comes to pass through a certain trick of sense
That all things which we look at appear then
To be doubled as we look; double the lights
For each flame-flowering lamp; the furniture
Double throughout the mansion in twin sets;
Men's faces double with two bodies each.
Moreover, when sleep has bound fast our limbs
In sweet slumber, and our whole body is sunk
In profound rest, yet it then seems to us
As though we were awake and moved our limbs,
And in the blind darkness of night we think
That we behold the daylight and the sun,
And though confined within a room, we seem
To be changing sky and sea, rivers and mountains,
And to cross plains on foot, to hear noises
Though night's austere silence prevails all round,
And to be uttering speech though we say nothing.
Many things of this sort we see besides
In marvellous fashion, which all as it were
Seek to destroy the credit of our senses:
But all in vain; because the greatest number
Of these illusions cheat us on account
Of mental suppositions, which we add
Ourselves, holding as seen things which the senses
Have never seen. For nothing is more hard
Than to distinguish clear from doubtful facts,
Which straightway the mind adds on of itself.

Furthermore, if a man believe that nothing
Is known, he does not know whether this even
Can be known, since he admits that he knows nothing.
I decline then to argue against one
Who puts his head where his feet ought to be.

Yet even were I to grant that he knows this,
I would still ask him: since he has never yet
Seen any truth in things, whence does he know
What either knowing or not knowing are?
What has produced the concept[1] of the true
And of the false? and what has proved the doubtful
To differ from the certain? You will find
That from the senses first has been produced
The concept of the true, and that the senses
Can never be refuted. For that thing
Must first be found which is more worthy of trust
And of itself is able to confute
Things that are false by true things. Well now, what
Ought we to deem more worthy of our trust
Than sense? Shall reason, founded on false sense,
Have power to contradict those very senses
On which it is wholly founded? For unless
They are true, all reason likewise becomes false.
Or shall the ears be able to disprove
The eyes, or the touch the ears? Again shall taste
Question this touch, or the nostrils confute,
Or the eyes convict it? Not so, I presume.
For each sense has its separate faculty
Assigned to it apart, each its own power;
And therefore it must be that we perceive
By one sense what is soft or cold or hot,
By another sense the various colours of things,
And so see all that goes along with colour.[2]
Taste also has its faculty apart;
Odours arise from one sense, sounds from another.
And therefore it must needs be that the senses
Cannot convict each other. Nor again
Will they be able to disprove themselves,
Since always equal credit must be allowed them.
What therefore has at any time appeared

[1] See note on II. 744, p. 70.
[2] Form, outline, volume, etc.

True to the senses, *is* true. And if reason
Shall prove unable to explain the cause
Why things, that close at hand were square, should seem
To be round at a distance, still 'tis better,
Failing to find the reason, to account
Erroneously for the cause of either shape,
Than to let slip anywhere from your grasp
Facts that are manifest, and so, destroying
The origins of all belief, tear up
The whole of those foundations whereon rest
Life and existence. For then would not only
All reason come to ruin; life itself
Would collapse straightway, unless you should resolve
To trust the senses, avoiding precipices
And all else of this sort that should be shunned,
And following what is opposite to such things.
Thus all those hosts of words are empty of meaning
Which have been ranked and marshalled against the senses.
Lastly, as in a building, if the rule
First used be warped, if the square be untrue
And swerve from the straight line, if anywhere
Your level sag the least jot, the whole house
Must needs be faultily built, crooked and warped,
Sloping, leaning forwards, leaning backwards,
Without symmetry, so that some parts seem
Already about to fall, others are falling,
All ruined by the first wrong measurements;
In the same way your reasoning about things
Will of necessity prove warped and false,
Whenever it is based upon false senses.

And now to show you how the other senses
Perceive each its own object, is the path,
By no means stony, that awaits me still.

First of all, every sound and voice is heard
When they have made their way into the ears

And struck the sense of hearing with their body.
For voice also and sound you must admit
Are bodily, since they can strike the senses.
Moreover the voice often scrapes the throat,
And a cry, passing forth, will make the windpipe
More rough; for when first elements of voices,
Gathering in greater throngs, begin to issue
Abroad through the strait passage, you must know
The door too of the mouth, so crammed, is scraped.
Thus beyond doubt voices and words consist
Of bodily elements, with power to hurt.
Nor can you fail to notice how much body
Is taken away, and how much is withdrawn
From a man's strength and sinews by a speech
Continued without pause from the first gleam
Of morning to the shadow of black night,
And most of all when it has been poured forth
With the whole force of his lungs. Therefore a voice
Must needs be bodily, since by much speaking
A man will lose a portion from his body.
Roughness of voice moreover comes from roughness
Of atoms, just as smoothness is begotten
Of smoothness. Nor are the atoms of like shape
Which pierce the ears, when with deep hollow murmur
The trumpet bellows, and when the barbarous
Berecynthian pipe re-echoes with harsh din,
And when swans from the rushing streams of Helicon
With mournful voice raise their melodious dirge.

When therefore from deep down within our body
We force these voices forth, and shoot them abroad
Straight through the mouth, then does the mobile tongue,
That deft artificer of words, divide
And mould them, and the structure of the lips
In its turn gives them shape. So when the space
Traversed from start to finish by each voice
Is not too long, the words themselves must also

Be clearly heard, and syllable by syllable
Distinguished; for each sound will then preserve
Its structure and its shape. But if too wide
Be the intervening distance, then the words
Must be tangled together, as they pass
Through much air, and the voice must be disordered
In its flight through the breezes. Thus it is
That you can hear a sound, yet not distinguish
What is the meaning of the words; so tangled
And hampered is the voice when it arrives.
Again one word, sped from the herald's mouth,
Often awakes the ears of a whole crowd.
Thus one voice suddenly into many voices
Becomes dispersed, since it divides itself
Among the many separate ears, imprinting
On each the form and clear sound of the word.
But of the voices, some, that do not fall
Directly on the ears, are carried past
And perish scattered fruitlessly in the air;
While others, striking upon solid places,
Rebound and give the sound back, and at times
Delude us with the echo of a word.
When you perceive this clearly, you may explain
To yourself and others, how in lonely places
Rocks may give back similar forms of words
In the same order, when among darkened hills
We seek straying companions, with loud shouts
Calling upon them scattered on all sides.
I have known places give back even six
Or seven voices, when but one was uttered;
In such wise to and fro did hill to hill
Toss back the words and iterate the echo.
Such haunts the neighbours fancy that goat-footed
Satyrs and Nymphs inhabit; and they tell
How there are Fauns, by whose night-wandering clamour
And jocund revels, so they assert, the voiceless
Silences oft are broken; and sounds of strings

Are heard, and sweet sad ditties, which the pipe,
Touched by the fingers of the melodist,
Pours forth. They tell too how the peasant-folk
Through the whole countryside listen, while Pan,
Tossing the pine-crown wreathed about his head,
That is half-man's, half beast's, with curved lip oft
Runs o'er the open reeds, that ceaselessly
The pipes may pour their woodland music forth.
Of many such-like prodigies and portents
They tell, lest they should haply be supposed
To inhabit solitudes, which even the Gods
Have abandoned. For this reason, or may be
Moved by some other cause, they bandy about
Such fabulous wonders, even as all mankind
Are over-greedy of ear-tickling tales.

Lastly, we need not wonder how it is
That voices penetrate and strike the ears
Through places which prevent the eyes from seeing
Visible things. Thus often we perceive
A conversation even behind closed doors,
Doubtless because a voice can pass uninjured
Through tortuous passages in things, while idols
Refuse to pass: for they are torn to shreds,
Unless they glide through passages that are straight,
Like those of glass through which every image flies.
A voice moreover is distributed
In all directions, since sounds are begotten
One from another, once a single sound,
Issuing, has sprung asunder into many;
As often a spark of fire will scatter itself
Into fragments of fire. And so places,
Though hidden far from sight, are filled with voices,
Vibrating on all sides and stirred with sound.
But all idols proceed in a straight course
When once discharged; and therefore none can see
Beyond a wall, but can hear voices through it.

And yet even this voice, while through the walls
Of houses it is passing, becomes blunted
And penetrates our ears confusedly,
And we seem to hear sound rather than words.

Nor do the tongue and palate, by whose means
We perceive flavour, cause more difficulty
Or need fresh explanation. First of all
We perceive flavour in the mouth, whenever
We press it forth while we are chewing food,
Just as if one were squeezing with the hand,
Till it be dry, a sponge soaked full of water.
And then whatever we press forth is all
Distributed through the cavities of the palate
And intricate passages of the porous tongue.
So when the particles of oozing flavour
Are smooth, then do they touch caressingly
And stroke caressingly all round about
The moist exuding chamber of the tongue.
But on the other hand, just in proportion
As each particle is endowed with roughness,
They prick the sense and tear it in their onslaught.
Next, the pleasure that comes from flavour reaches
The palate, but no further: when the food
Has dropped right down the throat, there is no pleasure
While it is all distributing itself
Throughout the frame. Nor does it make the least
Difference with what food the body is nourished,
So long as what you take you can digest
And distribute throughout the frame, preserving
An even state of moisture in the stomach.

Now will I make clear and intelligible
How there are different foods for different creatures,
And why that which for some is bitter and nauseous,
May yet seem to be passing sweet to others;
And why in such things the discrepancy

And difference is so great, that what to one
Is food, to others may be virulent poison.
Thus there is also a serpent, that when touched
By human spittle, wastes away and perishes
By gnawing itself to death. Again, to us
Hellebore is rank poison, but makes goats
And quails grow fat. That you may understand
How this can happen, first you must remember
What we have said already, that the seeds
Contained in things are mixed in manifold ways.
Further, all living creatures that take food,
Even as to outward view they are unlike,
And as the external contour of their limbs
Bounds each diversely according to its kind,
So too they are formed of seeds of varying shape.
Since further the seeds differ, so likewise
Must the intervals be different, and the channels,
Which we call passages, in all the limbs,
And therefore in the mouth and palate too.
Some then must needs be smaller, some more large,
Triangular in some creatures, square in others,
While many must be round, some many-angled
In many ways. For just as the proportion
And motions of the atomic shapes require,
So the shapes of the passages must differ;
And as the texture varies of the walls
That bound them, so too must the channels vary.
When therefore what is sweet to some, to others
Proves bitter, then for one to whom 'tis sweet,
It must be that the smoothest bodies enter
The palate's cavities with caressing touch,
Whereas with those to whose taste the same food
Seems bitter, doubtless it is the rough barbed atoms
That penetrate the pores. From these examples
It should be easy now to understand
Each separate case. Thus when from superabundance
Of bile someone has been attacked by fever,

Or a violent disease has been aroused
In any other way, then the whole body
Is deranged, and the positions of the atoms
Are then all changed; so that the particles
Which once were suitable to cause sensation,
Are now no longer suitable; while those others
Are better fitted which can penetrate
The pores, and there beget a sour sensation.
Both kinds indeed are mingled in the flavour
Of honey, as I have shown you often before.

Now listen, and I will show you how the impact
Of smell touches the nostrils. First there must be
Many things whence a varying flux of scents
Rolls and streams on; and these we must believe
Are sent forth streaming and scattered on all sides.
But some smells better suit some creatures, others
Suit others, owing to their unlike atoms.
And therefore by the scent of honey, bees
Are drawn from any distance through the air,
As vultures are by carrion: and so too
The onward reaching power of scent in dogs
Leads them whithersoever the wild beasts
Have fled on cloven hoof; and the white goose,
Preserver of the citadel of Rome's race,
Perceives from far away the scent of man.
Thus diverse smells assigned to diverse creatures
Lead each to its own food, and compel each
To recoil from nauseous poison; and thus it is
That all the tribes of wild beasts are preserved.

Nor yet is this found only in smells and flavours,
But the forms of things also, and their colours
Are not all so well suited to the senses
Of all, that some will not distress the sight
More than will others. Ravening lions indeed
Cannot confront and gaze upon the cock,

Who is wont to clap the night out with his wings
And with shrill voice to summon dawn: so surely
Do they at once bethink themselves of flight,
Doubtless because in the body of a cock
Are certain seeds, which, when they have been discharged
Into the eyes of lions, pierce right through
Their pupils, causing a pain so sharp, they cannot,
Fierce though they are, endure to face those seeds.
And yet they have no power to hurt our eyes,
Either because they do not enter in,
Or because, though they enter, a free passage
Out of the eyes is given them, that they may not
By lingering hurt the eyes in any part. 721

Now of all the various smells that stir the nostrils 687
One may well reach much further than another;
Yet is no smell carried so far as sound,
Or as a voice, to say naught of those things
Which strike the eyeballs and stir vision there.
For scent comes wandering slowly on, and soon
Dies away, yielding itself gradually
To be dispersed into the winds of air;
First because, issuing from deep down within,
Not easily from each thing may it be discharged
(For the fact that odours stream off and depart
From the inner parts of things, is shown by this,
That all are found to have a stronger smell
When broken, when pounded, when dissolved by fire);
Next because it is evident that smell
Is formed of larger elements than voice,
Since odours do not penetrate stone walls,
Which voice and sound will commonly pass through.
So also you will find it not so easy
To trace out in what quarter a thing which smells
Is situated; for the blow grows cool
As it loiters through the air, nor does it rush
Hot to the senses with its news of things.

For this cause dogs will often lose the scent
And search in vain for the traces of their prey.

Listen and learn now what things move the mind,
And in a few words hear whence come those things
That enter into it. First of all I say
That idols of things are wandering about
Many in many ways on all sides round,
So thin that, when they meet, they easily
Unite in the air, like cobweb or gold-leaf.
For these are of a texture far more thin
Than are those idols which assail the eyes
And provoke vision; since these enter in
Through the pores of the body, and arouse
The tenuous substance of the mind within,
And so provoke sensation. Thus it is
We behold Centaurs and the limbs of Scyllas,
And Cerberus-like faces of dogs, and idols
Of those who are dead, whose bones the Earth embraces;
Since idols of all kinds are everywhere
Travelling about, some that spontaneously
Are formed within the air, some that are all
Thrown off from various things, others again
Made and compounded from the shapes of these.
For certainly no image of a Centaur
Is formed from one that lives, since there has never
Existed living creature of such kind:
But when the images of a horse and man
Have chanced to meet, they at once easily
Cling to each other, as I said before,
Because of their fine substance and thin texture.
In the same way are formed all other things
Of this kind. And when these, through exceeding lightness,
Are travelling swiftly, as I showed before,
Any one of these subtle images
Easily stirs the mind by a single stroke;
For mind too is thin, and marvellously mobile.

That this must be what happens, you may learn
Easily from what follows. Since the one
Is like the other—what with the mind we see,
And what with the eyes—they both must come about
In a like way. Now therefore since I have shown
That I perceive a lion, let us say,
By means of idols that provoke the eyes,
We may be sure that the mind too is moved
In a like way, and that by means of idols
It sees a lion, or aught else, neither more
Nor less than do the eyes, save that the idols
Which it perceives are thinner. Nor when sleep
Has prostrated the body, does the mind's
Intelligence wake for any other cause
But that these idols that provoke our minds
Are the same that provoke them when we are waking;
So much so that we seem in very truth
To look on him who has abandoned life,
Whom death and the earth hold now within their power.
Now Nature constrains this to come to pass
Because the bodily senses are all checked
And at rest then throughout the limbs, and so
Cannot refute what is false by true facts.
In sleep moreover memory lies inert
And torpid, nor does it protest that he
Whom the mind deems it is beholding alive,
Has long been in the power of death and lethe.
For the rest, it is not wonderful that idols
Should move, and rhythmically toss their arms
And other limbs; for in our sleep an image
Seems at times to do this; because in truth
When the first image vanishes, and then
A second has been born in a different pose,
That former seems now to have changed its gesture.
We must of course conceive this to take place
Quite rapidly; such is the speed, so great
The store of things, so great in any single

Perceptible moment is the store of particles
Out of which the supply may be renewed. 776

Moreover it sometimes happens that an image 818
Of the same kind is not supplied, but what
Before was a woman, seems changed to a man
There in our grasp; or else that face and age
Have become different. But sleep and oblivion
See to it that we feel no wonder at this. 822

And here there are many problems, many doubts 777
To make clear, if we wish to explain the truth.
First we must ask, why, when we have the fancy
To think of anything, straightway our mind
Thinks of that very thing. Do the idols wait
Upon our will, and so soon as we will it
Does some image present itself to us,
Be it sea, or earth, or heaven that we desire?
Gatherings of men, processions, banquets, battles—
Does Nature create and make ready for us
All such things at command? and that although
In the same place there may be other minds
Thinking of things that are all quite different.
Then again, when in dreams we behold idols
Advance in rhythm and move their supple limbs,
Flinging out swiftly each supple arm in turn
And with foot answering hand see them repeat
The same gesture—why then, these idols doubtless
Are steeped in art, and wander about well-trained
So that at night-time they can play such games.
Or will not rather this be the true reason?
Because within one time-space which our senses
Perceive, that is, while but one sound is uttered,
Many latent time-spaces are contained,
Which reasoning discovers to exist,
Therefore at once, within however small
A space of time you like, the various idols

Are at hand ready in each several place:
Such is the speed, so great the store of things;
For when a first image vanishes, and then
A second has been born in a different pose,
The former seems now to have changed its gesture.
And since they are thin, the mind can see distinctly
Those alone which it strains itself to see;
So all the others vanish, save those only
For which the mind has been preparing itself.
Moreover it prepares itself expecting
To behold that which follows on each thing;
Which therefore it does behold. Do you not see
How the eyes also, when they are endeavouring
To perceive something that is tenuous,
Strain themselves and prepare themselves, and how
We cannot without this perceive distinctly?
And even when things are plainly visible,
You may observe that, if you do not turn
Your mind that way, it will be just as though
The object all the time were far away
In the remote distance. What wonder then
If the mind loses all else save those things
In which its whole attention is absorbed?
Moreover from small evidence we draw
Deductions far too large, and so entangle
Our minds within the snare of self-delusion.

Herein you should most earnestly desire
To escape the fault, and with foresighted fear
Shun the error of supposing the bright lights
Of the eyes to have been created to the end
That we might see; or that the sloping shins
And thighs, based on the feet, have power to bend
Only that we may step out with long strides;
Or again that on sturdy upper arms
Forearms were fitted, and on either side
Ministering hands were given us, that so

We might perform whatever life should need.
These and other conjectures of like sort
Are all due to fallacious reasoning
And put effect for cause; since in our bodies
Nothing was ever born that we might use it,
But that which has been born begets the use.
For neither before eyes were born did seeing
Exist, nor speech before the tongue was made;
But rather the creation of the tongue
Was long anterior to discourse, and ears
Were made a great while before sound was heard;
And all the limbs existed, I suppose,
Before a use for them was known, and so
Could not have grown in order to be used.
But on the other hand exchanging blows
In the close strife of battle, mangling bodies
And fouling limbs with gore, all this began
Long before gleaming missiles ever flew;
And Nature prompted men to avoid a wound
Or ever the left arm had learnt the art
Of using the protection of a shield.
Aye, and yielding to rest the tired body
Is older far than a soft-cushioned bed;
And quenching thirst began before cups were.
So these things, which through experience of life's needs
Were first discovered, we may well believe
To have been invented that they might be used.
Far otherwise are all those things which first
Themselves were born, then afterwards revealed
Their usefulness. Chief among these we find
The senses and the limbs. Wherefore again
And yet again I say, it is impossible
You should believe they could have been created
For the purpose of performing useful service.

Nor need we think it strange that it should be
The nature of every living creature's body

To require food. For indeed I have shown
That atoms stream off and depart from things
Many in many ways: but most numerous
Must those be that stream off from living creatures.
For because these are often in active motion,
And many particles are pressed forth in sweat
From deep within, many breathed out through their mouths
When they pant from exhaustion, for these causes
The body is rarefied, and its whole substance
Is undermined; and on this follows pain.
Food therefore is taken that it may support
The frame through which it spreads, and recreate
The strength, and so close up that open-mouthed
Desire for eating throughout limbs and veins.
Moisture too passes into all the parts
That demand moisture; and those particles
Of heat, crowding in multitudes, that set
Our belly ablaze, by the incoming liquid
Are scattered and extinguished like a fire,
So that dry heat may no more parch the frame.
Thus then is panting thirst washed from our body;
Thus is the hungry craving satisfied.

Now will I tell how it is we are able
To step out when we please, and how we have power
To move our limbs diversely, and what cause
Is wont to thrust forward the so great load
Of this our body. Do thou mark well my words.
Idols of walking first present themselves
To our mind and strike it, as we have said before.
Next comes the will; for no one can begin
To act in any way until his mind
Has seen beforehand what it wills to do.
What the mind sees beforehand, of that thing
Is formed an image. Therefore when the mind
Bestirs itself so that it wills to walk

And step forward, straightway it strikes the soul
Whose force is spread over the whole body
Through limbs and frame. And this is easily done,
For the soul is in close union with the mind.
Next the soul strikes the body in its turn,
And so little by little the whole mass
Is pushed forward and moves. Moreover then
The body becomes rarefied, and the air
(As it must do of course, being always mobile)
Passes and penetrates abundantly
Through the opened passages, and is thus dispersed
Into all the most minute parts of the body.
Here then two causes acting severally
Bring about that the body is carried on
As a ship by sails and wind. Nor yet herein
Need it cause wonder that such tiny bodies
Can steer so great a body and turn about
Our whole weight. For indeed the wind, though fine
And of a subtle substance, drives and pushes
A mighty ship of mightily moving mass;
And one hand rules it, however swiftly it goes;
One helm steers it to any point you please.
Also by means of pulleys and tread-wheels
Machines can move many things of great weight
And lift them with slight effort from the ground.

Now in what ways sleep floods rest through our limbs,
And sets our bosoms free from the mind's cares,
In verses few indeed yet sweetly tuned
Will I set forth, even as the swan's brief song
Is better than the clamouring of cranes
Spread through the cloudy sky of the south wind.
Then give me subtle ears and a keen mind,
Lest you deny that what I say is possible,
And turn from me with a spirit that rejects
The words of truth, though it be you yourself
That are in error yet perceive it not.

First then sleep comes to pass when the soul's force
Has been dispersed throughout the frame, in part
Having been cast abroad and gone elsewhere,
While in part it has been thrust back, retreating
Deeper within the body; and then it is
That our limbs are unknit and fall relaxed.
For without doubt sensation exists in us
By the soul's operation: so when slumber
Hinders our sense from functioning, we then
Must suppose that our soul has been disturbed
And cast abroad: yet not all; else the body
Would lie steeped in the eternal chill of death.
Indeed, if no part of the soul were left
Hidden within the limbs, as fire lies hidden
Smothered under thick ash, whence could sensation
Suddenly be rekindled through the limbs,
As flame can spring up from a secret fire?

But in what manner this change comes to pass,
And by what cause the soul can be disturbed
And the body grow languid, I will unfold.
See to it lest I waste words on the winds.
First then the body on its outer side,
Being touched by breaths of the surrounding air,
Must needs be beaten upon and buffeted
By the air's repeated blows; and for this cause
All things almost are covered by a hide,
Or else by shells or callous skin or bark.
And when we breathe, this air at the same time,
As it is drawn in and exhaled, must beat
On the inner side no less. So since the body
Is buffeted from both sides, and since the blows
Make their way in through the small passages
To our body's primal parts and elements,
There takes place gradually throughout our limbs
A kind of breaking up: for the positions
Of the first elements both of body and mind

Become disordered. Next it comes to pass
That of the soul a part is forced abroad,
And a part retreats inward and hides there,
A third part too, dispersed throughout the frame,
Cannot remain united, nor by motion
Act and react; for nature barricades
All paths of meeting: therefore sense withdraws
Deep within, since the motions are all changed.
And as there is nothing to support the frame,
The body becomes feeble, and all the limbs
Grow languid: arms and eyelids droop; and often,
Even when a man is lying down, his hams
Give way beneath him and relax their strength.
Sleep follows also on food, because while food
Is being distributed through all the veins,
It operates with the same effect as air.
And that slumber is far the heaviest
Which you fall into when replete or tired,
Because the largest number of atoms then,
Bruised by much effort, have become disordered.
And for the same causes the soul in part
Is thrust more deeply inward, and likewise
Is forced out more abundantly, and becomes
More self-divided and dispersed within.

And generally to what pursuits soever
Each of us is attached and closely tied,
Or on whatever tasks we have been used
To spend much time, so that therein the mind
Has borne unwonted strain, in those same tasks
We mostly seem in sleep to be engaged.
Lawyers imagine they are pleading causes
Or drafting deeds; generals that they are fighting
In some pitched battle; mariners that they still
Are waging with the winds their lifelong war;
And I that I am toiling at my task,
Questioning evermore the nature of things,

And setting these discoveries forth in books
Written in our native tongue. And thus in general
Do all other pursuits and arts appear
To fill men's minds and mock them during sleep.
And with those who for many days together
Have watched stage shows with unremitting zeal,
We generally find that when they have ceased
To apprehend them with their senses, yet
Passages remain open in the mind
Through which the same idols of things may enter.
Thus the same sights for many days keep passing
Before their eyes, so that even when awake
They seem to be beholding figures dancing
And moving supple limbs; also their ears
Seem to be listening clear-toned melodies
Of the lyre's eloquent strings, while they behold
In fancy the same audience, the stage too,
Glowing with all its varied scenery.
So great is the influence of zeal and pleasure,
And of those tasks whereon not only men
Are wont to spend their energies, but indeed
All living animals. Thus you will see
Strong horses, when their limbs are lying at rest,
Nevertheless in slumber sweat and pant
Continually, and as though to win some prize
Strain their strength to the utmost, or else struggle
To start, as if the barriers were thrown open.
And often hunters' hounds while softly slumbering
Will yet suddenly toss their legs about
And utter hurried yelps, sniffing the air
Again and again, as though following the trail
Of wild beasts they have scented: and roused from sleep
They often chase the empty images
Of stags, as if they saw them in full flight,
Till having shaken their delusions off
They come back to themselves. But the mild brood
Of dogs reared in the house, will shake themselves

And start up from the ground, as if they saw
Unknown figures and faces. And the more savage
Each breed is, the more fierce must be its dreams.
Also in the night-time birds of various kinds,
Suddenly taking flight, trouble with wings
The groves of deities, when in gentle sleep
Hawks have appeared threatening them with havoc
Of battle, flying after them in pursuit.
Again the minds of men, which greatly labouring
Achieve great aims, will often during sleep
Act and perform the same. Kings take by storm,
Are made captive, join battle, cry aloud
As though assassinated then and there.
Many men struggle and utter groans in pain,
And as though mangled by a panther's fangs
Or savage lion's, fill the whole neighbourhood
With vehement clamourings. Many in their sleep
Discourse of great affairs, and often so
Have revealed their own guilt. Many meet death:
Many, as though falling with all their weight
From high cliffs to the ground, are scared with terror,
And like men reft of reason, hardly from sleep
Come to themselves again, with beating heart
And trembling limbs. Likewise a man will sit
Thirsting beside a river or pleasant spring
And gulp almost the whole stream down his throat.
Innocent children also, slumber-bound,
Often believe they are lifting up their dress
By a basin or earthen jar, and so will pour
The liquid, drained from their whole body, forth,
Soaking the gorgeous-hued magnificence
Of Babylonian coverlets. Then too,
To those into the currents of whose youth
For the first time seed is entering, when the ripe
Fulness of time has formed it in their limbs,
From without there come idols emanating
From some chance body, announcing a glorious face

And beautiful colouring, that excites and stirs
Those parts that have grown turgid with much seed,
So that oft, as if all things had been done,
The full tide overflows and stains their vesture.

This seed whereof we spoke is stirred in us
When first ripening age confirms our frame.
For different causes move and stimulate
Different things: from man the influence
Of man alone rouses forth human seed.
So soon as, thus dislodged, it has retired
From its abodes throughout the limbs and frame,
It withdraws from the whole body, and assembling
At certain places in the system, straightway
Rouses at last the body's genital parts.
These places, irritated, swell with seed;
And so the wish arises to eject it
Towards that whereto the fell desire tends;
While the body seeks that by which the mind
Is smitten by love. For all men generally
Fall towards the wound, and the blood will spirt forth
In that direction whence the stroke was dealt us;
And if he is at close quarters, the red drops
Sprinkle the foe. Thus he who has been struck
By the missiles of Venus (whether a boy
With womanish limbs launches the shaft, or else
Some woman darting love from her whole body),
Yearns towards that whereby he has been wounded,
And longs to unite with it, and shoot the stream
Drawn from the one into the other body;
For dumb desire gives presage of the pleasure.

This desire we call Venus: from it comes
Our Latin name for love;[1] and from this source
Has trickled first into the heart that drop
Of Venus' honeyed sweetness, followed soon

[1] Cupido.

By chilling care. For though that which you love
Be absent, yet are images of it present,
And its sweet name still haunts within your ears.
But it is wise to shun such images,
And scare off from you all that feeds your love,
Turning your mind elsewhere, and vent instead
Your gathering humours on some other body,
Rather than hold them back, set once for all
Upon the love of one, and so lay up
Care and unfailing anguish for yourself.
For the wound gathers strength and grows inveterate
By feeding, while the madness day by day
Increases, and the misery becomes heavier,
Unless you heal the first wounds by new blows,
And roving in the steps of vagrant Venus
So cure them while yet fresh, or can divert
To something else the movements of your mind.

Nor does the man who shuns love go without
The fruits of Venus; rather he makes choice
Of joys that bring no after-pain: for surely
The pleasure of intercourse must be more pure
For those that are heart-whole than for the love-sick.
For in the very moment of possession
The passion of lovers fluctuates to and fro,
Wandering undecidedly, nor know they
What first they would enjoy with eyes and hands.
What they have sought, they tightly press, and cause
Pain to the body, and often print their teeth
Upon the lips, and kiss with bruising mouths,
Because the pleasure is not unalloyed,
And there are secret stings which stimulate
To hurt that very thing, whate'er it be,
From which those germs of madness emanate.
But easily, while love lasts, Venus allays
Such pains; and soft delight, mingled therein,
Bridles their bites. For herein lies their hope,

That from that very body whence proceeds
Their burning lust, the flame may in turn be quenched,
Although Nature protests the opposite
Must happen, since this is the one sole thing
Whereof the more we have, so much the more
Must the heart be consumed by fell desire.
For food and drink are taken within the body;
And since they are wont to settle in fixed parts,
In this way the desire for water and bread
Is easily satisfied: but from the face
And beautiful colouring of man there enters
Nothing into the body to enjoy
Save tenuous images, a love-sick hope
Often snatched off by the wind. As when in sleep
A thirsty man seeks to drink, and no liquid
Is given to quench the burning in his limbs,
Yet he pursues the images of water,
Toiling in vain, and still thirsts, though he drink
In a rushing river's midst; even so in love
Venus deludes lovers with images:
For neither, gaze intently as they may,
Can bodies satiate them, nor with their hands
Can they pluck anything off from the soft limbs,
Aimlessly wandering over the whole body.
And when at last with limbs knit they enjoy
The flower of their age, when now the body
Presages rapture, and Venus is in act
To sow the fields of woman, eagerly
They clasp bodies and join moist mouth to mouth
With panted breath, imprinting lips with teeth—
In vain; for naught thence can they pluck away,
Nor each with the whole body entering pass
Into the other's body; for at times
They seem to wish and struggle so to do:
So greedily do they cling in the bonds of Venus,
While their limbs melt, enfeebled by the might
Of pleasure. Finally, when the gathered lust

Has burst forth from the frame, awhile there comes
A brief pause in their passion's violent heat.
Then returns the same madness: the old frenzy
Revisits them, when they would fain discover
What verily they desire to attain;
Yet never can they find out what device
May conquer their disease: in such blind doubt
They waste away, pined by a secret wound.

Consider too how they consume their strength
And are worn out with toiling; and consider
How at another's beck their life is passed,
How duties are neglected, reputation
Totters and grows sick. Meantime their substance
Vanishes and is changed to Babylonian
Coverlets; while upon the loved one's feet
Elegant Sicyonian slippers laugh.
Then doubtless big green-flashing emeralds
Are set in gold; and the sea-purple dress,
Worn out by constant use, imbibes the sweat
Of love's encounters. The wealth which their fathers
Had nobly gathered, becomes hair-ribbons
And head-dresses, or else maybe is turned
Into a long Greek gown, or stuffs of Alinda
And Ceos. Feasts with goodly broideries
And viands are prepared, games, numerous cups,
Unguents, crowns and festoons; but all in vain;
Since from the well-spring of delights some touch
Of bitter rises, to give pain amidst
The very flowers; either when the mind
Perchance grows conscience-stricken, and remorse
Gnaws it, thus to be spending a life of sloth,
And ruining itself in wanton haunts;
Or else because she has launched forth some word
And left its sense in doubt, some word that clings
To the hungry heart, and quickens there like fire;
Or that he fancies she is casting round

Her eyes too freely, or looking on some other,
And on her face sees traces of a smile.

When love is assured and fully prosperous,
These evils are experienced; but if love
Be crossed and hopeless, there are evils such
That you might apprehend them with closed eyes,
Beyond numbering; so that it is wiser,
As I have taught you, to be vigilant
Beforehand, and watch well lest you be snared.
For to avoid being tripped up in love's toils
Is not so difficult as, once you are caught,
To issue from the nets and to break through
The strong meshes of Venus. None the less,
Even when you are tangled and involved,
You may escape the peril, unless you stand
In your own way, and always overlook
Every defect whether of mind or body
In her whom you pursue and long to win.
For this is how men generally behave
Blinded by lust, attributing to women
Good qualities which are not truly theirs.
So we see those in various ways misformed
And ugly, to be fondly loved and held
In highest favour. And a man will mock
His fellows, urging them to placate Venus,
Because they are troubled by a degrading love;
Yet often the poor fool will have no eyes
For his own far worse plight. The tawny is called
A honey brown;[1] the filthy and unclean,
Reckless of order; the green-eyed, a Pallas;
The sinewy and angular, a gazelle;
The tiny and dwarfish is a very Grace,
Nothing but sparkle; the monstrous and ungainly,
Stupendous and composed of majesty.
She stammers, cannot talk, why then she lisps;

[1] Most of the predicates in this list are Greek words.

The mute is bashful; but the fiery-tongued
Malicious gossip becomes a brilliant torch.
One is a slender darling, when she scarce
Can live for lack of flesh; and one half dead
With cough, is merely frail and delicate.
Then the fat and full-bosomed is Ceres' self
Suckling Iacchus; the snub-nosed, a female
Silenus, or a Satyress; the thick-lipped,
A kiss incarnate. But more of this sort
It were a tedious labour to recite.
Yet be she noble of feature as you will,
And let the might of Venus emanate
From every limb; still there are others too;
Still we have lived without her until now;
Still she does, and we know she does, the same
In all things as the ugly, and, poor wretch,
Perfumes herself with evil-smelling scents,
While her maids run and hide to giggle in secret.
But the excluded lover many a time
With flowers and garlands covers tearfully
The threshold, and anoints the haughty posts
With oil of marjoram, and imprints, poor man,
Kisses upon the doors. Yet when at last
He has been admitted, if but a single whiff
Should meet him as he enters, he would seek
Specious excuses to be gone, and so
The long-studied, deep-drawn complaint would fall
To the ground, and he would then convict himself
Of folly, now he sees he has attributed
More to her than is right to grant a mortal.
Nor to our Venuses is this unknown:
Wherefore the more are they at pains to hide
All that takes place behind the scenes of life
From those they would keep fettered in love's chains;
But all in vain, since in imagination
You yet may draw forth all these things to light,
Discovering every cause for ridicule:

Then if she be of a nature that can charm,
And not vexatious, you may in your turn
Overlook faults and pardon human frailty.

Nor always with feigned love does a woman sigh,
When with her own uniting the man's body
She holds him clasped, with moistened kisses sucking
His lips into her lips. Nay, from the heart
She often does it, and seeking mutual joys
Woos him to run to the utmost goal of love.
And nowise else could birds, cattle, wild beasts,
And sheep and mares submit to males, except
That their exuberant nature is in heat,
And burning draws towards them joyously
The lust of the covering mates. See you not also
That those whom mutual pleasure has enchained
Are often tormented in their common chains?
How often on the highroads dogs desiring
To separate, will strain in opposite ways
Eagerly with all their might, yet the whole time
They are held fast in the strong bonds of Venus!
Thus they would never act, unless they had
Experience of mutual joys, enough
To thrust them into the snare and hold them bound.
Therefore I assert, the pleasure must be common.

Whenever, mingling her seed with the man's,
The woman with sudden force has overwhelmed
And mastered the man's force, then children are born
Like to the mother from the mother's seed,
As from the father's seed like to the father.
But those whom you see sharing the form of both,
Mingling their parents' features side by side,
Grow from the father's body and mother's blood,
When mutual ardour has conspired to fling
The seeds together, roused by the goads of Venus
Throughout the frame, and neither of the two

Has gained the mastery nor yet been mastered.
Moreover sometimes children may be born
Like their grandparents, and will oft recall
The forms of their remoter ancestors,
Because the parents often hold concealed
Within their bodies, mingled in many ways,
Many first elements which, handed down
From the first stock, father transmits to father.
And out of these Venus produces forms
With ever-varying chances, and recalls
The look and voice and hair of ancestors:
Since these qualities can no more result
From a fixed seed than do our faces, limbs,
And bodies. Also children of female sex
May spring from a father's seed, and males be born
Formed from a mother's body: for the birth
Is always fashioned out of the two seeds.
Whichever of the two that which is born
Is most like, of that parent it will have
More than an equal share; as you may observe,
Whether it be a male or female offspring.

Nor is it the divine powers that can thwart
A man's begetting, so that he may never
Receive from sweet children the name of father,
But must live out his days in sterile wedlock;
As men in general fancy, and so sprinkle
The altars sorrowfully with much blood,
And heap the shrine-tables with offerings,
To make their wives pregnant with copious seed.
But vainly they importune the divinity
And sortilege of the gods. For they are sterile
Sometimes from too great thickness of the seed,
Or else it is unduly thin and fluid.
Because the thin cannot adhere and cleave
To the right spots, it forthwith flows away
Defeated, and departs abortively.

Others again discharge a seed too thick,
More solid than is suitable, which either
Does not shoot forth with so far-flung a stroke,
Or cannot so well penetrate where it should,
Or having penetrated, does not easily
Mix with the woman's seed. For harmonies
Are found to be most various in love's rites;
And some men will more readily fertilize
Some women, and other women will conceive
More readily and grow pregnant from other men.
And many women, sterile hitherto
In several marriages, have yet at last
Found mates from whom they could conceive children,
And so become enriched with a sweet offspring.
And for those men to whom their wedded wives,
However fruitful, had failed so far to bear,
A well-matched nature has been often found
That they might fortify their age with children.
So important is it, if seeds are to agree
And blend with seeds for purposes of birth,
That the thick should encounter with the fluid,
And the fluid with the thick. And herein too
It is of moment on what diet life
Is nourished; for the seed within the limbs
By some foods is made solid, and by others
Is thinned and dwindled. Also in what modes
Love's bland delight is dealt with, that likewise
Is of the highest moment. For in general
Women are thought more readily to conceive
After the manner of beasts and quadrupeds,
Since so the seeds can find the proper spots,
The breasts being bent downward, the loins raised.
Nor have wives the least need of wanton movements:
For a woman thwarts conception and frustrates it,
If with her loins she joyously lures on
The man's love, and, with her whole bosom relaxed
And limp, provokes lust's tide to overflow;

For then she thrusts the furrow from the share's
Direct path, turning the seed's stroke aside
From its right goal. And thus for their own ends
Harlots are wont to move, because they wish
Not to conceive nor lie in childbed often,
Likewise that Venus may give men more pleasure.
But of this surely our wives should have no need.

Nor is it by divine interposition,
Nor through the shafts of Venus, that sometimes
A girl of inferior beauty may be loved.
For sometimes she herself by her behaviour,
Her gentle ways and personal daintiness,
Will easily accustom you to spend
Your whole life with her. Besides it is custom
That harmonizes love. For what is struck
However lightly by repeated blows,
Yet after a long lapse of time is conquered
And must dissolve. Do you not likewise see
That drops of water falling upon stones
After long lapse of time will pierce them through?

BOOK V

Who is there that by energy of mind
Could build a poem worthy of our theme's
Majesty and of these discoveries?
Or who has such a mastery of words
As to devise praises proportionate
To his deserts, who to us has bequeathed
Such prizes, found and won by his own genius?
No man, I think, formed of a mortal body.
For if we are to speak as the acknowledged
Majesty of our theme demands, a god
Was he, most noble Memmius, a god,
Who first found out that reasoned plan of life
Which now is called philosophy, and whose skill
From such great billows and a gloom so dark
Delivered life, and steered it into a calm
So peaceful and beneath so bright a light.
For compare the divine discoveries
Of others in old times. 'Tis told that Ceres
First revealed corn to men, Liber the juice
Of grape-born wine; though life without these things
Might well have been sustained; and even now
'Tis said there are some peoples that live so.
But to live happily was not possible
Without a cleansed mind. Therefore all the more
Is this man justly deemed by us a god,
From whom came those sweet solaces of life,
Which still through mighty nations spread abroad
Have power to soothe our minds. Should you suppose
Moreover that the deeds of Hercules
Surpass his, then yet further will you drift
Out of true reason's course. For what harm now
Would those great gaping jaws of Nemea's lion
Do to us, and the bristly Arcadian boar?
What could the bull of Crete, or Lerna's pest

The Hydra fenced around with venomous snakes,
And threefold Gēryon's triple-breasted might,
Or those brazen-plumed birds inhabiting
Stymphalian swamps, what injury so great
Could they inflict upon us, or the steeds
Of Thracian Diomede, with fire-breathing nostrils,
Near the Bistonian wilds and Ismarus?
Also the serpent, guardian of the bright
Gold-gleaming apples of the Hesperides,
Fierce and grim-glancing, with huge body coiled
Round the tree's stem, how were it possible
He could molest us by the Atlantic shore
And those stern seas, which none of us goes near,
And no barbarian ventures to approach?
And all those other monsters which likewise
Have been destroyed, if they had not been vanquished,
What harm, pray, could they do, though now alive?
None, I presume: for the earth even now abounds
With wild beasts to repletion, and is filled
With shuddering terror throughout its woods, great mountains
And deep forests, regions which we have power
For the most part to avoid. But if the mind
Has not been purged, what tumults then, what dangers
Must needs invade us in our own despite!
What fierce anxieties, offspring of desire,
Rend the distracted man, what mastering fears!
Pride also, filthy greed, and insolence,
Of what calamities are not they the cause!
Luxury too, and slothfulness! He therefore
Who could subdue all these, and banish them
Out of our minds by force of words, not arms,
Is it not right we should deem such a man
Worthy to be numbered among the gods?
The more that he was wont in beautiful
And godlike speech to utter many truths
About the immortal gods themselves, and set
The whole nature of things in clear words forth.

I, in his footsteps treading, follow out
His reasonings and expound in my discourse
By what law all things are created, how
They are compelled to abide within that law
Without power to annul the immutable
Decrees of time: and first above all else
The mind's nature was found to be composed
Of a body that had birth, without the power
To endure through a long period unscathed;
And it was found to be mere images
That are wont to deceive the mind in sleep,
Whenever we appear to behold one
Whom life has abandoned. Now, for what remains,
The order of my argument has brought me
To the point where I must show both that the world
Is composed of a body which must die,
Also that it was born; and in what ways
That confluence of matter from all sides
Established earth sky sea the stars the sun
And the moon's globe; then too what living creatures
Rose from the earth, and which were those that never
At any time were born; next in what way
Mankind began to employ varied speech
One with another by giving names to things;
In what ways also that fear of the Gods
Entered their breasts, which now through the whole world
Give sanctity to shrines and lakes and groves,
Altars and images of Gods. Moreover
I will make plain by what force and control
Nature pilots the courses of the sun
And journeyings of the moon, lest we perchance
Deem that they traverse of their own free will
Their yearly orbits between heaven and earth,
Obliging us by furthering the increase
Of crops and living things, or should suppose
They move by any forethought of the Gods.
For those who have been rightly taught that Deities

Lead a life free from care, if yet they wonder
By what means all things can be carried on,
Such above all as are perceived to happen
In the aethereal regions overhead,
They are borne back again into their old
Religious fears, and adopt pitiless lords,
Whom these unhappy men believe to be
Almighty; for they are ignorant of what can
And what cannot exist; in fine they know not
Upon what principle each thing has its powers
Limited, and its deep-set boundary stone.

But now, lest I delay you more with promises,
In the first place consider, Memmius,
The seas, the lands, the sky, whose threefold nature,
Three bodies, three forms so dissimilar,
Three such marvellous textures, a single day
Shall give to destruction, and the world's vast mass
And fabric, for so many years upheld,
Shall fall to ruin. Nor am I unaware
How novel and strange, when first it strikes the mind,
Must appear this destruction of earth and heaven
That is to be, and for myself how difficult
It will prove to convince you by mere words;
As happens when one brings to a man's ears
Some notion unfamiliar hitherto,
If yet one cannot thrust it visibly
Beneath his eyes or place it in his hands;
For the paved highway of belief through touch
And sight leads straightest into the human heart
And the precincts of mind. Yet none the less
The truth will I speak out. The event itself
It may be will bring credence to my words,
And you will see the earth terribly quaking,
And the whole world within a brief hour's space
Shattered to ruins. But may pilot fortune
Steer far from us such disaster, and may reason

Convince us rather than the event itself
That the whole universe may well collapse
Tumbling together with a dread crash and roar.

But before I attempt concerning this
To announce fate's oracles in more holy wise,
And with far surer reasoning than those
Delivered by the Pythian prophetess
From the tripod and laurel leaves of Phoebus,
Many consolatories will I first
Expound to you in learned words, lest haply
Curbed by religion's bit you should suppose
That earth and sun and sky, sea stars and moon,
Their substance being divine, must needs abide
Eternally, and should therefore think it just
That, after the manner of the Giants, all
Should suffer penance for their monstrous guilt,
Who by their reasoning shake the world's firm walls
And fain would quench the glorious sun in heaven,
Shaming with mortal speech immortal things;
Though in fact such objects are so far removed
From any share in divine energy,
And so unworthy to be accounted Gods,
That they more reasonably may be deemed
To offer us the conception[1] of what is quite
Devoid of vital motion and of sense.
For truly by no means can we suppose
That the nature and judgment of the mind
Can exist linked with every kind of body;
Even as in the sky trees cannot exist,
Nor clouds in the salt sea, nor in the fields
Can fishes live, nor blood reside in timber,
Nor sap in stones. Where each one thing may grow
And reside, is determined and ordained.
Thus the mind's nature cannot come to birth

[1] See note on II. 744, p. 70.

Alone without a body, nor exist
Separated from sinews and from blood.
Nay, were this possible, far more easily
Could the mind's force reside in head or shoulders
Or right down in the heels, and would be born
In any part you choose, and thus at least
Would abide in the same man as its home.
But since even in our body it is seen
To be determined and ordained where soul
And mind can separately dwell and grow,
All the more strongly must it be denied
That mind could dwell wholly outside a body
And living form, in crumbling clods of earth,
In the sun's fire, or water, or aloft
In the domains of aether. Such things therefore
Are not endowed with divine consciousness,
Because they cannot be quickened into life.

This too you cannot possibly believe,
That there are holy abodes of Deities
Anywhere in this world. For so tenuous
Is the nature of Gods, and from our senses
So far withdrawn, that hardly can the mind's
Intelligence perceive it. And since always
It has eluded touch or blow of hands,
It must touch nothing which for us is tangible:
For naught can touch that may not itself be touched.
So even their abodes must be unlike
Our own, tenuous as their bodies are.
All this hereafter I will prove to you
By plentiful argument. Further, to say
That for the sake of mankind the Gods willed
To frame the wondrous nature of the world,
And that on this account we ought to extol
Their handiwork as worthy of all praise,
And to believe that it will prove eternal
And indestructible, and to think it sin

Ever by any effort to subvert
What by the ancient wisdom of the Gods
Has been established everlastingly
For mankind's benefit, or by argument
To assail and overthrow it utterly
From top to bottom—to invent such errors
And others like them, all this, Memmius,
Is folly. For what advantage could our thanks
Bestow upon immortal and blessed beings
That for our sakes they should bestir themselves
To perform any task? Or what new fact
Could have induced them, tranquil hitherto,
After so long to change their former life?
For it seems fitting *he* should take delight
In a new state of things, to whom the old
Was painful: but for him whom in past times,
While he was living in felicity,
No evil had befallen, for such a one
What could have kindled a desire for change? 173
Must we imagine that their life was sunk 175
In darkness and in misery till the birth
And origin of things first dawned for them? 176
Besides, what evil had it been to us 174
Not to have been created? For whoever
Has once been born, must wish to abide in life
So long as luring pleasure bids him stay:
But one who has never tasted the love of life,
Nor even been numbered in life's ranks, what harm
Were it for him not to have been created?
Again, whence first was implanted in the Gods
A pattern for begetting things? Whence too
The preconception[1] of what men should be,
So that they knew and imagined in their minds
What they desired to make? And by what means
Could they have ever learnt the potency

[1] See note on II. 744, p. 70.

Of primal atoms, or have known what forms
Might be produced by changes in their order,
Unless Nature herself had given them first
A sample of creation? For indeed
These primal atoms in such multitudes
In so many ways through infinite past time
Impelled by blows and moved by their own weight,
Have been borne onward so incessantly,
Uniting in every way and making trial
Of every shape they could combine to form,
That 'tis not strange if they have also fallen
Into such groupings and acquired such motions
As those whereby this present world of ours
Is carried on and ceaselessly renewed.

But even were I ignorant of the truth
Concerning the first elements of things,
Yet this would I still venture to affirm,
And prove both from the system of the heavens
And from much other evidence, that Nature
Has by no means been fashioned for our benefit
By divine power; so great are the defects
Which are her bane. First, of the whole space
Covered by the enormous reach of heaven,
A greedy portion mountains occupy
And forests of wild beasts; rocks and waste swamps
Possess it, or the wide land-sundering sea.
Besides, well-nigh two-thirds are stolen from men
By burning heat and frost ceaselessly falling.
All that is left for husbandry, even that
The force of Nature soon would overspread
With thorns, unless resisted by man's force,
Ever wont for his livelihood to groan
Over the strong hoe, and with down-pressed plough
To cleave the earth. For if we do not turn
The teeming clods with coulters, and so labouring
The soil of earth, summon the crops to rise,

They could not of their own accord spring up
Into the bright air. Even then sometimes,
When answering our long toil throughout the land
Every bud puts forth its leaves and flowers,
Either the sun in heaven scorches them
With too much heat, or sudden gusts of rain
Or nipping frosts destroy them, or wind-storms
Shatter them with impetuous whirling blasts.
Furthermore why does Nature multiply
And nourish terrible tribes of savage beasts
By land and sea, dangerous to mankind?
Why do the seasons of the year bring maladies?
Why does untimely death range to and fro?
Then again, like a mariner cast ashore
By raging waves, the human infant lies
Naked upon the ground, speechless, in want
Of every help needful for life, when first
Nature by birth-throes from his mother's womb
Thrusts him into the borders of the light,
So that he fills the room with piteous wailing,
As well he may, whose fate in life will be
To pass through so much misery. But flocks
And herds of divers kind, and the wild beasts,
These, as they grow up, have no need of rattles;
To none of them a foster-nurse must utter
Fond broken speech; they seek not different dresses
To suit each season; no, nor do they need
Weapons nor lofty walls whereby to guard
What is their own, since all things for them all
The Earth herself brings forth abundantly,
And Nature, the creatress manifold.

First of all, since the substance of the earth,
Moisture, and the light breathings of the air,
And burning heats, of which this world of ours
Is seen to be composed, have all been formed
Of a body that had birth and that will die,

Of such a body must we likewise deem
That the whole nature of the world is made.
For things whose parts and members we see formed
Of a body that had birth and shapes that die,
These we perceive are themselves always mortal,
And likewise have been born. Since then I see
That the chief parts and members of the world
Decay and are reborn, I may be sure
That heaven also and earth once had a time
Of origin, and will have of destruction.

Herein lest you should think that without proof
I have seized this vantage, in that I assume
Earth and fire to be mortal, and do not doubt
That moisture and air perish, and maintain
That these are reborn too and grow afresh,
Consider first how no small part of the earth,
Ceaselessly baked by the sun's rays and trampled
By innumerable feet, gives off a mist
And flying clouds of dust, which the strong winds
Disperse through the whole atmosphere. Part too
Of the earth's soil is washed away by rains,
And scouring rivers gnaw their banks away.
Also, whate'er earth gives for nourishment
And increase, is restored to her in due course.
And since beyond doubt the all-mother Earth
Is seen to be no less the general tomb,
You thus may see how she is ever lessened,
And with new growth increases evermore.

Next, that the sea, the rivers and the springs
Are always overflowing with new supplies
Of water welling up perennially,
It needs no words to explain. The vast down-flow
Of waters from all sides is proof of this.
But as the water that is uppermost
Is always taken away, it comes to pass

That on the whole there is no overflow;
Partly because strong winds, sweeping the seas,
Minish them, and the sun in heaven unweaves
Their fabric with his rays; partly because
The water is distributed below
Throughout all lands. For the salt is strained off,
And the moisture's pure substance, oozing back,
All meets together at the river-heads,
Thence, as a current of fresh water, flows
Over the land along some course that once
Was cleft for it to stream down with liquid foot.

Now must I speak of air, which every hour
Is changed through its whole body in countless ways.
For always whatever flows away from things
Is all borne into the vast sea of air:
And if it were not in its turn to give
Particles back to things, recruiting them
As they flow off, all would have been long since
Disintegrated and so changed to air.
Therefore air never ceases to be born
Out of things, and to pass back into things,
Since, as we know, all are in constant flux.

Likewise that bounteous fountain of clear light,
The sun in heaven, ceaselessly floods the sky
With fresh brightness, and momently supplies
The place of light with new light: for each foremost
Emission of his radiance perishes,
On whatsoever spot it falls. This truth
You may thus learn. So soon as clouds begin
To pass below the sun, and as it were
To break off the light's rays, their lower part
Forthwith perishes wholly, and the earth
Is shadow-swept wherever the clouds move.
Thus you may know that things have need always
Of fresh illumination, and that each

Foremost discharge of radiance perishes;
Nor in any other way could things be seen
In sunlight, if the fountain-head itself
Did not send forth a perpetual supply.
Also those lights we use here upon earth
At night-time, hanging lamps, and torches bright
With quivering beams, rich with abundant smoke,
Are in haste in like fashion to supply
New radiance with ministering glow;
Their flickering flames follow and follow and follow,
Nor ever does the unbroken stream of light
Appear to quit the spots whereon it plays;
So suddenly is its perishing concealed
By the swift birth of flame from all these fires.
Therefore you must suppose that in this way
The sun and moon and stars shoot their light forth
Out of supplies continually renewed,
And that they always lose whatever beams
Come foremost; lest perchance you should believe
Their energy to be imperishable.

Again, is it not seen that even stones
By time are vanquished, that tall towers fall
And rocks crumble away, that shrines and idols
Of Gods grow worn out and dilapidate,
Nor may the indwelling holiness prolong
The bounds of destiny or strive against
The laws of Nature? Then do we not see
The monuments of men fallen to ruin;
Brazen statues moreover growing old,
And crags of flinty stone? See we not rocks
Split off from mountain heights fall crashing down
Unable more to endure the powerful stress
Of finite age? Surely they would not fall
Thus suddenly split off, if through the lapse
Of infinite past years they had withstood
All the assaults of time without being shattered.

Now contemplate that which around and above
Compasses the whole earth with its embrace.
If it begets all things out of itself,
As some have told us,[1] and receives them back
When they have perished, then the whole sky is made
Of a body that had birth and that must die.
For whatsoever nourishes and augments
Other things from itself, must needs be minished,
And be replenished when it receives them back.

Moreover, if there never was a time
Of origin when earth and heaven were born,
If they have always been from everlasting,
Why then before the Theban war and Troy's
Destruction have not other poets sung
Of other deeds as well? Whither have vanished
So many exploits of so many men?
Why are they nowhere gloriously inscribed
On the eternal monuments of fame?
But in truth, as I think, this sum of things
Is in its youth: the nature of our world
Is recent and began not long ago.
Wherefore even now some arts are being wrought
To their last polish, some are still in growth.
Of late many improvements have been made
In navigation, and musicians too
Have given birth to new melodious sounds.
Also this theory of the nature of things
Has been discovered lately, and I myself
Have only now been found the very first
Able to turn it into our native words.
Nevertheless, if you perchance believe
That long ago all these same things existed,
But that the generations of mankind
Perished by scorching heat, or that their cities
Fell in some great convulsion of the world,

[1] The Stoics.

Or else that flooded by incessant rains
Devouring rivers broke forth over the earth
And swallowed up whole towns, so much the more
Must you admit that there will come to pass
A like destruction of earth and heaven too.
For when things were assailed by such great maladies
And dangers, if then some more fatal cause
Had overwhelmed them, they would have been dissolved
In havoc and vast ruin far and wide.
And in no other way do we perceive
That we are mortal, save that we all alike
In turn fall sick of the same maladies
As those whom Nature has withdrawn from life.

Again, whatever things abide eternally,
Either, since they are of solid body,
Must repel strokes, nor suffer anything
To penetrate them which might disunite
The close-locked parts within, like those material
Atoms whose nature we have described before;
Or they must be able to endure throughout
All time, because they are exempt from blows
(As void is, which abides untouched, nor suffers
One whit from any stroke), or else because
There is around them no supply of space
Into which things might as it were depart
And be dissolved; even as the sum of sums
Is everlasting, nor is there any space
Outside, into which things might spring asunder,
Nor are there bodies which might fall upon them
And so dissolve them with a violent blow.
But neither, as I have shown, is this world's nature
Solid, since there is void mixed up in things;
Nor yet is it like void; nor verily
Are atoms lacking that might well collect
Out of the infinite and overwhelm
This sum of things with violent hurricane,

Or threaten it with some other form of ruin;
Nor further is there any want of room
And of deep space, into which the world's walls
Might be dispersed abroad; or they may perish
Shattered by any other force you will.
Therefore the gates of death are never closed
For sky or sun or earth or the deep seas,
But stand open, awaiting them with huge
Vast-gaping jaws. So you must needs admit
That all these likewise once had birth: for things
Of mortal body could not until now
Through infinite past ages have defied
The strong powers of immeasurable time.

Again, since the chief members of the world
So mightily contend together, stirred
By unhallowed civil warfare, see you not
That some end may be set to their long strife?
It may be when the sun and every kind
Of heat shall have drunk all the waters up
And gained the mastery they are struggling for;
Though they have failed as yet to achieve their aim,
So vast are the supplies the rivers bring,
Threatening besides to deluge every land
From out the deep abysses of the ocean;
All in vain, since the winds, sweeping the seas,
Minish them, and the sun in heaven unweaves
Their fabric with his rays; and these are confident
They will be able to dry all things up
Before moisture can achieve its end.
So fierce the warlike spirit they breathe out
As they strive with each other for mighty issues
In equal contest: though indeed fire once
Obtained the mastery, so the fable tells,
And water in the fields once reigned supreme.
For fire prevailing licked up and consumed
Many things, when the ungovernable might

Of the Sun's horses, swerving from their course,
Through the whole sky and over every land
Whirled Phaëthon. But then the almighty Father,
Stirred to fierce wrath, with sudden thunder-stroke
Dashed great-souled Phaëthon from his car to the earth;
And as he fell the Sun-god meeting him
Caught from him the world's everlasting lamp,
And brought back tamed and trembling to the yoke
The scattered steeds; then on their wonted course
Guiding them, unto all things gave fresh life.
So forsooth the old Grecian poets sang,
Though straying from true reason all too far.
For fire can only gain the mastery
When an excess of fiery particles
Have flocked together out of infinite space;
And then its strength fails, vanquished in some way,
Or else things perish, utterly consumed
By scorching gusts. Also, as the fable tells,
Water gathering together once began
To gain the mastery, when it overwhelmed
Living men with its waves. But afterwards,
When all its force, which out of infinite space
Had been gathered together, was in some way
Diverted and withdrew, the rains ceased then,
And the violence of the rivers was abated.

But in what ways that confluence of matter
Established earth and sky and the sea's deeps,
The sun's course and the moon's, I will set forth
In order. For in truth not by design
Did the primordial particles of things
Arrange themselves each in its own right place
Intelligently; nor indeed did they bargain
What motions each should follow; but because
These primal atoms in such multitudes
In so many ways through infinite past time
Impelled by blows and moved by their own weight,

Have been borne onward so incessantly,
Uniting in every way and making trial
Of every shape they could combine to form,
Therefore it is that after wandering wide
Through vast periods, attempting every kind
Of union and of motion, they at last
Collect into such groups as, suddenly
Flocking together, oftentimes become
The rudiments of mighty things, of earth
Sea and sky and the race of living creatures.

Then, in that chaos, neither could the sun's disk
Be seen flying aloft with bounteous light,
Nor the stars of great heaven, nor sea, nor sky,
Nor yet earth nor the air, nor anything
Resembling those things which we now behold,
But only a sort of strange tempest, a mass
Gathered together out of primal atoms
Of all kinds, which discordantly waged war
Disordering so their interspaces, paths,
Connections, weights and blows, meetings and motions,
Since with their unlike forms and varied shapes
They could not therefore all remain united,
Nor move among themselves harmoniously.
Then next, portions began to fly asunder,
And like things to unite with like, and so
To separate off the world, and to divide
Its members, portioning out its mighty parts;
That is, to mark off the high heaven from earth,
And the sea by itself, that it might spread
With unmixed waters, and likewise the fires
Of aether by themselves, pure and unmixed.

Now first the several particles of earth,
Since they were heavy and intertangled, met
Together in the middle, and all took up
The lowest places: and the more they met

Thus intertangled, the more did they squeeze out
Those particles which were to form sea stars
Sun and moon and the walls of the great world.
For all these are of smoother rounder seeds
And of much smaller elements than earth.
So first through openings in the porous soil
The fire-laden aether here and there
Bursting forth rose and lightly carried off
Many fire atoms; much in the same way
As often we may see when first the beams
Of the radiant sun with golden morning light
Blush through the grasses gemmed with dew, and lakes
And ever-flowing rivers exhale mist;
Or as earth itself is sometimes seen to smoke:
And when floating aloft these vapours all
Unite on high, then taking bodily shape
As clouds, they weave a veil beneath the heavens.
Thus then the light diffusive aether once
Took bodily shape, and arched round on all sides,
Far into every quarter spreading out,
So with its greedy embrace hemmed in all else.

Next came the rudiments of sun and moon,
Whose globes turn in the air midway between
Aether and earth; for neither did the earth
Nor the great aether claim them for itself,
Since they were not so heavy as to sink
And settle down, nor so light as to glide
Along the topmost borders: but their course
Between the two is such, that as they roll
Their lifelike bodies onward, they are still
Parts of the whole world; even as with us
Some of our members may remain at rest
While at the same time others may be in motion.

Now when these things had been withdrawn, the earth,
Where now the ocean's vast blue region spreads,

Sank suddenly down and flooded with salt surge
Its hollow parts. And day by day the more
The encircling aether's streams and the sun's rays
Compressed the earth into a closer mass
By constant blows upon its outer surface
From every side, so that thus beaten upon
It shrank and drew together round its centre,
The more did the salt sweat, squeezed from its body,
Increase by its oozings the sea's floating plains,
And the more did those many particles
Of heat and air escaping fly abroad,
Till far away from earth they densified
The lofty glittering mansions of the sky.
The plains sank lower, the high mountains grew
Yet steeper; for the rocks could not sink down,
Nor could all parts subside to one same level.

Thus then the earth's ponderous mass became
Solid with close-packed body, and all the slime,
So to speak, of the world by its own weight
Slid down together to the lowest plane
And at the bottom settled there like dregs.
Then the sea, then the air, then the fire-laden
Aether itself, all these were now left pure
With limpid bodies. Some indeed are lighter
Than others; and most limpid and light of all
Over the airy currents aether floats,
Not blending with the turbulent atmosphere
Its limpid substance. All below, it suffers
To be embroiled by violent hurricanes,
Suffers all to be tossed with wayward storms,
While itself gliding on with changeless sweep
Bears its own fires along. For that the aether
May stream on steadily with one impulse,
The Pontos demonstrates, that sea which streams
With an unchanging current, evermore
Preserving as it glides one constant pace.

Now let us sing what is the cause that gives
The stars their motions. First, if the great globe
Of heaven revolves, then we must say that air
Presses upon the axis at each end,
And holds it from outside, closing it in
At both poles; also that there streams above
Another current, moving the same way,
In which the stars of the eternal world
Roll glittering onward; or else that beneath
There is another stream, to drive the sphere
Upwards the opposite way, just as we see
Rivers turn wheels round with their water-scoops.
It likewise may well be that the whole sky
Remains at rest, and yet the shining signs
Are carried onwards; either because within them
Are shut swift tides of aether, that whirl round
Seeking a way out, and so roll their fires
On all sides through the sky's nocturnal mansions;
Or else that from some other source outside
An air-stream drives and whirls the fires along;
Or else they may be gliding of themselves,
Moving whithersoever the food of each
Calls and invites them, nourishing everywhere
Their flaming bodies throughout the whole sky.
For it is hard to affirm with certainty
Which of these causes operates in this world:[1]
But what throughout the universe both can
And does take place in various worlds, fashioned
In various ways, this I teach, then describe
What divers causes there may be throughout
The universe for the motions of the stars:
And one of these in our world too must be
The cause which to the heavenly signs imparts
Their motive vigour; but dogmatically
To assert which this may be, is in no wise
The duty of one who advances step by step.

[1] See note on ἰσονομία, or "equal distribution", II. 535, p. 62.

Now if we ask why the earth is at rest
In the world's midst, it would seem probable
That its weight gradually diminishing
Should disappear, and that the earth should have
Another nature underneath, conjoined
And blent in union from its earliest age
With those aerial portions of the world
Wherewith it lives embodied. For this cause
It is no burden, nor weighs down the air,
Just as to a man his own limbs are no weight,
Nor is the head a burden to the neck,
Nor do we feel that the whole body's weight
Is resting on the feet; yet every weight
Annoys us that is laid on us from outside,
Though often it is far lighter than ourselves.
Of such great moment is it what the properties
Are of each thing. So then the earth is not
An alien body intruded suddenly,
Nor thrust from elsewhere into an alien air,
But was conceived together with the world
At its first birth as a fixed portion of it,
Just as our limbs are seen to be of us.
Moreover the earth, when shaken suddenly
With violent thunder, by its trembling shakes
All that is over it; which in no wise
Could happen if it were not closely bound
With the world's airy parts, and with the sky.
For earth and heaven by common roots cohere
One with another, from their earliest age
Conjoined and blent in union. See you not too
That heavy as our body's weight may be,
Yet the soul's force, though exceeding tenuous,
Sustains it, being so closely joined and blent
In union with it? Further, what has power
To lift the body with a nimble leap,
Except the soul's force that controls the limbs?
Do you not now perceive how great the power

May be of a tenuous substance, when 'tis joined
With a heavy body as closely as the air
Is joined with earth, and the mind's force with us?

Nor can the size and heat of the sun's disk
Be much greater or smaller than to our senses
They appear to be. For from whatever distance
Fires can fling light, and breathe upon our limbs
Their warming heat, these intervening spaces
Take away nothing from the body of flame;
The fire is not shrunken visibly.
So since the sun's heat and the light it sheds
Reach our senses and throw light everywhere,
The form and size too of the sun must needs
Be seen by us from the earth in their true scale
With neither addition nor diminishment.
Also the moon, whether it moves along
Illuminating earth with borrowed light,
Or throws out its own rays from its own body,
Howe'er that be, moves with a shape no larger
Than seems that shape which our eyes contemplate.
For all things which we look at from far off
Through much air, seem to grow blurred in their shapes
Before their size lessens. Therefore the moon,
Seeing that it presents a clear aspect
And definite shape, must needs by us from the earth
Be seen on high just as it is defined
By its outlines, and of its actual size.
Lastly consider all those fires of aether
You see from the earth. Since fires which here below
We observe, for so long as their flickering light
Remains distinct and their heat is perceived,
Appear to change their size to less or greater,
But only a very little now and then
According to their distance, you may thence
Know that the fires of aether can be smaller
By no more than a very slight degree,
Or larger by the tiniest minute fraction.

This also is not wonderful, how the sun,
Small as it is, can shed so great a light,
As with its flood to fill all seas and lands
And sky, with warm heat bathing everything.
For it may be that hence the single well
For the whole world opens and gushes out,
Shooting forth an abundant stream of light,
Because from everywhere throughout the world
In such wise do the particles of heat
Gather together, and their uniting mass
Converges in such wise, that a blazing glow
Streams forth here from a single fountain-head.
See you not too how wide a meadow-land
One little spring of water sometimes floods,
Overflowing whole fields? It may be also
That from the sun's flame, though it be not great,
Heat seizes on the air with scorching fires,
Should the air chance to be susceptible
And ready to be kindled when 'tis struck
By tiny heat-rays: thus we sometimes see
A wide-spread conflagration from one spark
Catch fields of corn or stubble. Perhaps too
The sun shining on high with ruddy torch
May be surrounded by much fire and heats
Invisible, fire which no radiance
Reveals, so that it merely reinforces
The heat-discharging stroke of the sun's rays.

Nor is there any simple theory,
Certain and obvious, of how the sun
Out of his summer stations passing forth
Approaches the midwinter turning-point
Of Capricorn; and how coming back thence
He bends his course to the solstitial goal
Of Cancer; also how the moon is seen
To traverse every month that space whereon
The journeying sun spends a year's period.
For these events, I say, no simple cause

Can be assigned. It seems most probable
That the revered opinion of the sage,
Democritus, should be the truth: the nearer
The several stars are to the earth, the less
Can they be borne on with the whirl of heaven:
For in the lower portions of this whirl
He says its speed and energy diminish
And weaken; so that gradually the sun
Is left behind among the rearward signs,
Since he is far beneath those burning stars.
And the moon, so he says, more than the sun.
Her course being lower and farther from the sky
And nearer to the earth, just so much less,
He says, can she keep even with the signs.
For since more languid is the whirl whereby
She is borne along, being lower than the sun,
So much the more do all the signs around her
Overtake and pass by her. Thus it is
That she seems to move backward to each sign
More rapidly than the sun, because the signs
Are coming up to her more rapidly.
It may be also that two streams of air
Cross the sun's path at fixed times, each in turn,
Flowing from opposite quarters of the world,
Whereof the first may thrust the sun away
Out of the summer signs, until he comes
To his winter turning-point and the icy frost;
While the other from the freezing shades of cold
Sweeps him right back to the heat-laden regions
And the torrid constellations. And just so
We must suppose that the moon and the planets,
Which roll in their huge orbits through huge years,
May move on streams of air alternately
From opposite quarters. Do you not also see
How clouds are shifted by opposing winds,
The lower in directions contrary
To those above? Why should not yonder stars

Be likewise carried by opposing currents
Upon their mighty orbits through the heavens?

But night covers the earth with vast darkness,
Either when after his long course the sun
Has entered on the uttermost parts of heaven,
And now grown languid has breathed forth his fires,
That by their journey are shaken and worn out
With traversing much air; or else because
That same force which has borne his orb along
Above the earth, compels him now to turn
His course backward and pass beneath the earth.

Likewise at a fixed time Matuta[1] spreads
The rosy dawn abroad through the aether's regions
And opens out her light, either because
The same sun, travelling back below the earth,
Seizes the sky while yet unrisen, and fain
Would kindle it with his rays; or else because
Fires meet together, and many seeds of heat
Are wont at a fixed time to stream together
Causing new sunlight each day to be born.
Even so 'tis told that from the mountain heights
Of Ida at daybreak scattered fires are seen,
Which then unite as if into one globe
And make up the sun's orb. Nor yet herein
Should it cause wonder that these seeds of fire
Can stream together at a time so fixed,
Repairing thus the radiance of the sun.
For everywhere we see many events
Happening at fixed times. Thus trees both flower
And shed their blossoms at fixed times; and age
At a time no less fixed bids the teeth drop,
And the boy clothe his features with the down
Of puberty, and let a soft beard fall

[1] The ancient Roman Goddess of the Dawn.

From either cheek. Lastly lightning and snow
Rains clouds and winds happen at more or less
Regular seasons of the year. For since
Causes from the beginning have been such,
And things from the first origin of the world
Have so fallen out, they still repeat themselves
In regular sequence after a fixed order.

The cause too why days lengthen and nights wane,
While daylight shortens as the nights increase,
May either be because, when the same sun
Journeys beneath and above the earth, he parts
The coasts of aether in curves of unlike length,
And into unequal halves divides his orbit:
(Whatever he has subtracted from one half,
Just so much, as he comes round, does he add
On to the opposite half, till he has reached
That sign of heaven where the year's node makes
The shades of night equal to the daylight;
For in the sun's mid course between the blasts
Of south wind and of north, the heaven holds
His turning-points apart at distances
Now equalised, since such is the position
Of the whole starry circle, to glide through which
The sun takes up the period of a year,
Lighting the earth and sky with slanting rays,
As is shown by the arguments of those
Who have mapped out all the quarters of the sky,
Adorned with their twelve signs spaced out in order):
Or it may be the air in certain parts
Is thicker, therefore the trembling lamp of fire
Is hindered in its course beneath the earth,
Nor can it easily force a passage through
And emerge at the place where it should rise;
And so in winter the nights are long and lingering
Ere the day's radiant oriflamme comes forth:
Or else those fires which cause the sun to rise

From a particular point, for a like reason
Are wont to stream together slower or quicker
In alternating periods of the year.
And so perhaps those speak the truth who hold
That every morning a new sun is born.

It may be the moon shines because she is struck
By the sun's rays, and turns towards our eyes
A larger portion of this light each day
The further she recedes from the sun's orb,
Until over against him with full light
She has shone forth, and as she rises up
Has looked upon his setting from on high:
Thereafter in her gradual backward course
In the same manner she must hide her light
The nearer she now glides to the sun's fire
Travelling through the circle of the signs
From the place opposite to him:[1] as those hold
Who fancy that the moon is like a ball,
And moves along a course below the sun.
It is also possible that she revolves
With her own light, and yet shows varying
Phases of brightness: for there may well be
Another body, which glides on beside her
Obstructing and occulting her continually,
And yet cannot be seen because it moves
Without light. Or perhaps she may turn round
Like a ball, let us say, whose sphere is tinged
With glowing light over one half its surface;
And as she turns her sphere, she may present
Varying phases, till she has turned that side
Which glows with fire towards our gazing eyes;
Then she twists gradually back once more
And hides the luminous half of her round ball:
As the Chaldean sages seek to prove,
Refuting with their Babylonian doctrine

[1] From the West.

The opposing science of the astronomers;
Just as though what each sect is fighting for
Might not be true, or there were any reason
Why you should risk embracing the one creed
More than the other. Again, why every time
There should not be created a fresh moon
With fixed succession of phases and fixed shapes,
So that each day each new-created moon
Would perish and another be produced
To take its place, this were no easy task
To prove by argument convincingly,
Since there can be so many things created
In fixed succession. Thus Spring goes its way,
And Venus, and the wingèd harbinger
Of Venus leads them on; while treading close
On Zephyr's footsteps, mother Flora strews
The path before them, covering it all over
With every loveliest colour and rich scent.
Next in procession follows parching Heat
With dusty Ceres in his company,
And the Etesian blasts of the North winds.
After these Autumn comes, and by his side
Advances Euhius Euan,[1] following whom
The other Seasons with their winds appear,
Volturnus loudly thundering, and Auster[2]
Terrible with his lightnings. Then at length
December brings snow and renews numb frost.
Winter follows with teeth chattering for cold.
Wherefore it seems less wonderful that the moon
Should be begotten and destroyed again
At fixed times, seeing that so many things
Can come to pass at times so surely fixed.

Likewise the obscurations of the sun
And the moon's vanishings you must suppose

[1] Bacchus.
[2] Volturnus was a South-east, Auster a South wind.

May be produced by many different causes.
For why should the moon be able to shut out
The earth from the sun's light, and lift her head
On high to obstruct him from the earthward side
Blocking his fiery beams with her dark orb,
And yet at the same time some other body
Gliding on without light continually
Should be supposed unable to do this?
Why too should not the sun at a fixed time
Grow faint and lose his fires and then again
Revive his light, when he has had to pass
Through tracts of air so hostile to his flames
That for a time his fires are quenched and perish?
And why should the earth have power in turn to rob
The moon of light, and likewise keep the sun
Suppressed, while in her monthly course the moon
Glides through the clear-cut shadows of the cone,
And yet at the same time some other body
Should not have power to pass under the moon,
Or glide above the sun's orb intercepting
The beams of light he sheds? And after all,
If the moon shines with her own radiance,
Why in a certain region of the world
Might she not grow faint, while she makes her way
Through tracts unfriendly to her unborrowed light?

Now since I have demonstrated how each thing
May come to pass throughout the azure spaces
Of the great heaven, how we may know what force
Causes the varying motions of the sun
And journeyings of the moon, and in what way
Their light being intercepted they may vanish
Covering with darkness the astonished earth,
When as it were they close their eye of light,
And opening it again, survey all places
Radiant with shining brightness—therefore now
To the world's infancy and the tender age

Of the earth's fields will I go back, and show
What in their first fecundity they resolved
To raise into the borders of the light
And give in charge unto the wayward winds.

In the beginning Earth brought forth all kinds
Of plants and glowing verdure on hillsides
And over all the plains: the flowering meadows
Shone with green colour: next to the various trees
Was given a mighty emulous impulse
To shoot up into the air with unchecked growth.
As on the limbs of quadrupeds and the bodies
Of winged fowl the first growths are feathers, hairs
And bristles, so the new Earth then put forth
Grasses and brushwood first, and afterwards
Gave birth to all the breeds of mortal creatures,
That rose up many in number in many modes
And divers fashions. For no animals
Can have dropped from the sky, nor can land-creatures
Have issued from the salt depths of the sea.
Hence with good reason the Earth has won the name
Of Mother, since from the Earth all things were born.
And many living creatures even now
Spring from the soil, formed by rains and the sun's
Fierce heat: therefore the less strange it appears
If then they arose more numerous and more large,
Since they grew up when earth and air were young.
So first of all the varied families
And tribes of birds would leave their eggs, hatched out
In the spring season, as now the cicadas
In summer-time leave of their own accord
In quest of life and livelihood their sleek skins.
Then came the time when first the Earth produced
The race of mortal men. For in the fields
Plenteous heat and moisture would abound,
So that wherever a fit place occurred,
Wombs would grow, fastened to the earth by roots:

And when the growth of the infants in due time,
Avoiding moisture and demanding air,
Had broken these wombs open, then would Nature
Turn to that place the porous ducts of the Earth,
Compelling her to exude through open veins
A milk-like liquid; just as nowadays
After child-bearing every woman is filled
With sweet milk; since with her too that whole flow
Of nutriment sets streaming towards her breasts.
Earth to these children furnished food, the heat
Clothing, the grass a bed well lined with rich
Luxuriance of soft down. Moreover then
The world in its fresh newness would give rise
Neither to rigorous cold nor excessive heats
Nor violent storms of wind, for in a like
Proportion all things grow and gather strength.

Therefore again and yet again I say
That with good reason the Earth has won and keeps
The name of Mother, since she of herself
Gave birth to humankind, and at a period
Well-nigh determined shed forth every beast
That roams o'er the great mountains far and wide,
Likewise the birds of air many in shape.
But because she must have some limit set
To child-bearing, she has ceased, like a woman
Worn out by lapse of years. For Time transforms
The whole world's nature, and all things must pass
From one condition to another: nothing
Continues like itself. All is in flux:
Nature is ever changing and compelling
All that exists to alter. For one thing
Moulders and wastes away grown weak with age,
And then another comes forth into the light,
Issuing from obscurity. So thus Time
Changes the whole world's nature, and the Earth
Passes from one condition to another:

So that what once she bore she can no longer,
And now can bear what she did not before.

And many monsters too did the Earth essay
To produce in those days, creatures arising
With marvellous face and limbs, the Hermaphrodite,
A thing of neither sex, between the two,
Differing from both; some things deprived of feet;
Others again with no hands; others dumb
Without mouth, or else blind for lack of eyes,
Or bound by limbs that everywhere adhered
Fast to the body, so that they could perform
No function, nor go anywhere, nor shun
Danger, nor take what their need might require.
Other such monstrous prodigies did Earth
Produce, in vain, since nature banned their growth,
Nor could they reach the coveted flower of age,
Nor find food, nor be joined in bonds of love;
For we see numerous conditions first
Must meet together, before living things
Can beget and perpetuate their kind:
First they must have food; then a means by which
The seeds of birth throughout the frame may stream
From the relaxed limbs; also that the male
And female may unite, they must have that
Whereby each may exchange mutual joys.

And many breeds of animals in those days
Must have died out, being powerless by their offspring
To perpetuate their kind. For all those creatures
Which now you see breathing the breath of life,
'Tis either cunning, or courage, or again
Swiftness of movement, that from its origin
Must have protected and preserved each race.
Moreover many by their usefulness
Commended to us, continue to exist
Consigned to our protection. The fierce breed

Of lions first, and the other savage beasts,
Their courage has preserved, foxes their craft,
Stags their swift flight. But the light-slumbering hearts
Of faithful dogs, and the whole family
Born from the seed of burden-bearing beasts,
Woolly flocks too, and hornèd herds, all these,
Memmius, to man's protection are consigned.
For their desire has always been to escape
Wild beasts and to live peaceably, obtaining
Without toil of their own the abundant food
Which to reward their services we give them.
But those whom nature has not thus endowed
With power either to live by their own means
Or else to render us some useful service
For which we might allow their race to feed
And dwell safe under our guardianship, all those,
'Tis plain, would lie exposed a prey and spoil
To others, trammelled in their own fatal bonds,
Till nature had extinguished their whole kind.

But Centaurs there have never been, nor yet
Ever can things exist of twofold nature
And double body, moulded into one
From limbs of alien kind, whose faculties
And functions from the two sides cannot be
Sufficiently alike. That this is so,
From what follows the dullest wit may learn.
Consider first that a horse after three years
Is in his flower of vigour, but a boy
By no means so: for often in sleep he still
Will seek the milky paps of his mother's breasts.
Afterwards, when the horse's lusty strength
Fails him in old age, and his limbs grow languid
As life ebbs, only then, when the boy's age
Is flowering, youth begins, and clothes his cheeks
With soft down. Do not then believe that ever
From man's and burden-bearing horse's seed

Centaurs can be compounded and have being;
Nor yet Scyllas with half-fish bodies, girdled
With raging dogs, and other suchlike things,
Whose limbs we see discordant with each other;
Since neither do they reach their flower together,
Nor acquire bodily strength, nor in old age
Lose it at the same time: dissimilar
In each the love that burns them, and their modes
Of life incongruous: nor do the same foods give
Their bodies pleasure. Thus we may often see
Bearded goats thrive on hemlock, which for man
Is virulent poison. Since moreover flame
Is wont to scorch and burn the tawny bodies
Of lions no less than every other kind
That exists on the earth and is composed
Of flesh and blood, how could it come to pass
That one, yet with a triple body, in front
A lion, behind a serpent, in the midst
Its goat's self, a Chimaera should breathe forth
From such a body fierce flame at the mouth?
Therefore he who can fable that when earth
Was new and the sky young, such animals
Could have been propagated, resting alone
Upon this vain term, newness, he no doubt
Will babble out many follies in like fashion,
Will say that rivers then throughout the earth
Commonly flowed with gold, that trees were wont
To bloom with jewels, or that men could once
Be born with limbs so mighty, they could stalk
With giant strides across deep seas and turn
The whole heaven round about them with their hands.
For the fact that there were many seeds of things
Within the earth at that time when it first
Shed living creatures forth, is yet no proof
That beasts could have been born of mingled kinds,
Or limbs of different animals joined together;
Because the various families of plants,

The crops and thriving trees, which even now
Teem upward from the soil luxuriantly,
Can yet never be born woven together;
But each thing has its own process of growth;
All must preserve their mutual differences,
Governed by nature's irreversible law.

But that first race of men in the open fields
Was hardier far (small wonder, since hard Earth
Had brought it forth), built on a frame of bones
More large and solid, while the flesh was knit
By powerful sinews: nor did they easily
Suffer from heat or cold, nor from strange foods,
Nor yet from any bodily disease.
And during many revolving periods
Of the sun through the sky, they lived their lives
After the roving habit of wild beasts.
No one was then the curved plough's stalwart guide,
None yet had knowledge how to till the fields
With iron, or plant young saplings in the soil,
Nor how to lop old boughs from the tall trees
With pruning-hooks. What suns and rains had given,
What of her own free will Earth had brought forth,
Was enough bounty to content their hearts.
Neath acorn-bearing oak-trees their wont was
To recreate their bodies; and those berries
Which now upon the arbutus you see
Ripening to scarlet hues in winter-time,
The Earth then bore plentifully and larger
Than in these days. Then too many other kinds
Of coarse food did the world's luxuriant youth
Give birth to, ample enough for wretched men.
But to allay their thirst rivers and springs
Invited, as now waters, tumbling down
From the great mountains with clear-sounding plash,
Summon from far the thirsting tribes of beasts.
Furthermore in their roamings they would haunt

The familiar silvan precincts of the Nymphs,
Caverns wherefrom they knew that gliding streams,
Bounteously gushing forth, bathed the wet rocks—
The wet rocks, over green moss dripping down—
Or welled up bubbling over the level plain.
As yet they knew not how to employ fire,
Or to make use of skins and clothe their bodies
With spoils of wild beasts; but inhabiting
Woods, mountain-caves and forests, they would shelter
Their squalid limbs in thickets when compelled
To shun the buffeting of winds and rains.
No regard could they have to a general good,
Nor did they know how to make use in common
Of any laws or customs. Whatsoever
Fortune might set before him, that would each
Take as his prize, cunning to thrive and live
As best might please him, for himself alone.
And in the woods Venus would join the bodies
Of lovers, whether a mutual desire,
Or the man's violence and vehement lust
Had won the woman over, or a bribe
Of acorns arbute-berries or choice pears.
Trusting in marvellous strength of hands and feet
They would pursue the woodland tribes of beasts
With showers of stones or ponderous club; and many
They overcame; some few they would avoid
In hiding-places. And like bristly boars,
When night-time overtook them, they would fling
Their savage limbs naked upon the ground,
Enveloping themselves with leaves and boughs.
Nor did they call for daylight and the sun
Wandering terror-stricken about the fields
With loud wails through the shadows of the night,
But silently, buried in sleep they lay
Waiting until the sun with rosy torch
Brought light into the sky. For since from childhood
They had been wont to see darkness and light

Alternately begotten without fail,
Never could they feel wonder or misgiving
Lest night eternal should possess the earth
And the sun's light for ever be withdrawn.
Rather what caused anxiety was that often
Wild beasts made sleep unsafe for these poor wretches;
And driven from their homes in sheltering rocks
They fled at the entrance of a foaming boar
Or strong lion, yielding up at dead of night
Their leaf-strewn beds in panic to fierce guests.

And yet scarcely more often then than now
Would mortal men leave the sweet light of life
With lamentation. Each one of them indeed
Would doubtless be more likely in those days
To be seized and devoured by wild beasts' teeth,
A living food, and with his groans would fill
Mountains and forests, while he saw his own
Live flesh in a live monument entombed;
And those whom flight had saved with mangled body,
From that time forth would hold their trembling hands
Over their noisome scars, with dreadful cries
Invoking death, till agonising throes
Rid them of life, with none to give them aid,
Ignorant of what wounds required. But then
A single day did not consign to death
Thousands on thousands marshalled beneath standards,
Nor did the turbulent waters of the deep
Shatter upon the rocks both ships and men.
At that time vainly, without aim or result
The sea would often rise up and turmoil,
Then lightly lay aside its empty threatenings;
Nor could the treacherous wiles of the calm deep
Lure men to destruction with laughing waves;
For reckless seamanship was then unknown.
Moreover lack of food would then consign
Their fainting limbs to death: now rather plenty

Sinks men to ruin. Often for themselves
Would they pour poison out unwittingly:
To others now with subtler skill we give it.

Afterwards, when they had learnt the use of huts
And skins and fire; when woman, joined with man
In wedlock, dwelt apart in one abode,
And they saw offspring born out of themselves,
Then first the human race began to soften.
For fire made their chilly bodies now
Less able to endure the cold beneath
The roof of heaven; Venus impaired their strength;
And children easily by their blandishments
Broke down the haughty temper of their parents.
Then too neighbours began to join in bonds
Of friendship, wishing neither to inflict
Nor suffer violence: and for womankind
And children they would claim kind treatment, pleading
With cries and gestures inarticulately
That all men ought to have pity on the weak.
And though harmony could not everywhere
Be established, yet the most part faithfully
Observed their covenants, or man's whole race
Thus early would have perished, nor till now
Could propagation have preserved their kind.

But it was nature constrained men to utter
The tongue's various sounds; and need wrung from them
The names of things, in the same way almost
As impotence of tongue is in fact seen
To teach gesture to infants, prompting them
To point at things around them. For all creatures
Divine by instinct how far they can use
Their natural powers. Thus before horns are born
And stand out on the forehead of a calf,
When he is angry he butts and charges with it.
Then panther cubs and lion whelps will fight

With claws and feet and teeth, even at a time
When teeth and claws have hardly yet been formed.
Also we see how the whole race of birds,
Trusting their wings, will seek a fluttering succour
From new-fledged pinions. Therefore to suppose
That somebody once apportioned names to things,
And that from him men learnt to use words first,
Is mere folly. For why should this one man
Be able to denote all things by words
And utter the tongue's varied sounds, yet others
At the same time be deemed incapable
To have done the like? Besides, if others too
Had not made use of words among themselves,
Whence was the preconception[1] of their use
Implanted in this man, and whence was given
The original power to know and comprehend
What he desired to do? Again, one man
Could not subdue by force the wills of many,
Compelling them to learn his names for things.
It is not easy in any way to teach
And persuade deaf men what they ought to do;
Since never would they endure his voice for long,
Nor suffer unintelligible sounds
Fruitlessly to be dinned into their ears.
Lastly what should there be to wonder at
So much in this, that mankind, when their voice
And tongue were in full vigour, should denote things
By different sounds as different feelings bade,
Since dumb cattle and even the wild beasts
Are wont to emit distinct and varied sounds,
When they feel fear or pain, and when joy moves them?
This indeed may be learnt from manifest facts.
When the large soft mouths of Molossian dogs
Begin to growl, angrily laying bare
Their hard teeth, then far different is the tone
In which they threaten, savagely thus drawn back,

[1] See note on II. 744, p. 70.

From the clear sound which, when they bark outright,
Fills the whole neighbourhood. But when they essay
In gentle mood to lick their cubs, or when
They toss them with their paws, and snapping at them
Tenderly make as though they would devour them
With half-closed teeth, thus fondling them they yelp
With a quite different sound from their deep bay
When left alone in houses, or from the whimper
With which crouching they shrink away from blows.
Furthermore does not a young stallion's neigh
Seem different when he rages among the mares
Pierced in his flower of age by winged love's goads,
From when with wide-stretched nostrils he snorts out
The battle signal, or when at other times
He is merely whinnying with limbs atremble?
Lastly the varied families of winged birds,
Hawks, and ospreys, and gulls that seek their living
In the salt waters of the ocean waves,
Utter at other times quite other cries
Than those they make when they fight over food
Or struggle with their prey. And some will change
Their harsh notes in accordance with the weather,
As do the long-lived tribes of crows, and flocks
Of rooks, when they are said to call for rain
Or sometimes to be summoning winds to blow.
Since therefore various feelings can compel
Animals, speechless though they be, to utter
Such varying sounds, how much more natural
Is it that in those days men could denote
Dissimilar things by many different sounds!

In answer to your silent questioning here,
I say it was the lightning first brought fire
Down to the earth for men; and thence it is
All other flames have spread. Thus we behold
Many things, sowed with flames from heaven, blaze forth
When the sky's stroke has charged them with its heat.

Yet when a branching tree, tossed by the wind,
Chafing the branches of another tree,
Sways to and fro, then fire is forced out
By violent stress of friction; and at times
Hot flames are kindled and flash forth from boughs
And stems rubbing together. Of these two chances
Either may first have given fire to men.
Next the sun taught them to cook food, heating
And softening it with flame; since they would note
Many things mellowing about the fields
Smitten and conquered by his scorching rays.

And ever more and more men who excelled
In subtlety and power of mind, would show them
How for new methods and for the use of fire
To exchange their former life and livelihood.
Kings began to found cities and build forts
As refuges and strongholds for themselves,
Dividing cattle and lands, and portioning
To each his share according to his beauty,
His strength, and intellect; for comeliness
Was much esteemed, and strength was paramount.
Afterwards property was devised, and gold
Discovered, which with ease robbed both the strong
And beautiful of their honours: for most men,
However brave and beautiful by birth,
Follow the fortunes of the richer man.
But whosoever by true reason's rule
Governs his days, for him plain frugal living
And a contented spirit is mighty wealth;
For of a little never is there lack.
Yet men wished to become renowned and powerful,
That so their fortunes on a stable base
Might rest, and, being wealthy, they might lead
A tranquil life—but all in vain; for while
They strove to mount to the highest pitch of honour,
They rendered their path perilous; nay, even when

They have reached the summit, envy will sometimes
Strike like a thunderbolt and hurl men down
Contemptuously to noisome Tartarus:
Since highest things, lifted above all else,
Are most wont as by lightning to be blasted
By envy; so that quietly to obey
Is better than to crave sovereign power
And lordship over realms. Therefore let men
Sweat drops of blood, wearying themselves in vain,
Struggling along ambition's narrow road;
Since from the mouths of others comes their wisdom,
And 'tis from hearsay, rather than their own
Authentic feelings, they pursue such aims:
Nor does this happen now, nor will it happen
Hereafter, any more than once it did.

And so men slew their kings, and the ancient majesty
Of thrones and haughty sceptres was laid low.
The glorious symbol of the sovereign head,
Trodden bloodstained beneath the people's feet,
Mourned its proud honour lost; for that is greedily
Trampled down which before was too much feared.
Thus to the very lees of anarchy
All things would be reduced, when each man grasped
At lordship and dominion for himself.
Then some among them taught how to create
Magistrates, and established codes, that all
Might learn to obey laws. For now mankind,
Utterly wearied of a violent life,
Lay languishing by reason of its feuds;
Therefore the sooner of their own free will
Did they submit to laws and stringent codes.
For seeing that each, when anger prompted him,
Strove more severely to avenge himself
Than just laws now permit, for this cause men
Grew tired of a life of violence.
'Tis thus that fear of punishment infects

The enjoyment of life's prizes: for the nets
Of violence and wrong entangle all those
Who inflict them, and most often they recoil
On such as used them first: nor is it easy
For him to pass a quiet and peaceful life,
Whose deeds transgress the bonds of public peace.
For though he should elude both gods and men,
Yet he must needs mistrust whether his guilt
Will remain veiled for ever; since 'tis said
That many often by talking in their dreams
Or in delirious sickness have betrayed
Their secrets, and revealed long-hidden crimes.

Now what may be the cause that has spread wide
The cult of deities over mighty nations,
And filled cities with altars, and prescribed
The observance of such festal rites as now
At solemn times and places are performed,
Whence even now is implanted in men's minds
Religious awe, that over the whole earth
Raises new temples to the Gods and prompts
Worshippers to frequent them on feast-days—
Why this should be, it is easy to explain.
For even in early times mortals would see
With waking mind, and yet more often in sleep,
Deities with aspects of surpassing beauty
And marvellous bodily stature. To these then
They attributed sensation, since they appeared
To move their limbs and utter stately speech
Worthy of their noble aspect and vast strength.
Also they deemed eternal life was theirs,
Because their images continually
Would reappear, and their form did not change,
But most because men could not well conceive
How beings who seemed gifted with such strength
Could lightly be subdued by any force.
And they believed that their felicity

Must be beyond compare, since none of them
Seemed ever troubled by the fear of death,
Because moreover in sleep they beheld them
Performing many marvels, yet therein
Showing no sign of effort on their part.
Again they saw how the orderings of heaven
And the year's varying seasons would come round
According to fixed law, yet could they not
Discover from what causes this took place.
Therefore they found a refuge from such doubts
In handing all things over to the Deities
And deeming all to be guided by their nod.
The abodes and mansions of the Gods they placed
In heaven, because they saw night and the moon
Progressing through the sky, moon, day and night,
The severe constellations of the night,
The sky's night-wandering torches[1] and gliding fires,
Clouds and sun, rains and snow, winds, lightnings, hail,
Thunder's swift crash and mightily threatening murmurs.

O unhappy race of men, that could assign
Such functions to the Deities, and thereto
Add cruel wrath! What groans then for themselves
Did they beget, what wounds for us, what tears
For our children's children! It is no piety
To be seen often with veiled head to turn
Towards a stone, visiting every altar,
Nor to fall grovelling with outspread palms
Prostrate before the temples of the Gods,
Nor sprinkling altars with much blood of beasts
To add to votive offering votive offering;
But this rather is piety, to have power
To survey all things with a tranquil mind.
For when we lift our eyes to the celestial
Temples of the great universe, and the aether

[1] Meteors.

Studded with glittering stars, and contemplate
The paths of sun and moon, then against our hearts,
Burdened with other evils, this fear too
Begins to lift its reawakened head,
Lest we should find it true that with the Gods
Resides a boundless power which can move
Upon their various courses the bright stars.
For ignorance of cause troubles the mind,
So that it doubts whether there ever was
A birth-time and beginning for the world,
And likewise whether there shall be an end,
Till which the world's walls can endure this strain
Of restless motion; or whether by the Gods
With eternal stability endowed
They can glide on through endless lapse of years,
Defying the strong powers of infinite time.
Again, whose mind shrinks not with awe of Gods,
Whose limbs cower not in terror, when beneath
The appalling stroke of thunder the parched earth
Shudders, and mutterings run through the vast sky?
Do not the peoples and the nations quake,
And proud kings stricken with religious dread
Sit quailing, lest for any wicked deed
Or overweening word the heavy time
Of reckoning and punishment be ripe?
Also when the full violence of a wind
Raging across the sea sweeps o'er the waves
The high commander of a fleet with all
His powerful legions and his elephants,
Does he not supplicate the Gods with vows
For mercy, and with craven prayers entreat them
To lull the storm and grant propitious gales?
But all in vain; since often none the less,
Seized by the violent hurricane, he is whirled
Onto the shoals of death. Thus evermore
Some hidden power treads human grandeur down,
And seems to make its sport of the proud rods

And cruel axes,[1] crushed beneath its heel.
Lastly, when the whole earth rocks under them,
And cities tumble with the shock or stand
In doubt, threatening to fall, what wonder is it
That mortal creatures should abase themselves,
Allowing vast dominion to the Gods,
And wondrous powers to govern the whole world?

Now must I tell how copper gold and iron,
And weighty silver also, and massive lead
Were first discovered when on mountain heights
Fire had consumed huge forests with its heat,
Kindled either by lightning from the sky,
Or because men waging some forest war
Had carried fire among their enemies
For terror's sake; or else because drawn on
By the soil's goodness they would wish to clear
Fat lands and turn them into pasturage,
Or to kill beasts and grow rich with the spoils.
For hunting with the pitfall and with fire
Came into use before woods were enclosed
With nets or drawn by dogs. Howe'er that be,
From whatsoever cause the heat of flame
With terrible crackling had devoured whole forests
Down to their deepest roots and thoroughly baked
The soil with fire, forth from the glowing veins
There would ooze and collect in cavities
Streams of silver and gold, of copper too,
And lead. When afterwards men found these metals
Cooled into lumps and glittering on the ground
With brilliant colours, they would pick them up
Attracted by their bright smooth loveliness;
And they would then observe how each was formed
Into a shape similar to the imprint
Of the hollow where it lay. Next it would strike them
That, melted down by heat, these could be made

[1] The insignia of the Roman magistrates.

To run into any form and mould they pleased,
And further could by hammering be wrought
Into points tapering as sharp and fine
As they might need, so furnishing themselves
With tools wherewith to cut down woods, hew timber
And plane planks smooth, to drill and punch and bore.
And this they attempted first with silver and gold
No less than with stout copper's masterful strength:
But in vain, since their force would yield and fail,
And they would prove less fit to endure hard toil.
For copper then was the more highly esteemed;
Gold lay despised as useless with its dull
And blunted edge: now copper lies neglected,
While gold has mounted to the pitch of honour.
Thus Time as it revolves is ever changing
The seasons of things. What was once esteemed
Becomes at length of no repute; whereon
Some other thing, issuing from obscurity,
Mounts up and daily is coveted more and more,
And, once discovered, blossoms out in praises,
Rising to wondrous honour among men.

Now, Memmius, you will easily of yourself
Understand in what way the nature of iron
Was first discovered. Hands nails teeth and stones
Were the earliest weapons, boughs also torn off
From forest trees, and flame and fire, so soon
As these became known. Later the force of iron
And copper was discovered. And the use
Of copper was known earlier than of iron,
Since it is easier to be worked, and found
More copiously. With copper they would till
The soil of earth, with copper they stirred up
The waves of war and dealt wide-gaping wounds
And seized on lands and cattle: for all else,
Being naked and unarmed, would at once yield
To those who had weapons. Then by slow degrees

The sword of iron made progress, while the type
Of the copper sickle came to be despised.
With iron they began to cleave the soil,
And through its use wavering war's conflicts
Were rendered equal. Earlier was the custom
Of mounting armed upon a horse's back
And guiding it with reins and dealing blows
With the right arm, long before men dared tempt
The risks of battle in the two-horsed car.
And they would learn the art to yoke two steeds
Earlier than to yoke four, or to mount armed
Upon scythed chariots. Next the Poeni taught
The grim Lucanian kine,[1] with towered backs
And snake-like hands, to endure the wounds of war
And rout great troops of martial chivalry.
Thus miserable discord brought to birth
One thing after another to appal
Mankind's embattled nations, every day
Making addition to war's frightfulness.

Also in warfare they made trial of bulls,
And sought to drive fierce boars against the foe.
And some sent mighty lions in their van
With armed trainers and savage guardians
To govern them and hold them in with chains;
In vain, for heated with promiscuous carnage,
Raging they put to flight squadrons of friends
And foes alike, tossing on every side
Their terrible crests; nor could the horsemen calm
Their horses panic-stricken by the roaring,
Or turn them by the bridle against their foes.
The she-lions would spring fiercely on all sides
Right in the faces of their adversaries,
Or from behind seizing them off their guard
Would clasp and tear them wounded down to the earth,

[1] Elephants, first seen by the Romans in Lucania in the army of Pyrrhus, 281 B.C.

Gripping them with their strong teeth and hooked claws.
The bulls would toss and trample underfoot
Their own friends, goring the horses from beneath
In belly and flank, tearing the soil up savagely.
Fierce boars would rend their allies with strong tusks,
Staining the broken weapons with their blood,
And put to rout both horse and foot together.
The steeds, to escape from the tusk's cruel push,
Would swerve aside or rearing paw the air;
In vain, for with severed tendons they would crash
Heavily down to earth and lie stretched out.
Beasts, by the keepers deemed to have been tamed
Sufficiently at home, they now would see
Heated to madness in the hour of battle
By wounds and shouts, flight, panic and uproar.
Of all the different kinds of savage beasts
None could they rally, once dispersed in flight;
As often nowadays the Lucanian kine,
Gashed cruelly with the steel, will fly dispersed,
Inflicting much grim havoc on their friends.
If indeed men ever acted thus. But scarcely
Can I believe that, ere this dire disaster
Befell both sides alike, they were not able
To imagine and foresee that this would happen.
And it were easier to maintain that this
Happened somewhere within the universe
Of various worlds fashioned in various ways,
Than upon any one determined earth.[1]
But men chose to act thus, not in the hope
Of victory so much, as from the wish
To give their foes cause to lament, and then
Perish themselves, being desperate through mistrust
Of their own numbers, or through lack of arms.

The plaited garment came before the dress
Of woven stuff. Weaving comes after iron,

[1] See note on ἰσονομία, or "equal distribution", II. 535, p. 62.

Since weaving tools need iron to fashion them.
By no means else can such smooth things be made
As heddles, spindles, shuttles and clattering yarn-beams.
Men before womankind did Nature prompt
To work wool; for in general the male sex
Is by far the more skilful and ingenious:
Till the rough husbandmen so chided them
That at length they consented to resign
Such lighter tasks into the hands of women,
And themselves took their share in heavier toils,
Hardening with hard labour limbs and hands.

And it was Nature, creatress of things,
Who first by her example taught mankind
How to sow, and first prompted them to graft;
For berries and acorns dropping from the trees
Would put forth in due season underneath
Swarms of seedlings: and hence the fancy came
To insert grafts into the boughs, and plant
Young saplings in the soil about the fields.
Next they would try another and yet another
Method of tilling their loved piece of land,
And so could watch how kindly fostering culture
Helped the earth to improve its own wild fruits.
And they would force the forests day by day
To retreat higher up the mountain-sides
And yield the ground below to husbandry,
That so meadows and ponds rivulets crops
And glad vineyards might cover hill and plain,
While grey-green boundary strips of olive trees
Might run between the fields, stretching far out
O'er hillock valley and plain; as now you see
Whole countrysides enriched with varied beauty,
Adorned with rows of sweet fruit-bearing trees
And enclosed round about with fertile groves.

But the art of imitating with their mouths

The liquid notes of birds, came long before
Men could delight their ears by singing words
To smooth tunes; and the whistlings of the zephyr
In hollow reeds first taught the husbandmen
To blow through hollow stalks. Then by degrees
They learnt those sweet sad ditties which the pipe,
Touched by the fingers of the melodist,
Pours forth, such as are heard mid pathless woods
Forests and glades, among the lonely haunts
Of shepherds, and the abodes of magic calm.
Thus would they soothe and gratify their minds,
When satiate with food; for all such things
Give pleasure then. So often, couched together
On the soft grass, beside a water-brook
Beneath a tall tree's boughs, at no great cost
They would regale their bodies joyously,
At those times chiefly when the weather smiled
And the year's seasons painted the green herbage
With flowers. Then went round the jest, the tale,
The merry laugh; for then the rustic muse
Was in full force; then frolick jollity
Would prompt them to enwreathe their heads and shoulders
With plaited garlands woven of flowers and leaves,
Or dancing out of measure to move their limbs
Clumsily, and with clumsy foot to beat
Their mother earth; whence smiles and jovial laughter
Would rise; since being more novel and admired,
All such sports then were held in high esteem.
And they would find solace for wakefulness
In giving voice to many varied notes
Of winding song, and running with curved lip
Over the reed-pipes: and from them this custom
Is handed down to watchmen nowadays,
Who though they have better learnt to observe time,
Yet not one whit more pleasure do they enjoy
Than once that silvan race of earth-born men.
For what is present, if we have never known

Anything more delightful, gives us pleasure
Beyond all else and seems to be the best;
But if some better thing be afterwards
Discovered, this will often spoil for us all
That pleased us once, and change our feelings towards it.
Thus it was acorns came to be disliked:
Thus were abandoned those beds of strewn grass
And heaped leaves: the dress too of wild beast skin
Fell thus into contempt—though I suppose
That when it was invented it would rouse
Such envy that the man who wore it first
Would be waylaid and slain: yet after all
It would be torn to pieces among the thieves
And with much bloodshed utterly destroyed,
So that it never could be turned to use.
Therefore skins then, now gold and purple vex
Men's lives with cares and wear them out with war.
And here, I think, the greater guilt is ours;
For the cold would torment those earth-born men
Naked without their skins; but us no harm
Whatever can it cause to go without
A purple robe broidered with large designs
In gold thread, so we have but on our backs
A plain plebeian cloak to keep us warm.
Therefore mankind is always toiling vainly,
Fruitlessly wasting life in empty cares,
Doubtless because they will not recognize
The limits of possession nor the bounds
Beyond which no true pleasure can increase.
And so by slow degrees this ignorance
Has carried life out into the deep seas,
And from the bottom stirred up war's huge waves.

But those vigilant watchers, sun and moon,
That circling round illumine with their light
The vast revolving temple of the sky,
Taught mankind how the seasons of the year

Return, and how all things are brought to pass
According to a fixed plan and fixed order.

And now men dwelt securely fenced around
By strong towers, and the land was portioned out
And marked off to be tilled; already now
The sea was gay with flitting sails, and towns
Were joined in league of friendship and alliance,
When first poets made record in their songs
Of men's deeds: for not long before this time
Had letters been invented. For which cause
Our age cannot look back to earlier things
Except where reasoning reveals their traces.

Shipping and agriculture, city-walls,
Laws, arms, roads, robes and other suchlike things,
Moreover all life's prizes and refinements,
Poems and pictures and the chiselling
Of fine-wrought statues, every one of these
Long practice and the untiring mind's experience
Taught men by slow degrees as they progressed
Step after step. Thus time little by little
Brings forth each several thing, and reason lifts it
Into the borders of the light; for first
One thing and then another must in turn
Rise from obscurity, until each art
Attains its highest pitch of excellence.

BOOK VI

In ancient days Athens of glorious name
Was first to spread abroad corn-bearing crops
Among unhappy mortals, and to frame
Their lives in a new mould and give them laws.
Also those kindly solaces of life
She first bestowed, when she gave birth to a man
Endowed with such great intellect, who once
Poured forth all wisdom from truth-telling lips;
Whose glory, even when his light was quenched,
Because of his divine discoveries
Was noised abroad in ancient times, and now
Is lifted high as heaven. For when he saw
How well-nigh all those things which need demands
For man's subsistence had been now provided;
And that so far as it seemed possible
Life was established in security;
That men had attained power and affluence
Of wealth honour and glory, and grown proud
In their children's good name; yet that not one
At home possessed a heart the less care-stricken,
But ceaselessly despite his wiser mind
Tormenting all his days, could not refrain
From petulant rage and wearisome complaint;
Then did he understand it was the vessel
Itself that was the cause of imperfection,
And by its imperfection all those things
That came within it, gathered from outside,
Though ne'er so excellent, were spoiled therein;
In part because he saw that there were holes
Through which it leaked, so that by no means ever
Might it be filled full; partly that he perceived
How as with a foul savour it defiled
All things within it which had entered there.
And so with truthful words he purged men's hearts

And fixed a limit to desire and fear;
Then setting forth what was the highest good
Which we all strive to attain, he pointed out
The path along which by a slender track
We might in a straight course arrive at it;
Likewise he showed what evils there must be
In mortal affairs on every side, arising
And flying this way and that, whether it were
By natural chance or force, since it was Nature
Which had ordained it so; and by what gates
To meet each evil, men must sally forth:
Also he proved how mostly without cause
Mankind set darkly tossing in their hearts
The sad billows of care. For just as children
In the blind darkness tremble and are afraid
Of all things, so we sometimes in the light
Fear things that are no whit more to be dreaded
Than those which children shudder at in the dark,
Imagining that they will come to pass.
This terror therefore and darkness of the mind
Must needs be scattered not by the sun's beams
And day's bright arrows, but by contemplation
Of Nature's aspect and her inward law.
So the more zealously will I weave the web
Of my discourse, completing my design.

And now that I have shown you how the sky's
Mansions are mortal, and that heaven is formed
Of a body that had birth, and since of all
That takes place and must needs take place therein
I have unravelled most, give further heed
To what remains. Since once I have made bold
To mount the glorious chariot of the Muses,
I will now tell how in the upper air
Tempests of wind arise; how all sinks down
To rest once more: the turmoil that has been
Vanishes when its fury is appeased.

And I will explain all else that mortals see
Coming to pass on earth and in the sky,
Such sights as often hold them in terrified
Suspense of mind, and through fear of the Gods
Abase their souls and crush them grovelling
Down to the ground, because they are compelled,
Through ignorance of the causes, to assign
All such things to the empire of the Gods,
Acknowledging their power to be supreme.
For those who have been rightly taught that Deities
Lead a life free from care, if yet they wonder
By what means all things can be carried on,
Such above all as are perceived to happen
In the aethereal regions overhead,
They are borne back again into their old
Religious fears, and adopt pitiless lords,
Whom these unhappy men believe to be
Almighty; for they are ignorant of what can
And what cannot exist; in fine they know not
Upon what principle each thing has its powers
Limited, and its deep-set boundary stone.
And therefore all the more they are led astray
By blind reasoning. Now unless you fling
Forth from your mind and banish far away
All such belief in falsehoods that degrade
The Deities and consist not with their peace,
Then, thus by you disparaged and profaned,
Oft will their holy godheads do you hurt;
Not that their sovereign power can be impaired,
So that in anger they should wish to exact
Fierce penalties, but because you yourself
Will fancy that those placid beings throned
In serene peace, can verily be tossed
By great billows of wrath: nor will you enter
With a calm breast the temples of the Gods,
Nor yet will you be able to receive
In tranquil peace of spirit those images

Which from their holy bodies, heralding
Their divine beauty, float into men's minds.
And to what kind of life these errors lead
May be imagined. Such credulity
The most veracious reasoning alone
Can drive far from us. And though to that end
I have set forth much already, yet more still
Remains for me to adorn in polished verses.
The inward law and aspect of the heavens
Must now be grasped: tempests and bright lightnings,
Their action and what cause sets them in motion,
Must be described; lest, when you have mapped the sky
Into augural divisions, you should then
Quake in dismay, questioning from what quarter
The flash sped in its flight, or on which side
It vanished; in what manner it pierced through
Into walled places, and how, having played
The tyrant there, it leapt forth and was gone.
Of all such operations by no means
Can men perceive the causes, and so fancy
That they must come to pass by power divine.
O Muse of knowledge, solace of mankind
And the delight of Gods, Calliope,
Point the track out before me as I speed
Towards the white line of my final goal,
That so with thee to guide me I may win
The glorious crown of victory and its praise.

First of all, when the azure heavens are shaken
By thunder, it is because clouds, as they fly
Through the upper air, rush violently together
Driven by conflicting winds. For no sound comes
From any serene quarter of the sky,
But wheresoever in a denser host
The clouds are gathered, thence more frequently
The crashing thunder bursts with a mighty roar.
Moreover clouds cannot be formed of substance

So dense as stones or logs, nor yet so thin
As mists or flying smoke; for they must then
Either fall dragged down by sheer weight like stones,
Or like smoke would be unable to cohere,
Or to contain cold snows and showers of hail.
Furthermore clouds give forth over the plains
Of the wide-spreading world just such a sound
As when at times a canvas, that lies stretched
Above some great theatre, tossing among
The poles and beams, cracks loudly, or sometimes torn
By a boisterous gale flaps wildly, and imitates
The noise of paper rent (for that sound too
You may observe in thunder); or when gusts
With buffeting blows are whirling through the air
A hanging cloth or flying sheets of paper.
And sometimes it may happen that the clouds
Cannot meet front to front, but each instead
Moves past the other's flank leisurely grazing
Body with body in opposite directions;
And thence comes that dry sound which on our ears
Grates harshly, and is long drawn out, until
The clouds have escaped from such close neighbourhood.

Often too in this manner all things appear
To tremble from the shock of heavy thunder,
And the vast walls of the capacious world
Seem to be suddenly riven and leap apart,
When gathering swiftly a storm of violent wind
Has hurled itself into the clouds, and there
Shut in, with whirling eddy compels a cloud
On all sides more and more to become hollow,
While the outer layers thicken all around;
Then, when the wind's force and impetuous rushing
Have weakened it, the cloud splits and explodes
With a terrifying crash. Nor is this strange;
Since often a small bladder filled with air,
When suddenly burst, will give forth a loud sound.

Also we can explain to you how it is
That winds make noises when they blow through clouds.
Often we see the clouds that move along
Are branching and rough in many ways. Just so,
When through a dense wood blasts from the north-west
Are blowing, the leaves give forth a similar roar
And the branches crash noisily. Sometimes too
A strong wind's violent force tears through a cloud
And breaks it asunder with a forthright charge.
For what must be a wind-storm's power there,
By manifest facts is shown; since here on earth,
Where it is gentler, it yet wrenches out
And plucks tall trees up from their deepest roots.
There are waves also that move through the clouds
And give a kind of hoarse roar as they break,
Just such as may be heard in deep rivers,
Or on the great sea when the surf is breaking.
Such too is the roar heard when the burning force
Of lightning falls from one cloud into another:
If haply that cloud which receives the fire
Contains much moisture, at once with a great din
It quenches the fire's life; just as white-hot
From a glowing furnace iron is wont to hiss
When we have plunged it quickly into cold water.
Or should a drier cloud receive the fire,
Then, kindled on a sudden, it will burn
With a huge noise; as though by whirlwinds driven
A flame should range o'er laurel-foliaged mountains
Consuming all things in its mighty rush:
And naught burns in the crackling flame with sound
More terrible than Apollo's Delphic laurel.
Again, loud crashing of ice and falling of hail
Is often heard in the vast clouds on high.
For when the wind into a narrow space
Packs them together, those mountains of cloud,
Congealed and mixed with hail, must then break up.

Moreover it lightens when by their collision
The clouds have struck out many seeds of fire;
Just as if stone or steel were to strike stone;
For then also a flash leaps out, and fire
Scatters bright sparks abroad. But we perceive
The thunder with our ears after our eyes
Have seen the lightning-flash, because things always
Travel more slowly to the ears than those
Which excite vision travel to the eyes.
This truth from another instance you may learn.
When from afar you watch some man who is cutting
A huge tree down with double-headed axe,
You will perceive the stroke before the blow
Sounds in your ears. Thus too we see the lightning
Before we hear the thunder, that is discharged
Together with the flash for a like cause,
Since from the same collision it was born.

Moreover thus it is that the clouds blazon
Whole regions with a winged flash, and the storm
Lightens with quivering vehemence. When the wind
Has forced its way into a cloud, and there
Whirling about, as I have shown before,
Has thickened the outer cloud by hollowing it,
Then with its own swift movement it grows hot.
Thus you see all things heated through and through
And fired by motion: nay, a ball of lead
Whirling through a long course will even melt.
When therefore it has torn through the black cloud,
This heated blast will seem by violence
Suddenly to press out and scatter abroad
The seeds of fire that cause those vibrating
Flashes of flame. Thereon follows the sound,
Which moves more slowly to assail our ears
Than do those things that travel towards our eyesight.
When this takes place, you must know that the clouds
Are thick, and at the same time piled up high

In marvellous masses one above the other;
Nor should you be deceived because we see
From below rather how great is their breadth
Than to how great a height they stand piled up.
For do but look, when winds are carrying
Clouds in mountainous shapes athwart the sky,
Or when you see them banked along the sides
Of mighty mountains one above the other,
Pressing down from above, while they remain
Motionless, and the winds on every side
Are slumber-bound: then you will comprehend
How vast must be their masses, and perceive
Caverns built as it were of hanging rocks;
Which when, a tempest gathering, the winds
Have filled, imprisoned in the clouds they chafe
With loud roaring, and bluster within their dens
Like wild beasts. Now from this side now from that
They send abroad their mutterings through the clouds,
And seeking a way out whirl round, and roll
Together from the clouds the seeds of fire;
And so, when they have gathered a large number,
They cause within the hollow furnaces
Flame to rotate, till they have burst the cloud
Asunder, and flashed in bickering lightning forth.

Another reason why yon golden colour
Of liquid fire flies swiftly down to the earth,
Is that the clouds themselves must have within them
Numberless seeds of fire; for when the clouds
Are without any moisture, they are mostly
Of a bright flame-like colour. And in truth
It needs must be that the clouds should receive
Many such seeds from the sun's light; and so
With good cause they are ruddy and shed forth fires.
When therefore a wind has driven these clouds together,
Crowding and crushing and compelling them
Into one place, they press out and shed forth

The seeds that cause lightning's flame-coloured flash.
Also it lightens when the clouds of heaven
Are rarefied: for when the wind is gently
Dispersing and dissolving them as they move,
Those seeds that make lightning must fall perforce.
Then without hideous terrifying din
It lightens, and with no tumultuous uproar.

Furthermore, with what nature thunderbolts
Are endowed is made manifest by their strokes,
And by the encaustic traces of their heat,
And the marks which exhale the noisome vapours
Of sulphur: for all these are signs of fire,
Not of wind nor of rain. Besides, they often
Set roofs on fire, and with nimble flame
Will play the tyrant even within the house.
This fire, most subtle among all fires, has nature
Formed of minute and mobile particles,
Such that nothing whatever can withstand it.
For the strong thunderbolt passes through walls
Of houses, even as sounds and voices do;
Passes through stones, through brass, and in an instant
Melts brass and gold. Also it causes wine
To disappear suddenly, though the jars
Remain untouched, doubtless because its heat
The moment it arrives will easily loosen
And make the earthenware of the vessel porous
On every side, then forcing a way within it
Will swiftly separate and disperse abroad
The wine's first elements. Yet this, we see,
The sun's heat cannot accomplish in long years
With all the potence of its quivering blaze:
So much more swift and masterful is this force.

And now in what way thunderbolts are begotten,
How they acquire such speed and violence
That they can split towers open with a stroke,

Throw down houses, tear out beams and rafters,
Demolish or displace the monuments
Of heroes, strike men lifeless, on all sides
Lay cattle low—by what force they have power
To do such things as these, I will set forth,
And detain you with promises no longer.

Thunderbolts we must deem to be begotten
From thick clouds piled on high; for none are ever
Discharged from a serene sky, nor when clouds
Are of slight density. The truth of this
Is proved beyond all doubt by manifest fact:
Since clouds grow to huge masses at such times
Throughout the sky, so that we might imagine
That all its darkness had abandoned Acheron
From all sides, and filled full the sky's great caverns;
So rapidly does the hideous night of clouds
Gather together, and faces of murk horror
Hang over us on high, whene'er the tempest
Is purposing to forge its thunderbolts.
Often moreover a black cloud out at sea
Falls, like a stream of pitch poured down from heaven,
Afar off onto the waves, heavily charged
With darkness, drawing with it a murky tempest
Big with lightnings and hurricane—a cloud fraught
With fires and winds to the utmost, in such wise
That even on land men shudder and seek shelter.
Thus then we must believe such storms tower high
Above our heads. For neither would the clouds
Whelm the earth in such blackness, were they not
Built high above each other, multitudes
On multitudes, robbing us of the sun;
Nor, falling, could they drown the earth in rain
So great as to make rivers overflow
And flood whole plains, if the sky were not packed
With clouds piled up on high. At such times then
All things with winds and fires are filled; and therefore

Rumblings and lightnings take place on all sides.
For I have shown already that hollow clouds
Contain innumerable seeds of heat;
Also from the sun's rays, and from their warmth,
They must take many in. And for this cause,
When the same wind, that chances to collect
These clouds into some one place, has pressed out
Many seeds of heat, and likewise mixed itself
With this fire, then will an eddy find its way
Inside, and whirl round in that narrow space,
Till in the glowing inner furnaces
It has sharpened the thunderbolt. For the wind
Is kindled in two ways: it grows hot both
By its own speed and through contact with fire.
After that, when the vehement wind is heated
To the utmost, and the impetuous power of fire
Has entered, then the thunderbolt, as it were
Fully forged, on a sudden cleaves the cloud;
So forth, rapidly darting, leaps the flame
Illumining all things round with quivering flashes.
Close thereon follows a clap so violent
That, bursting asunder suddenly, the mansions
Of heaven appear to crush us from above.
Thereupon trembling violently assails
The earth, and mutterings run through the lofty sky;
For then it seems as though the whole tempest
Quaked with the shock, and rumbling sounds break forth.
And from this shock there follows rain so heavy
And so abundant, that the whole sky above
Seems to be turning into rain, and tumbling
Thus headlong, to be summoning the world back
To a deluge: so great is the flood discharged
By the bursting of the cloud and the wind's fury,
When with the fiery stroke flies forth the thunder.
There are times also when the rushing force
Of wind falls from without upon a cloud

Hot with a thunderbolt now fully forged;
And so soon as the wind has burst the cloud,
Straightway that eddying whirl of fire falls
Which we call thunderbolt in our native speech.
The same takes place in other directions too
Wherever the wind's violence has inclined.
Also it sometimes happens that the wind's
Violence, though it sets forth without fire,
Catches fire in the course of its long travel,
Losing, as it advances, certain particles
That are too large to make their way through the air
So speedily as the rest; gathering too
Out of the air itself and sweeping along
Other very small particles, that mix
With the wind and create fire as they fly;
In much the same way as a ball of lead
Will often become hot during its course,
When casting from it many particles
Of coldness, it has taken up fire in the air.
Sometimes again, when the wind's violence,
Though cold and without fire at setting forth,
Has struck its stroke, the mere force of the blow
May arouse fire; doubtless because no sooner
Has the wind smitten the cloud with a fierce blow,
Than elements of heat can stream together
Both from the wind and likewise from that thing
Which then receives the blow. Thus when with iron
We strike stone, fire flies out: nor do its seeds
Of hot flame run together at the blow
Any the slower because the iron that strikes
Is cold. Thus in like manner a thing must needs
Be kindled by the thunderbolt, should it chance
To be prepared and suitable for flames.
Besides, we have small reason to suppose
That the wind's might can be entirely cold
When it has rushed with such force from above;
Nay, if it be not kindled on its course

With fire already, it must yet arrive
At least in a warm state and mixed with heat.

But the cause of the speed and powerful stroke
Of thunderbolts, and of the rapid fall
With which they are wont to reach their aim, is this:
First in the clouds their violent force collects
Gathering mighty energies for flight;
Then when the cloud no longer can contain
The thunderbolt's increasing fury, its force
Is pressed forth, and so flies with marvellous speed
Like missiles hurled from powerful catapults.
Furthermore it is formed of elements
Both small and smooth; and such a substance nothing
Can easily withstand; for slipping in
Between, it penetrates through the open pores:
Wherefore it is not hindered and delayed
By many obstacles, and for this cause
Flies onward, gliding with impetuous speed.
Again, all weights whatsoever by their nature
Press downwards; but when a blow is given as well,
The speed is doubled, and the impetus
Grows stronger, so that the more violently
And swiftly does the lightning strike aside
Whatever obstacle would hinder it,
And so pursues its journey. Furthermore,
Since it comes rushing onward from far off,
It must acquire greater and greater speed,
Which grows with moving and augments the lightning's
Mighty strength, giving vigour to its stroke.
For this speed causes all the seeds of the bolt
To be borne onward in a direct line
Towards one place, driving them all together,
As on they rush, into that single path.
And maybe, as it goes, the lightning draws
Certain particles out of the air itself,
And these kindle its swiftness by their blows.

Also it passes right through many things,
And yet leaves them undamaged and intact,
Because the liquid fire finds its way
By the open pores. And many it pierces through,
When the atoms of the thunderbolt have fallen
On the atoms of these things just at the points
Where they are interlaced and held together.
Moreover brass it easily dissolves,
And fuses gold in a moment, for its mass
Is formed of particles minutely small
And of smooth elements, which easily
Make their way in and, being there, at once
Dissolve all knots and loosen every bond.

It is in Autumn mostly that the sky's
Mansion, studded with glittering stars, is shaken
On all sides, and the whole earth too; or else
When the Spring's flowery season is disclosed.
For when it is cold the elements of fire
Are lacking, and winds fail during the heat,
Nor are the clouds then of so dense a body.
When therefore the sky's temperature stands
Between the two extremes, the different causes
Of lightning all combine; for then the year's
Cross-currents mingle together cold and heat
(And each of these for forging thunderbolts
A cloud has need of), so that there is a discord
Among things, and the air with fires and winds
In a mighty tumult billows furiously.
For the beginning of heat is the end of cold;
That is the Spring: therefore unlike things then
Mingling must fight together and turmoil.
And when the last heat mixed with the first cold
Comes round, that season which we call the Autumn,
Then too with Summer fierce Winter conflicts.
So this is why these seasons must be called
The year's cross-currents; and it is not strange

If at that time thunderbolts come most often
And turbulent storms are stirred up in the sky,
Since both sides then meet in tumultuous strife
Of doubtful battle, the one armed with flames,
The other with commingled winds and water.

By reasoning thus may we understand the true
Nature of the fire-carrying thunderbolt,
And so learn by what force it does each thing,
Not by unrolling scrolls of Tyrrhene charms
In vain search there for evidence of the Gods'
Concealed designs, questioning from what quarter
The flash sped in its flight, or on which side
It vanished; in what manner it pierced through
Into walled places; and how, having played
The tyrant there, it leapt forth and was gone;
Or what dire bane the thunderstroke from heaven
Has power to execute. But if Jupiter
And other deities with frightful din
Shake the resplendent mansions of the sky
And hurl fire whither each may have a mind,
Why strike they not all such as make no scruple
To commit some abhorrent crime, and cause them
From breast pierced through and through to breathe forth flames
Of lightning, a dread lesson to mankind?
Why rather is one who is conscious of no guilt,
Innocent though he be, wrapped and involved
In flames, seized in a moment by the whirlwind
And fire of heaven? Why too do they aim
At solitudes, and spend their toil in vain?
Are they at such times practising their arms
And strengthening their sinews? Why permit they
The weapon of the Father to be blunted
Against the earth? Wherefore does he himself
Allow this, and not spare it for his enemies?
Why furthermore does Jupiter never hurl

A bolt on the earth nor shed his thundering forth,
When the sky is unclouded on all sides?
Or, so soon as beneath him clouds have gathered,
Does he himself then go down into them,
That he may thence direct from close at hand
The strokes of his weapon? Aye, and for what reason
Does he hurl into the sea? For what offence
Does he arraign its waves, its watery masses
And floating plains? Again if he would have us
Avoid the thunderstroke, why is he loath
To give us power to behold it when 'tis hurled?
But if he wish to o'erwhelm us with his fire
Ere we are ware of it, why thunders he
From the same quarter, so that we can shun it?
Wherefore beforehand does he stir up darkness,
Rumblings and mutterings? Then how believe
That he should hurl his bolt on many sides
At the same time? Or would you be so bold
As to maintain that never has this happened,
That at one moment several strokes took place?
Nay, surely often and often has this happened,
And must needs happen, that even as it rains
And as showers fall in many different regions,
So at one time many thunderbolts are formed.
Lastly why does he shatter the holy shrines
Of Deities with destroying thunderbolt,
Nay, his own glorious temples? Why does he break
The fine-wrought idols of the Gods, and spoil
His own images of their majesty
By a violent wound? Why does he oftenest aim
At lofty spots; and why do we behold
Most traces of his fire on mountain-tops?

To proceed, it is easy from these facts
To understand how it is that those things
Which the Greeks from their nature named *presters*,[1]

[1] Fiery whirlwinds (πίμπρημι).

Come down into the sea, shot from on high.
For a kind of column sometimes is thrust down
From heaven and descends upon the sea,
While all round it the surges boil, stirred up
By violent blasts of wind; and all ships then
Caught in that turmoil, are tossed wildly about,
And so brought into utmost jeopardy.
This happens when at times the impetuous force
Of some wind has not power to burst a cloud,
As it essays to do, but weighs it down,
So that it seems like to a column thrust
Downward from sky to sea, little by little,
As though from above something were being forced
By a fist and push of arm, and so stretched out
Towards the waves. But when it has rent this cloud,
The wind's force bursts out thence into the sea,
And causes a wondrous boiling in the waves.
For the eddying whirl descends and carries down
Along with it that limber-bodied cloud;
And then this wind, as soon as it has thrust
The pregnant cloud down to the ocean's surface,
With a sudden swoop plunges itself entire
Into the water and stirs up the whole sea,
Compelling it to boil with a huge roar.
Sometimes moreover a whirling eddy of wind
Enwraps itself in clouds, sweeping together
The seeds of cloud out of the air, and seems
To imitate the *prester* that is thrust
Down from the sky. Whenever one of these
Has thrust itself down onto the earth, and there
Has burst, it vomits forth a monstrous fury
Of whirlwind and of storm. But because this
Rarely takes place at all, and because mountains
On land must needs obstruct it, such a sight
Is to be seen more often upon the sea
With its wide prospect and expanse of sky.

Clouds are formed, when in the upper tracts of heaven
All at once many flying particles
Have met together, of a rougher kind,
Such that, although the links that tangle them
Be slight, they yet can grasp and cling to each other.
These particles first cause little clouds to form;
Then the clouds grasp each other and congregate,
Increasing as they unite, and by the winds
Are borne on till at last a fierce storm gathers.
Also the nearer to heaven a mountain's crests,
The more continually at a height so great
Do they smoke with a tawny cloud's thick darkness,
Because, so soon as the clouds form, before
The eyes can see them yet, so thin they are,
The winds will drive together and carry them
To the highest mountain-crests. And here at last,
Thronging in greater crowds, they grow so dense
That they can become visible as they rise
From the very mountain-top into the aether.
For the evidence of fact, and our sensations
When we climb lofty mountains, make it clear
That the open spaces on the heights are windy.
Moreover, when clothes hung out on the shore
Absorb the clinging moisture, it is clear
That nature takes up numberless particles
From over the whole sea. Therefore it seems
The more likely that many particles
May also rise up out of the billowing
Of the salt ocean to increase the clouds;
For water is kin to water in every way.
Moreover from all rivers and likewise
Out of the earth itself we behold mists
And vapour rising; and these like a breath
Being thence forced out, are then carried aloft
Overcasting the heavens with their darkness,
And little by little as they flock together
Build up the clouds on high. For the stream also

Of the star-bearing aether from above
Presses down, and condensing them appears
To weave a web of clouds under the blue.
Also sometimes into this heaven of ours
There come from outside those bodies which form
Clouds and the flying rack; for I have shown
Their number to be numberless, and the sum
Of deep space to be infinite, and have proved
With what velocity such bodies fly,
And how in a moment they are wont to traverse
A space inexpressible. So 'tis not strange
If often storm and darkness in a brief time
Cover up seas and lands, brooding above them
With such great clouds; since everywhere through all
The passages of aether, and as it were
Through all the breathing-holes of the great world
Around us, power to issue forth and enter
Has been accorded to the elements.

Now listen; I will set forth in what manner
Rainy moisture is formed in the high clouds,
And thence descending falls to the earth in showers.
First you will grant that many seeds of water
Rise up together with the clouds themselves
From things of all kinds, so that both the clouds
And all the water that is within the clouds
Increase at the same time, just as our body
Increases at the same time with the blood,
As also does the sweat and all the moisture
That is within the limbs. Moreover clouds,
When winds carry them over the great sea,
Often imbibe, like hanging fleeces of wool,
Much moisture from the waves. And in like manner
Is moisture raised to the clouds from every stream.
And when the seeds of water, from all sides
Augmented, many in number in many ways
Have met together there, the close-packed clouds

Strive to discharge their moisture for two causes:
First the wind's force drives the rain-clouds together;
And then their very mass, when a great throng
Has been collected, thrusts and presses down
From above, and so makes the rain stream out.
Furthermore, when the clouds are rarefied
Or dispersed by the winds, being smitten too
By the sun's heat, they discharge rainy moisture
And trickle down, as over a hot fire
Wax melts away and quickly turns to liquid.
But a violent downpour follows when the clouds
Are violently pressed by either force,
By their own piled up mass, or by the wind's
Impetuous onrush. Also rains are wont
To last on and continue a long while
When many seeds of water are in motion,
And cloud piled upon cloud and rack on rack
Down-streaming are swept on from every side,
And when the whole earth smokes and breathes back moisture.
If at such times the sun mid the dark tempest
Has shone forth with his rays over against
The showering rain-mists, then in the black clouds
The colours of the rainbow stand revealed.

Those other things which have their birth and growth
In the upper air, and those things that are formed
Within the clouds, all, beyond question all,
Snow, winds and hail, cold hoar-frosts and the strength
Of ice, that mighty hardener of waters,
That curb which bridles every running stream—
How all these are produced and why they are formed,
Is yet most easy to find out and view
With the mind's eye, when you have fully learned
What properties belong to the elements.

Now listen and learn what is the cause of earthquakes.
And first you must consider that the earth,

Both below and above, in every part
Is full of windy caves, and that she bears
Many lakes in her bosom, many pools,
Rocks and precipitous cliffs; and you must think
That many rivers hidden beneath earth's crust
Are rolling violently onward waves
And submerged stones; for the clear facts demand
That everywhere she should be like herself.
Since therefore such things are found lying close
Beneath her surface, the earth quakes above
Shaken by mighty falls of rock, when time
Has caused those huge caves to subside below.
Indeed whole mountains fall, and straightway tremblings
From the great shock steal abroad far and wide:
And with good cause, since houses by the roadside
Tremble throughout when shaken by a wagon
Of no great weight; nor do they fail to rock
Whenever a sharp stone on the road jolts up
The iron tires of the wheels on either side.
Sometimes also, when a huge mass of soil,
Loosened by lapse of time, slides from the land
Down into great wide pools of water, the earth
Rocks quavering with the water's undulation,
Just as a jar at times cannot stand still
Unless the liquid in it has ceased to sway
With restless undulation to and fro.

Moreover when a wind, gathering together
Throughout the cavernous places underground,
Blows hard in one direction, pushing and thrusting
Into the deep caves with its mighty strength,
The earth will bend towards that side whereto
The headlong violence of the wind is pressing.
Then every structure built above the ground,
The more each towers skyward, the more it leans
Suspended, bending in the same direction
With beams wrenched forth and hanging ready to fall.

Yet men have not the courage to believe
That some destroying hour, some ruinous end
Awaits this great world's frame, though they behold
So great a mass of earth threatening to fall.
Why, if the winds did not abate, no force
Could ever rein things in, or as they crashed
Pull them back from destruction. But in fact,
Because by turns they abate, and then increase
Their violence, and rallying as it were
Return to the charge, and then retire defeated,
Therefore the earth more often threats to fall
Than it does fall; for it leans out, and then
Sways back again, and after lurching forward
Restores its masses to their old positions.
So from this cause all houses rock, the top
More than the middle parts, the middle parts
More than the base, and the base scarce at all.

Moreover for the same mighty earth-trembling
There is this other cause: that suddenly
A wind or some enormous force of air,
Which has arisen either from without
Or else within the earth, has flung itself
Into the hollow places of the earth,
And there at first among those mighty caves
Growls turbulently and rushes whirling round,
Till soon the wind's vehement force, worked up
To fury, bursts abroad, and therewith cleaving
The deep earth, opens a huge yawning chasm.
This it was that befell at Syrian Sidon,
Likewise at Aegium in the Peloponnese,
Towns that just such a breaking forth of wind,
And the earthquake that was caused thereby, threw down.
And many another walled city has fallen
Through great quakings on land, and many towns
Have sunk together with their habitants
Engulphed within the sea. And even though

Naught breaks forth, yet the air's impetuous rush
And the wind's savage violence spread out,
Ague-like, through the numerous pores of the earth,
And thereby inflict a trembling; as when cold
Has penetrated deep within our limbs,
It sets them shivering in their own despite,
Constraining them to tremble and be convulsed.
Therefore in towns men quake with a twofold terror:
They fear the roofs above them, and they dread
The caverns underneath, lest suddenly
The earth should break them up, lest torn asunder
She open a wide-gaped maw, then pell-mell tumbling
Endeavour to fill it up with her own ruins.
Wherefore let men imagine as they please
That heaven and earth will be indestructible,
To eternal stability consigned;
And yet from time to time the present force
Of danger is sure to apply within some soul
This further goad of terror, lest the earth,
Snatched away suddenly from beneath their feet,
Plunge into the pit, and lest the sum of things
Utterly giving way should follow after,
And the whole world become one shapeless ruin.

[In the first place they find it strange that nature
Does not enlarge the sea's bulk, though so great
A downflow of waters enters it, and though
All rivers fall therein from every side.
To these add wandering showers and flying storms
That sprinkle all seas and drench every land;
Add its own springs: yet in comparison
With the whole ocean, all these will scarce seem
Able to augment it by one single drop.
So it is hardly strange that the great sea
Should not increase in bulk. The sun moreover
Draws away a large portion by his heat:
For indeed we see how with his burning rays

The sun will dry soaked garments. But we know
That seas are many and stretch far and wide;
Therefore however small the amount of moisture
Sucked by the sun at any single place
From the sea's surface, yet in a space so vast
He will draw copiously from its waves.
Then again winds too, as they sweep the surface,
Can lift away great quantities of moisture,
Since very often we may see how roads
Grow dry beneath the winds in a single night,
And the soft mud congeals into hard crusts.
Moreover I have shown that the clouds too
Take up much moisture gathered from the sea's
Great surface, and then scatter it everywhere
Over the whole wide world, when it is raining
On land, and the winds sweep the clouds along.
Lastly, since earth is of a porous body,
And being contiguous with the sea girds in
Its shores on every side, it needs must be
That just as from the land the moisture of water
Passes into the sea, so it should likewise
Ooze out of the salt sea into the land.
For when the salt is strained off, and the moisture's
Pure substance has oozed back, all of it flows
Together to the river-heads, and thence
As a current of fresh water passes back
Over the land along some course that once
Was cleft for it to stream down with liquid foot.]

And now will I explain why fires at times
Breathe forth in such great eddies from the throat
Of Aetna's mountain. For with no mere common
Violence of destruction arose the storm
Of flame, that o'er the fields of Sicily
Playing the tyrant drew to itself the gaze
Of neighbouring nations, when seeing all the quarters
Of heaven flashing through dark smoke, men filled

Their hearts with terror, doubting what dread change
Nature might be in travail to bring forth.

To explain what here takes place, you must look wide
And deep, with a far survey on all sides;
So will you be reminded how the sum
Of all things is unfathomable, and see
How very small, how infinitesimal
A part of the whole sum must be one heaven,
Not even so large a part of it as one man
Is of the whole earth. If you set this truth
Firmly before your mind, survey it clearly,
And clearly comprehend it, you will cease
To wonder at many things. For who among us
Feels wonder if a man's limbs be possessed
By a fever that breaks out with burning heat,
Or by the pain of any other malady
Vexing his body? A foot will suddenly swell;
Sharp pain will often seize upon the teeth,
Or else invade the eyes; the "accursèd fire"[1]
Breaks out, and creeping about the body, burns
Whatever part it seizes, and so crawls
Over the limbs, doubtless because there exist
Seeds of many things, and this earth and heaven
Bring to us evil enough, whence may grow forth
Immeasurable fecundity of disease.
Therefore we must believe that in this way
Seeds of all kinds out of the infinite
Are supplied to the whole heaven and earth, enough
To cause the earth to quake with sudden shock,
The swift whirlwind to scour o'er sea and land,
The fire of Aetna to overflow, the sky
To glow with flames—for that too sometimes happens:
The quarters of heaven are on fire, and rain-storms
Appear in heavier masses, when perchance

[1] Erysipelas.

Sufficient seeds of water have come together.
"Aye, but this conflagration's turbulent blaze
Is too gigantic." Why, so is the river
Which is the greatest seen by him who never
Has before seen a greater; and so a tree
Or man may seem gigantic; and with all things
Of every kind, the greatest each has seen,
He will imagine those to be gigantic:
Yet all of them together, with the heavens
And earth and sea besides, will be as nothing
To the whole sum of the whole universe.

Yet now I will explain to you in what ways
This flame, stirred up suddenly to fury,
Blows forth from the vast furnaces of Aetna.
First the whole mountain is hollow underneath,
Supported everywhere on basalt arches.
Moreover in all caverns there is wind
And air, for air becomes wind when 'tis stirred
And driven about. When this wind has grown hot,
And in its fury, wheresoever it touches,
Has heated all the rocks and soil around,
And from these has struck out a fire, hot
With swift flames, then it rises and flings itself
Forth and aloft straight through the mountain's throat.
Thus does it carry its heat afar, and scatter
Afar its ashes, rolling thick black smoke,
And therewith hurls forth rocks of marvellous weight.
Doubt not, this is the turbulent force of air.
Besides over this mountain's roots the sea
For a great distance breaks its waves and sucks
Its tide back. From this sea are caverns reaching
Underground to the deep throat of the mountain.
By this path it is clear that water enters;
And the plain fact compels us to believe
That from the sea water mingled with wind
Penetrates deep within, and then blows forth,

And so lifts high the flame, and casts up rocks
And raises clouds of dust. For on the summit
Of the mountain there are craters, as the Greeks
Term them; whereas we call them throats or mouths.

Now there are various facts to explain which
'Tis not sufficient to assign one cause:
We must give several; though of these one only
Will be the actual cause. Thus should you see
A man's dead body lying at some distance,
It would be right to name all possible
Causes of death, that so the one true cause
Of this death might be mentioned. For although
You could not prove that he had died by steel,
Or by cold, or disease, or it may be poison,
Yet we know it was something of this kind
That has befallen him. There are many cases
Whereof similar statements might be made.

Alone in the whole world, the Nile, that river
Of all Egypt, rises when summer comes,
And overflows the plains. Thus it is wont
To water Egypt during the hot season,
Perhaps because against its mouths in summer
North winds prevail, which at that time of year
Are called the Etesian. Blowing against the stream
They check and drive its waters back, and filling
The channel, force the river to stand still.
For beyond doubt these blasts, that take their rise
From the icy constellations of the pole,
Blow right against the current: the river comes
Out of the southern lands where heat is born,
Rising from the inmost region of noon-day
Among black tribes of men tanned by the sun.
Or it may be that a great congestion of sand
Blocks up the mouths against the opposing waves,
When stirred by winds the sea washes the sand

Inside the channel; whereby less free becomes
The outlet of the river, and its waters
Less rapid likewise in their downward flow.
Also it well may happen that more rains
Fall in that season near the river's source
Because the Etesian blasts of the north winds
Drive all the clouds together at that time
Into those quarters. Doubtless when the clouds,
Swept afar to the region of noon-day,
Have flocked together, there on the mountain heights
At last they are packed and crowded in one mass
And violently compressed. Or else perhaps
The stream grows to full flood high up within
The mountains of the Ethiops, when the sun,
Shining on all with melting rays, compels
The white snows to flow down into the plains.

Now listen; with what nature are endowed
All the Avernian regions and their lakes,
I will unfold to you. First of all the name
Avernian has been given them from this fact,
That they are baneful to all kinds of birds:[1]
For when birds have arrived in flight directly
Above such places, forthwith they forget
The oarage of their wings, and slackening sail
Fall headlong with limp neck outstretched to the earth
If such should be the nature of the land,
Or into water if an Avernian lake
Should chance to spread below. There is a region
Near Cumae of this kind, where mountains smoke
Teeming with acrid sulphur and abounding
With hot springs. There is likewise such a place
Within the walls and on the very summit
Of the Athenian citadel, hard by
The temple of bountiful Tritonian Pallas,

[1] Avernus was supposed to be derived from a Greek word *ἄορνος* which means "birdless".

Whither no croaking crows will ever wing
Their flight, not even when the altars smoke
With offerings: so warily do they flee—
Not from the bitter wrath of Pallas against
Their spying vigilance, as Greek poets have sung—[1]
But of itself the nature of the place
Brings this about. In Syria too, we are told,
There is known to be a place such that, so soon
As even four-footed beasts have entered in,
It forces them by its peculiar power
To fall down heavily, as though sacrificed
By a sudden stroke to the infernal gods.
Now all these things take place by natural law,
And it is plain from what source come the causes
Whereby they are brought to pass. Let us not then
Believe that in such regions can be found
The gateway of Orcus; nor imagine next
That from them the infernal deities
Draw souls below to the shores of Acheron;
Even as wing-footed stags are often thought
By the breath of their nostrils to draw out
The tribes of serpents from their holes. But learn
How far removed this must be from true reason;
For now will I try to set forth the real facts.

First of all, as I have often said before,
I say that in the earth are elements
Of things of every kind: many that serve
For food, friendly to life; many with power
To inflict diseases and so hasten death.
Also I have shown before how different things
Are better suited for life's purposes
To different animals, because unlike

[1] Athena had entrusted a chest containing the infant Erichthonios to the three daughters of Cecrops, forbidding them to open it, which very naturally they soon did. A spying crow reported them to the Goddess, who, indignant at such tale-bearing, banished crows for ever from her Acropolis.

In each kind are their natures, and unlike
Their textures and the shapes of their first atoms.
Many harmful elements pass through the ears,
And through the nostrils many make their way
That are noxious and rough; and not a few
Should be avoided by the touch, or shunned
By the sight; others have a nauseous taste.

Furthermore we may see how many things
Are virulently noxious to man's sense,
So loathsome are they and so dangerous.
First there are certain trees that spread a shade
So very dangerous that they often cause
Pains in the head when a man has lain down
Stretched on the grass beneath them. Then again,
Among the great mountains of Helicon
There grows a tree that with the noisome scent
Shed by its flower is able to kill a man.
All these things doubtless grow forth from the earth
Because its soil holds in it many seeds
Of many things mingled in many ways,
Which it first separates and then gives forth.
Again, a newly extinguished night-taper
Striking the nostrils with its acrid stench
Stupefies then and there a diseased man
Who is wont to fall down foaming at the mouth.[1]
Put to sleep by the heavy scent of castor
A woman will sink back, and her gay broidery
Slips from her delicate hands, if she have smelt it
In the course of her monthly periods.
And many things there are besides that loosen
The fainting limbs throughout the frame, and cause
The soul to quake within its residence.
Again, if you should linger overlong
In the hot baths when you have eaten well,
How easily may you fall down in a faint

[1] An epileptic.

From your stool in the steaming water's midst!
How easily too may the oppressive fumes
Of charcoal make their way into the brain,
Unless we have taken a draught of water first!
And when a burning fever has laid hold
On a man's limbs, then will the odour of wine
Strike like a deadly blow. And have you not
Also observed how even within the earth
Sulphur is generated, and bitumen
Hardens into a noisome-smelling crust?
And indeed, when they are following up the veins
Of silver and gold, searching with iron tools
Deep in the secret places of the earth,
What smells Scaptensula[1] breathes from below!
Then what mischief do not gold-mines exhale!
How they ravage men's faces and complexions!
Have you not seen or heard how they are wont
To perish in a short time, and how soon
Their vital power fails those who are held fast
In such employment by necessity's
Strong duress? Therefore all such exhalations
The earth sends steaming forth, and breathes them out
Into the open air beneath the skies.

Thus too the Avernian regions must send up
Some power deadly to birds, which from the earth
Rises into the air, so as to poison
Some part or other of the atmosphere;
And soon as a bird has thither winged its way,
It is arrested there by the unseen poison,
And so, its flight being checked, it drops straight down
Over the place where the exhalation rises.
When there it has fallen, that same exhalation
Robs all its limbs of what remains of life.
For at first it merely causes in these birds
A kind of dizziness; but afterwards,

[1] Scaptensula, in Thrace, was famous for its silver-mines.

When they have tumbled into the very sources
Of poison, in that place their life itself
Must needs be vomited forth, because all round them
There is so large a store of poisonous air.

Also those exhalations from Avernus
May sometimes have such force that they dispel
All air that lies between the birds and the earth,
So that an almost void space is left there.
No sooner have the birds arrived in flight
Over this place, the energy of their wings
Is crippled and frustrated: on either side
Wasted is all the effort of their pinions.
So when they can sustain themselves no more
On lifting wings, nature of course compels them
To sink down by their weight to the earth, where lying
In almost empty void, they now disperse
Their souls through all the openings of their body.[1]

. . . .

Moreover during summer-time the water
In wells becomes colder, because the earth
Grows porous with the heat, and sends forth rapidly
Into the air whatever seeds of warmth
It may chance to contain. Therefore the more
The soil is drained of heat, the more cold grows
The moisture that is hidden within the earth.
Again, when the earth is everywhere compressed
And contracts and solidifies with cold,
Doubtless it must press forth, as it contracts,
All the heat it contains into the wells.

A spring there is near Ammon's fane,[2] 'tis said,
Cold in the daylight, and at night-time warm.
This spring men marvel at exceedingly,
And suppose that it suddenly grows hot
Because of the fierce sun below the earth,

[1] A leaf of the archetype is here lost.
[2] The temple of Jupiter Ammon in the Libyan desert.

When night has covered earth with dreadful darkness.
But this from true reasoning is far removed.
Why, the sun, acting upon the uncovered mass
Of water, had no power to make it warm
On the upper side, though from above his light
Possesses such great heat: how can he then
Below the earth, which has so dense a body,
Pervade with heat the water and make it boil—
And that when with his burning rays he scarce
Can make his warmth pierce through the walls of houses?
What is the cause then? Doubtless that the soil
Round the spring keeps more porous than elsewhere,
While near the water are many seeds of fire.
Therefore when with dew-laden shades the night
Has overwhelmed the earth, straightway the soil
Becomes cold through and through, and so contracts.
Thus, as though squeezed by a hand, it presses out
Into the spring whatever seeds of fire
It has within it; and these make warm the touch
And steam of the water. Next, when the risen sun
Has loosened with his rays the soil, and mingled
Therewith his heat, till he has made it porous,
The fire's primordial particles return
To their original stations, and thus all
The water's warmth retreats into the soil:
Wherefore the spring becomes cold in the daylight.
Besides, the water's liquid is perturbed
By the sun's rays, and through the quivering heat
Grows porous in the day-time; for which cause
It must give up whatever seeds of fire
It may contain; even as water often
Gives up the frost it holds within itself,
And melts the ice, loosening the bonds that bind it.

There is also a cold spring[1] whose nature is such
That tow, held over it, will often at once

[1] At Dodona in Epirus.

Catch fire and throw out flame; and in like manner
A pine-torch may be kindled and will shine
Over the stream wherever, as it floats,
The winds drive it. Doubtless the cause must be
That there are very many seeds of heat
Within the water; and from the earth itself
From deep down must rise up atoms of fire
Throughout the whole spring, and at the same time
Must be exhaled abroad and issue forth
Into the air, yet not so many of them
That the spring can grow heated. Furthermore
There is a force compels them to burst out
Suddenly through the water and disperse,
Then to unite when they have mounted up.
Just so within the sea at Aradus[1]
There is a spring that wells up with fresh water
And thrusts apart the salt waves all around it.
In many another region too the sea
Offers thirsting sailors a timely succour
By vomiting fresh waters amid salt.
In this way then those seeds of heat are able
To burst out through that cold spring and well up;
And when they are met together in the tow,
Or adhere to the body of the pine-torch,
They at once blaze up easily, because tow
And torches too have many seeds of fire
Latent within them. Do you not also see
How, when you move a newly extinguished wick
Close to some other night-lamp, it will kindle
Ere it has touched the flame, and a torch also
In the same way? And many things besides,
Touched merely by the heat, will at some distance
Blaze out before the fire is close enough
To invade them. And so this we must believe
To be what happens in that cold spring too.

[1] An island off the coast of Phoenicia. Just as the fresh water wells up through the salt at Aradus, so the seeds of fire well up through the cold spring water at Dodona.

To my next theme I now proceed, and tell
How, by what law of nature, it comes to pass
That iron can be attracted by that stone
Which the Greeks call the magnet, from the name
Of that place where it was discovered first
Within the land where the Magnētes dwell.
This stone men marvel at; for it often makes
A chain out of rings hanging from itself.
Thus you may sometimes see five rings or more
In pendent series swayed by gentle breezes,
One hanging from another as from beneath
It clings, and each one learning from its neighbour
The binding energy of the stone; so far
Does its compelling influence penetrate.

In matters of this kind many points first
Must be established ere you can assign
The reason of the fact to be explained;
And by a long circuitous road your aim
Must be approached. All the more urgently
Do I crave an attentive ear and mind.

In the first place from all things whatsoever
Which we behold, there must perpetually
Be streaming off, discharged and scattered thence,
Such bodies as have power to strike the eyes
And provoke vision there. Odours likewise
Perpetually stream off from certain things,
Just as from rivers cold, heat from the sun,
From the sea's waves devouring spray that eats
Into walls near the shore. Then various sounds
Are floating through the air unceasingly.
Moreover a salt-savoured moisture often
Comes into our mouth when we walk by the sea;
And when from close by we are watching wormwood
Being dissolved and mixed, a bitter taste
Assails our sense. In so constant a stream
From all things various effluences are passing

And being dispersed abroad on every side;
And no delay, no respite in this flow
Is ever granted, since continually
We have sensation, and at all times may see,
Smell, and perceive the sound of all such things.

And now I will remind you once again
Of how porous a body all things consist,
As was made clear in the first part of my poem.
For indeed, though the knowledge of this truth
Helps to solve many problems, yet above all
For just this question, whereon I intend
Now to discourse, I must at once establish
That nothing is perceptible to sense
Save body mixed with void. And first of all
In caves we see how the rocks overhead
Sweat with moisture, and trickle with oozing drops.
Sweat too from our whole body oozes out;
The beard grows, and over all our limbs
And frame hairs sprout; food is distributed
Through all the veins, increasing and nourishing
The body's very extremities and the nails.
Also we feel cold and heat pass through bronze;
Through gold and silver too we feel them pass
When we are holding full cups in our hands.
Again, through stone partition-walls of houses
Sounds flit, smell oozes, and cold, and fire's heat
That is even wont to penetrate strong iron.
Finally, though the breastplate of the sky
Encompasses the world, the seeds of clouds
And winds can enter through it, and therewith
The power of disease, when from without
It finds its way within: and it is natural
That storms, gathering from earth and sky, should hasten
To distant skies and lands; since there is nothing
That is not woven out of porous matter.

Furthermore not all particles that may be
Discharged from things, are such as to produce
The same sensations, nor are they adapted
In the same way to all things. Thus the sun
Bakes and dries up the earth; but it thaws ice,
And snows on the high mountains piled up high
It compels with its rays to waste away.
Wax also, placed in the sun's heat, grows liquid.
Moreover fire melts brass and fuses gold,
But shrivels and draws together hides and flesh.
Again water's liquidity hardens iron
Snatched from the fire, whereas it softens hides
And flesh, when these have been made hard by heat.
The wild olive delights the bearded she-goats
As though it verily breathed out a flavour
Of nectar and ambrosia; yet nothing
Bears leaves that are more bitter food for man.
Lastly, the pig shuns oil of marjoram,
And dreads all unguents; for to bristly swine
That is rank poison which to us sometimes
Appears to be restorative of life.
But on the other hand, though mire to us
Is foulest of all filth, it yet appears
To swine so pleasing that they wallow in it
All over with insatiable relish.

With this point also it would seem well to deal
Before I come to speak of our main theme.
Since many pores belong to various things,
These pores must needs possess differing natures,
Each with its own distinctive passages.
Thus there are various senses in living things,
And each takes into itself in its own way
Its special object; for we see that sounds
Penetrate to one sense, taste from flavours
To another, and to yet another smells.
Again one thing is seen to pierce through stones,

Another to go through wood, through gold another,
Yet others to pass out through silver and glass;
For through glass, so we find, stream images,
Through silver heat will travel, and one thing
Seems to pass through by the same way more quickly
Than other things. Assuredly the cause
Compelling all this to take place must be
The nature of the passages; for that
Varies (as we made clear a brief while since)
In manifold ways, because the things themselves
Are unlike in their nature and their textures.

Therefore, since all these truths have been established
And laid down ready for us in advance,
For what remains, out of them easily
Shall we explain the principle and make clear
The whole cause which attracts the strength of iron.
First of all from this stone there needs must flow
Innumerable seeds forming a current
Which beats away with blows all the air lying
Between the stone and the iron. When this space
Is emptied, and much room left void between,
Straightway into this void the primal atoms
Of iron fall headlong forward in one mass;
So the result is that the ring itself
Must follow, and thus move onward as one whole.
For there is nothing with first elements
More intertangled, or that clings linked together
More closely than the substance of strong iron
With its cold roughness. Therefore what I say
Is the less strange, that from among such elements
Numerous atoms starting from the iron
Cannot move forward into the void space
Unless the whole ring follows. This it does,
Following till it now has reached the stone
And clung to it by hidden fastenings.
The same process takes place in all directions:

Wherever a void is formed, whether above
Or on some side of the iron, immediately
The neighbouring atoms rush into the void;
For they are impelled by blows from other sides,
And are not able of their own accord
To rise up into the air. And furthermore,
To make the process easier, this fact also
Comes as a further aid to the ring's motion,
That so soon as the air in front of it
Has been made rarer and the space has grown
More empty and void, straightway it comes to pass
That all the air which lies behind the ring
Pushes and drives it forward from the rear.
For the air that lies round them is evermore
Beating on things; but only at such moments
Can it drive the iron forward, because then
On one side there is void space which receives
The ring within it. This air which I speak of,
Entering through the countless pores of the iron,
Penetrates subtly to its smallest parts,
Then thrusts and drives it onward, as the wind
Drives a ship under sail. Moreover all things
Must needs contain some air within themselves,
Since they are of porous substance, and the air
Surrounds all things and is in contact with them.
This air then, which in the iron's inmost parts
Lies hidden, is being tossed continually
In restless motion, and so past all doubt
Beats on the ring and stirs it from inside.
Thus, you will see, the ring is borne along
In that direction whither it first moved forward
Endeavouring to enter the void place.

There are times also when the nature of iron
Moves away from this stone, being wont to flee
And follow it turn by turn. I have even seen
Rings of Samothracian iron dance,

And iron filings leap madly about
Inside brass bowls, soon as this magnet stone
Is put beneath; so eager the iron seems
To escape from the stone. All that disturbance
Is brought about when the brass comes between,
Doubtless because, when a current from the brass
Has been the first to seize and take possession
Of the open passages within the iron,
Afterwards comes a current from the stone,
And finding all in the iron to be full
Has no passage to stream through as before:
Therefore it is compelled to dash against
And beat the iron texture with its wave.
Thus through the brass it spits off from itself
And drives away something which generally,
Were it not for the brass, it would suck in.

Herein refrain from wondering that the current
Issuing from this stone has not the power
To propel other things as well: for some
Stand firm by their own weight, gold for example;
Others again, because theirs is a body
So porous that the current unresisted
Flies through them, can in no wise be propelled;
And to this class wood, it is clear, belongs.
Between these two then lies the nature of iron:
So when it has absorbed certain minute
Bodies of brass, then the Magnesian stones
Are able to propel it with their stream.

Yet this case of the magnet stone and iron
Is not so singular, that I could not quote
A plentiful store of similar instances
Of things adapted solely for each other.
Thus you see how by mortar and naught else
Stones are cemented. By bull's glue alone
Is wood so firmly joined, that in its boards
The veins will gape more often into cracks

Than the glue's bindings will relax their hold.
Juices born of the grape consent to mingle
With streams of water, whereas heavy pitch
And light olive oil refuse. And with the substance
Of wool alone will the sea-purple dye
Of the murex unite in such a way
That in no wise can it be separated,
Not if you were at pains to renew its whiteness
With Neptune's flood, no, not if the whole sea
Should strive to wash it out with all its waves.
Then again is there not one thing alone
That unites gold to gold; and is not brass
Soldered to brass by tin? How many more
Such cases might one find! But to what purpose?
You have no need whatever of such long
Circuitous roads; nor were I wise to waste
So much pains on this point: but it seems best
To combine briefly in few words many things.
The closest unions are formed by those bodies
Whereof the textures mutually correspond
In such wise that the cavities of the one
Reciprocally fit the other's solids.
Moreover it is possible that some things
Are held together linked and interwoven
As though by rings and hooks; which seems more likely
To be what happens with this iron and stone.

Next, in what way diseases come about,
And from what cause gathering suddenly
The forces of disease may breathe a blast
Of death-bearing destruction on mankind
And on the tribes of beasts, I will unfold.
Firstly, I have shown above that there exist
Seeds of many things helpful to our life;
On the other hand, many that bring disease
And death, must needs be flying to and fro.
When these have flocked together by some chance

And so distempered the atmosphere, forthwith
The air becomes diseased. And all that throng
Of diseases and pestilence either comes,
Like clouds and vapours, from outside our world
Down through the sky; or else often they rise
Flocking together out of the earth itself,
When it has grown putrescent, being soaked through,
And smitten by untimely rains and suns.
See you not also how the novelty
Of climate and of water affects those
Who have travelled far from home and fatherland,
Just because there are wide discrepancies
In such things? For how much must we not think
The climate which the Britons know differs
From that of Egypt, where the pole of heaven
Leans aslant? Or how much must that of Pontus
Differ from that of Gades, and so onward
To the black tribes of men tanned by the sun?
Now just as we perceive how these four climates
At the four winds and quarters of the sky
Are different from each other, so likewise
The colour and faces of the men are seen
To differ widely, and diseases varying
In character attack the different races.
There is the elephant disease, whose origin
Is in mid Egypt by the streams of Nile,
And nowhere else. 'Tis the feet are attacked
In Attica, in Achaean lands the eyes.
Thus different regions are injurious
To different parts and members: and of this
The cause must be the varying kinds of air.
Therefore whenever an atmosphere, that chances
To be unfriendly to us, puts itself
In motion and a noxious air begins
To spread, like mist or cloud little by little
It creeps along, distempering and compelling
All things to change wherever it makes its way;

And thus it comes to pass that when at last
It comes to our atmosphere, it taints that too,
Making it like itself, and to us unfriendly.
And so this unforeseen destroying power
And pestilence on a sudden either falls
Upon the waters, or it settles down
Even on the crops, or other food of men
And provender of beasts; or else its force
Remains suspended in the atmosphere;
So when we inhale from it mixed breaths of air,
We needs must also absorb at the same time
These plagues into our body. In like manner
Pestilence often falls on cattle too,
And a distemper on lazy bleating sheep.
Nor does it matter much whether we travel
To places that are menacing to our health,
Changing the atmosphere that wraps us round,
Or whether nature brings on us where we are
A tainted atmosphere, or some infection
Whereof we have no experience, and whose first
Assault may therefore prove a danger to us.

Thus it was came that plague and death-fraught blast
That once within the land of Cecrops filled
The countryside with corpses, dispeopled
The streets, and drained the city of her burghers.[1]
For from the innermost frontiers of Egypt
This plague arose first and came traversing
Wide tracts of air and many floating plains,
Till over the whole people of Pandīon
At length it brooded: whereupon in troops
They were delivered to disease and death.
First with a burning heat the head would glow,
And the eyes redden and gleam with suffused light.
The livid throat within would sweat with blood,

[1] Lucretius here gives an account of the Plague of Athens in 430 B.C., following and often translating Thucydides II. 47–54.

The passage of the voice was blocked and choked
With ulcers, while the mind's interpreter,
The tongue, would exude gore, by sufferings
Enfeebled, heavy in movement, rough to the touch.
Thereafter, when descending by the throat
The force of the disease had filled the breast
And streamed together into the sick man's
Afflicted heart,[1] then verily would all
The fastnesses of life collapse. The breath
Would pour out from the mouth a noisome smell
Rank as the stench of fetid carcases
Thrown out unburied. And straightway the powers
Of the entire mind and the whole body too,
Now on death's very threshold, would grow faint.
And all the while torturing anxiety
And moanings mingled with complaining cries
Accompanied their unbearable sufferings.
A constant retching, often throughout whole nights
And days, compelling spasms perpetually
In sinew and limb, would utterly break men down,
Forwearying those already wearied out.
And yet in none could you perceive the skin
Burn on the body's surface with a heat
That seemed excessive; rather to the hand
The body would feel lukewarm; and likewise
Would appear red all over, as though with ulcers
Burnt into it, as when the "accursèd fire"[2]
Spreads o'er the limbs. But the inward parts of men
Would burn to the very bones: a flame would rage
Within the stomach as within a furnace.
Ne'er could you find aught light or thin enough

[1] Lucretius, apparently misunderstanding καρδίαν, the word used by Thucydides in the sense of "stomach", mistranslates it as *cor*, "heart", thus unduly hastening the progress of the disease. It is possible however, though hardly probable, that he uses *cor* in the sense of "stomach", as do some later Latin writers, e.g. Horace, *Sat.* II. 3. 28.

[2] Erysipelas.

To bring relief to the body—naught but wind
And the cool air. Some into cold rivers
Would fling their limbs on fire with disease,
Plunging within the waves their naked bodies.
Many leapt headlong down into deep wells,
Meeting the water with wide-gaping mouth;
Yet was the parching thirst that plunged them down
Still unquenched, for a flood of water seemed
No better than a few drops. From their suffering
There was no respite. Utterly wearied out
Their bodies lay. Low muttered the healing art
In voiceless fear, as ever and anon
They rolled around their staring eyes, aflame
With disease, and by sleep unvisited.
Then too were seen many symptoms of death:
The mind distraught in misery and terror;
A gloomy brow, frantic and violent looks;
The ears too, haunted and perturbed by noises;
The breath either drawn quickly, or in great gasps
At long intervals; glistening drops of sweat
Dewing the neck; the spittle in thin small flakes,
Tinged with saffron and salty, that with effort
Were forced up through the throat by a hoarse cough.
And all the time the tendons of the hands
Would contract, the limbs shiver, and coldness mount
Steadily from the feet by slow degrees.
Moreover, when the last moments drew near,
The nostrils became pinched, the tip of the nose
Grew sharp, the eyes deep-sunk, the temples hollow;
The skin was cold and hard; by a grin the mouth
Was writhen; tense and swollen was the forehead.
And no long time thereafter stiff in death
Would lie their limbs. For the most part, when the sun
Of the eighth day shone bright, or else the ninth,
They would yield up their life. And if perchance
Any among them had escaped death's doom,
Yet at some later time, through noisome ulcers

And a black flux of the bowels, wasting and death
Would still be awaiting him; or else the head
Would often ache with anguish, while a flow
Of purulent blood would pour from the gorged nostrils:
And through them would the whole strength of the man's
Body stream forth. Moreover, though he escaped
This violent discharge of noisome blood,
Yet would the plague pass into his joints and sinews,
And even into his body's genital parts.
And some, through grievous dread of death's threshold,
Bereaved of their virility by the knife
Would live on; some, though without hands and feet,
Remained alive, and some would lose their eyes:
So cruelly did the fear of death assail them.
Others too such forgetfulness of all things
Seized, that they could not even know themselves.
And though corpses piled upon corpses lay
In multitudes unburied on the ground,
Yet would the tribes of birds and of wild beasts
Either swerve quickly far away, to escape
The powerful stench, or else, when they had tasted,
They would sink fainting in a speedy death.
Yet in those days hardly would any bird
Appear at all, nor did the sullen breeds
Of wild animals come forth from the woods.
Many would sink faint with disease and die.
Above all faithful dogs would lie stretched out
In every street, and breathe reluctantly
Their spirit forth; for the power of disease
Wrenched the life from their limbs. Nor was there found
Any sure remedy for all alike;
For that which to one man had given the power
To breathe in the life-giving air, and gaze
Upon the regions of the sky, to others
Would be destruction and the cause of death.
But among all those miseries there was one
Most lamentable: when a man saw himself

Enmeshed by the disease, with sorrowing heart
He would lie down, as though to death condemned,
All courage lost; and looking for naught else
But death to come, would straightway abandon life.
For truly not for a moment did the infection
Of that ravening plague cease to lay hold
Of one after another, just as though
They had been woolly flocks or hornèd herds.
And this it was that above all heaped up
Death upon death: all who refused to visit
Their sick, neglect soon after would strike down
And punish for their too great greed of life
And fear of death, by a death foul and evil,
Abandoned and forlorn of help in turn.
But those who stayed to help the sick would perish
By the infection and by the toil which shame
And the entreaties of the sufferers,
Mingled with their lamenting cries, would then
Compel them to undergo. So thus it was
That those of noblest nature would meet death.
Lonely and unattended funerals
Were hurried through with emulous dispatch.
. . . .
And different bodies upon different pyres,
Struggling to bury the multitude of their dead.
Worn out with tears and grief they would go home,
Then for the most part take to their bed from sorrow.
Nor at a time so dire could one be found
Whom neither plague nor death nor grief assailed.

Moreover every shepherd by this time,
And herdsman, aye, and the curved plough's stalwart guide,
Were sickening, and their bodies would be huddled
In the corners of a sheiling, by disease
And poverty to death delivered over.
Sometimes over dead children you might see
The bodies of their parents stretched out dead,
Or again children breathing out their life

Over fathers and mothers. And this woe
In no small measure streamed in from the fields
Into the town, brought thither by the crowd
Of sickening countrymen, who from all sides
Flocked in plague-stricken. Every place and building
They filled full: wherefore all the more, thus packed
Within the city, death piled them in heaps.
Many bodies, that by thirst had been laid low,
Had crawled along the street and lay stretched out
Beside the fountains, where the breath of life
Was cut off through their too great lust for water;
And everywhere in open public places
And streets there might be seen many with bodies
Half-lifeless and with drooping limbs grown horrible
With filth, covered with rags, and perishing
From foulness of body, naught but skin and bones,
Now well-nigh buried in noisome sores and dirt.
Moreover death had filled with lifeless bodies
All the Gods' holy shrines, and everywhere
The temples of the heavenly powers were cumbered
With corpses; for the ministering priests
Had crowded all these buildings full with guests.
For now neither the worship of the Gods
Nor their divinities were much held in awe;
So dominant was the present misery.
Nor did those rites of sepulture, wherewith
This folk aforetime had been ever wont
To inter their dead, continue within the town;
For the whole people were in dismay and panic,
And each mourner would bury his own friend
As occasion might allow him. Furthermore
Sudden constraint and poverty would prompt
To many frightful acts. Thus with loud cries
They would lay their own kindred on pyres built
By others, and set torches underneath,
Wrangling and brawling often with much bloodshed
Sooner than leave the bodies unconsumed.

MACAULAY'S *MARGINALIA* TO LUCRETIUS

It happens that the translator has in his possession Macaulay's copy of Lucretius, which he took with him to India in 1834, and read through three times in the course of four years. It was Macaulay's habit to fill the margins of books which he was reading with copious notes and comments, and his Lucretius did not escape this disfiguring but human fate. These notes and scribbles are probably not worth publishing in full; yet they have certain virtues. They are often amusing; they give a glimpse of the writer's private mind, which is all the more interesting because most of what he wrote was so completely intended for the public, so lacking in intimacy; and they have at least an indirect bearing upon how to read Lucretius. It seems therefore not improper to take this opportunity of writing a little round about them, especially as they provide an excuse for giving some advice to the less erudite reader.

The most amusing of the marginalia are frankly nothing more than heckling with a pencil. They are pert, sometimes witty, sometimes almost impudent, always human and direct. Those who only know Macaulay's finished productions will be surprised to discover that he is capable of such things.

To begin with we find an almost incessant fire of wrathful ejaculations directed against the theories which Lucretius is explaining: "Stuff." "Nonsense." "Folly." "Idiocy." Sometimes these simple interjections are made more deadly by means of adjectives and adverbs: "Exceedingly absurd." "Wretched reasoning." "This is mere drivelling." "This is absolute drivelling." "All this is sad stuff." "Contemptible nonsense." "Unintelligible nonsense." "What an abyss of nonsense!"

From simple heckling such as this he passes to the elaboration of more complicated insults. For example, finding in the argument of the first book an *igitur* where nothing was proven, it occurs to him that Shakespeare's ironic "argal" would be a proper translation. So "argal" is written in the margin, and thereafter any *igitur* or *ergo* is in danger of similar treatment. By cumulative effect, this becomes a very deadly weapon.

Another of his tricks is to return the lie direct. When Lucretius states that he has explained something, Macaulay will margin him "Have you indeed!" And when his victim reports the theory that the sun which appears one day may not be the same as that which appeared the day before, he applauds contemptuously: "Bravo! a new sun every day."

The last two comments happen to make use of the exclamation mark, which is all the more effective in these notes for being so rare. Once he writes against a despised passage a simple!!!; and on one tremendous occasion uses no less than four: "Precious philosophy!!!!"

Sometimes he foregoes wit and pertness, appealing directly to the great deep prejudices by strongly emotive words: "Of all the absurdities of Epicurus, this is infinitely the most revolting." "This is more contemptible than anything in the Roman Catholic religion." "The absurdity of the whole theory of the simulacra is quite degrading." "This philosophy is beneath contempt."

So much for his anger. In these days of tolerance and restraint (I mean among the learned) it is odd, and rather charming, to find such an intensity of feeling aroused in private reading. Macaulay had a really tremendous hatred for the Epicurean system. On the other hand, for the poetry in Lucretius he had an equally passionate admiration, and praised it as warmly as he blamed the philosophy: "Beautiful writing." "Neat writing." "Very neat and clear." "Exceedingly neat and lucid writing." "Sublime beyond any passage of the kind in poetry." "The illustrations of Lucretius are the most beautiful that ever were used in didactic poetry." "There is nothing in Lucretius as admirable as these illustrations. They are in truth charming episodes which relieve the dullness of his lecture." "Nothing can be better than this series of illustrations. It is admirable, luminous, and picturesque."

With these specimens before him, the reader will perhaps have little difficulty in agreeing that we cannot learn much about Lucretius from Macaulay. There are longer notes which we have not quoted, but they suffer from the same faults as the smaller, more light-hearted scribbles. Altogether, they do no more than provide us with a little amusement, and some insight into the more private workings of Macaulay's mind and imagination.

That is the whole of their positive merit. But there is a quite sufficient further reason for publishing some of them here. Macaulay's way of reading Lucretius was not merely a wrong way of reading; it was a typically wrong way, in the sense that he made just those mistakes which the average reader today is most likely to make; and he made them very thoroughly. His notes teach us what to avoid; and that is no small merit in them, though a negative one.

His reading of Lucretius was wrong because it was incoherent and unintegrated. He made always this sharp distinction between the poetry and the philosophy, and while he loved the one, he hated the other. So he was left in a state of oscillation between pleasure and pain—surely not the effect that poetry ought to have. Thus he says: "I do not wonder that he repeats these lines. Absurd as the theory is, the expression is quite bewitching." "This whole passage, absurd as much of the reasoning is, seems to me a model of the kind, manly, modest, and at the same time lively and agreeable in a style fitted for didactic poetry." "Admirable poetry. But as to any real effect on the mind, these conceptions are worth no more than Mr Shandy's."

We have here the case of a man who cannot produce that "willing suspension of disbelief" which Coleridge thought essential to the reading of poetry; a man whose intellectual reaction to a poem is at odds with his emotional response. It would appear from recent arguments on this problem of poetry and intellectual belief, that some readers are capable of "suspending their disbeliefs" almost entirely; they can overlook the grossest errors if the quality of the poetry itself be high. Others are radically incapable of this spiritual agility. They can hardly enjoy any poetry the matter of which distresses them intellectually. Others again, and perhaps they are the majority, occupy the middle position. They are able to overlook a certain degree of intellectual discomfort in favour of good poetry, but find that the actual amount of their own disagreement with what they are reading may make a difference. A small amount of disagreement they can overcome; a large amount they cannot. If they think that the views of the poet are no worse than shallow and silly, they may be able to enjoy him; but if they think that his opinions are theoretically beneath contempt, and in practice highly pernicious, they will then be unable to do so. Probably most readers are in this middle class, and it is especially to them that Macaulay's reading of Lucretius may be a useful warning. The obstacle, evidently, to a full enjoyment of Lucretius does not lie in his art, but in the theories which he expounds. Can anything be said about these theories which will make them less of a stumbling-block, less destructive of poetic enjoyment, than they were to Macaulay?

In itself, the Epicurean system is more easily understood than any other of the great philosophies of antiquity. It offers few profound difficulties of interpretation; and thanks to Lucretius we have a very complete and clear exposition of it. Yet it has been gravely misunderstood and misrepresented. More than any other ancient philosophy it has aroused the controversial fervour of friends and the bitterness of enemies. In pre-Christian times it suffered severely; Cicero said some of his hardest things about it, and Horace more subtly yoked its name with the image of the swine, the man of brutish pleasures—an association which still remains strong in the popular mind. Christianity attacked it even more fiercely. Jerome took the trouble to put into circulation damaging statements about Lucretius himself; while in modern Europe, the Jesuits and the Inquisition tried to prevent the reading of Lucretius in the countries under their power. To some extent our feelings and thoughts on the subject of Epicureanism must be influenced by these controversies; and controversy always involves misrepresentation. Echoes of the old hates and prejudices ring in our own minds, however faintly, and make it harder to think freely and clearly for ourselves.

That is one difficulty. But there is another, even more serious, which applies more to us than to Macaulay and to readers before our time. It so happens that modern scientific theories about the constitution of matter, of the universe, and so on, coincide to some extent with those of Epicurus and the Greek Atomists. This coincidental similarity is underlined by the further accident that Dalton, when he advanced his atomic theory, chose the technical term for his particles from the Greeks. Thus it is easy to fall into the habit of thinking that Epicurus was in some sense a precursor of modern science. Nothing, in fact, could be farther from the truth; and nothing could give rise to more serious misunderstandings of the Epicurean system. In the first place, Epicureanism had no notion of experiment, no empirical method whatsoever. It could observe phenomena, as everyone can do, even those of us who are not scientists; but it never attempted, as empirical science must, to control the conditions of phenomena in such a way that hypothetical explanations could be proven or rejected. It was the product of thought and speculation, operating on the materials of ordinary observation. And there is a vast difference between such a collection of speculations, and a scientific system of hypotheses duly tested by a developed experimental technique.

There is another great difference between Epicureanism and modern science. Physicists, astronomers, and even biologists today are very much concerned with mathematics, as an essential part of their technique. An eminent contemporary physicist has said "the data of science, and the only data, are figures taken from measuring instruments". Epicurus, on the other hand, despised mathematics, which occupy not even the smallest place in his interpretation of the universe. This is a radical difference.

I should like to insist on the importance of these differences, because the results of regarding Epicurus as a forerunner of modern science are likely to be so unfortunate. Thus, when we consider some of his theories, we may find them remarkably good; and then we may come upon a development of them which shocks us profoundly. And we are more annoyed than we should be by the folly, because we find it mingled with good sense, and this shows that Epicurus need not have been so silly. That was to some extent Macaulay's experience, and it is even more likely to be the experience of the modern reader. But the reason why we are shocked, why we have this feeling of anger against Epicurus, is significant. As long as we are unduly impressed by a few accidental modernities of Epicureanism, we are liable to forget that it is, after all, a very ancient philosophy; and so we forget to treat it historically, as a thing of its own time, and as an attempt to respond to old needs in the old terms. We judge it, in fact, by totally wrong standards.

This is just what Macaulay did. Indeed one of the most interesting things about these marginalia is that they show so clearly his very deep lack of what we now call a historical sense. His method, like that of several other historians of his time, was to begin by forgetting that the past was past, and to transport himself back in time until he almost lived in the age about which he happened to be writing. Fortunately Macaulay's knowledge was immense, and his reconstructions of the past are always valuable and readable. They have, at their best, a kind of internal, imaginative truth, which places them above many studies by later historians who were more careful to remember that history is something past and done with. But in this particular case, Macaulay's lack of a historical sense was more disastrous. Judged as a modern philosophy, or as a philosophy of the nineteenth century, Epicureanism is all that he calls it, nonsense, stuff, and folly. And if the reader of Lucretius today judges his poem as twentieth-century philosophy, it will seem to him even more nonsensical, and so may trouble his reading even more than it did Macaulay's.

But there is, after all, a more truly historic way of regarding the past, which is to recognize that it is past, and that past thoughts and actions can only be understood if we take the trouble to consider them in their proper conditions, and in their relation to the whole of history. If we do this with the Epicurean system we shall be better able to enjoy the poetry in Lucretius, and shall not be tempted to regard his poem as a dull "lecture", helped out by occasional purple passages.

In the first place, the Epicurean system was not the work of one man, or of a few men. It was the culmination of a clearly defined line of speculation which had lasted for three centuries, beginning with Thales and the early monists, passing through the pluralists, such as Empedocles, and taking on a more polished form in the earlier atomists, Leucippus and Democritus. Many thinkers had contributed to the final outcome, some only by making significant errors, others by positive achievement; and it is clear from the historical survey of their work in the first book of Lucretius that the Epicureans acknowledged their debt to these early thinkers. Now in its very beginnings, with Thales, this line of speculation was not philosophy at all, as we now conceive it. It was archaic, primitive, crude in expression, and shadowy in meaning. Of Thales himself all that is left is the statement that the primary substance of everything is water. We cannot really know how much or how little he meant by this, and in the complete absence of further evidence, commentary must always remain doubtful. It is commonly assumed that he wished to propose that underlying all appearance there is a single real substance. If that be true, then certainly he had launched the human mind on one of its most exciting voyages.

The immediate followers of Thales elaborated his theory; but as they proceeded further it became obvious that the existence of this single real substance was difficult to reconcile with the infinite diversity in the actual forms of matter. Thus there emerged the problem of the One and the Many, the problem of the relation between some single simple reality and the ever-changing, ever-varied phenomena of the seen world. The earlier monism was broken down into pluralistic systems, which explained everything in terms of two or more elements. Empedocles best represents this line of thought. And finally, after further processes of advance and retreat, atomism emerges as a possible solution of the ultimate problem. Thus, for all its apparent modernity, Epicurean atomism had its roots in the crude, almost mythological, first efforts of the Western mind to explain the structure of the universe. And in spite of all the intervening work, some traces of this crudity remain to the end, and appear in the most complete and mature statements of the atomic school. Only if we remember these historical facts can we avoid the kind of misunderstanding which so disturbed Macaulay's reading of Lucretius.

I should like to take two examples from the marginalia to make this clear; one a criticism of an earlier pluralist, Anaxagoras, whose theories are reported by Lucretius, the other a criticism of a part of the Epicurean system itself.

In the history of speculation which concerns us here, Anaxagoras is to be regarded as the last of the pluralists, as the thinker who pushed the theory of pluralism to its uttermost limits, and thus imposed on those who came after him the necessity of finding a more moderate position. He held that the basis of reality is not one substance, or four substances, but an infinite number of particles. These particles moreover are not all alike, or slightly alike, but almost infinitely different. They are particles like the wholes which they form—a relation for which he coined the term *homœomerīa*. His views are thus described by Lucretius:

> First of all you must know that when he speaks
> Of this homœomerīa of things, he fancies
> That bones are made of other very small
> And minute bones, and flesh of very small
> And minute bits of flesh, while blood is formed

Of many drops of blood coming together;
And he believes that gold can be composed
Of grains of gold, that earth can grow together
From little particles of earth, that fires
Are made of fires, moisture of specks of moisture,
And all else he imagines and believes
To be formed on a like principle.
(Book I, lines 834–842.)

Against these lines Macaulay writes, with unusual moderation: "The doctrine of the *homœomeria* is false as applied to blood and to water. I suppose also as applied to gold. But it is not proved that it is not true of some substance which no human skill has been able to decompose." Now it is quite obvious to us that the theory is false, as Macaulay says. But its falseness is quite beside the point. If it happened to be correct, it would be almost equally beside the point, since its correctness could only be the result of pure accident. The theory of Anaxagoras is not to be judged as if it had been advanced last week in the columns of *Nature*, but as a stage in a particular line of ancient speculation. No doubt it can contribute nothing to modern science; but if it be judged by what it contributed to human knowledge in its own age, twenty-five centuries ago, then this theory must rank as one of the most brilliant developments of Ionian thought. By stating such an extreme form of pluralism, Anaxagoras revealed the limits of the possibilities of all pluralistic systems. He showed that pluralism, pushed to its logical conclusion, gave a full account of the Many, of the variety of phenomena, but that it utterly failed to explain the nature of the One, of the single underlying reality. Some factor of uniformity among the particles had to be reintroduced, and the atomists succeeded in doing this, at the same time retaining Anaxagoras' conception of particles. Speculative thought naturally proceeds by swinging from one extreme to another, in a series of actions and reactions, and some of the most useful contributions to philosophy have been extreme statements like that of Anaxagoras, not true themselves, but leading directly to syntheses of the highest rank. Ionian philosophy, in fact, is one of the clearest examples of the dialectical process. From the extreme monism of Thales and his followers we pass to the extreme pluralism of the *homœomeria*, and from this to the synthesis of the atomists, embracing and reconciling monism and pluralism. And no single stage in the whole process is irrelevant or useless. The *homœomeria* does not exist, and does not account for the forms of matter; but it led to a theory which was much more successful in explaining both the forms of matter and the single reality.

The other point which I would like to discuss concerns the Epicurean system itself, indeed the very centre of it, the famous "swerve" of the atoms. According to the general atomic theory—the theory of Leucippus, of Democritus, and finally of Epicurus—the physical universe was envisaged as an infinite void in which the atoms fell downwards. This was its primary and original condition, and the first problem to be solved was that of the cause of atomic combinations. For if all atoms simply fell through the void in straight paths, they would remain eternally separate. Democritus had suggested that some atoms, being heavier, fell faster, and collided with those which they overtook. But Epicurus was unable to accept this solution, because he realized that in the void all atoms, of whatever weight, must fall at equal speed, since there could be nothing to check their fall. Some other explanation had to be given, and he found it in the theory that the atoms at unpredictable times and places "swerve" out of their direct course to the least possible extent, but enough to cause collisions, from which the world of matter is created by combination of atoms.

No part of his theory has been attacked more violently than this. Cicero, for example, calls the idea "res ficta pueriliter"; and later critics have found innumerable objections. Macaulay himself is brief and forceful: "This is the most monstrous absurdity in all Epicurus' absurd theory." Certainly some of this criticism may be justified. It would appear that the "swerve", which is indistinguishable to the human eye, contradicts the fundamental principle of Epicurus that the senses are the only true judges of phenomena. Moreover it would seem to be causeless, accidental, and so a vital exception to the general Epicurean assumption that all things have causes. These and no doubt other criticisms might be made, all just, if we were judging the theory as though it were contemporary philosophy. But if we take it in its context, we see again that Epicurus had his reasons. The theory was invented to meet a genuine theoretical difficulty; and though we may find the theory itself a poor one, at least we must admit that it underlined the inconsistency in the theory of Democritus, and so advanced the general line of thought to some extent. It is also possible to show that the "swerve" is not such a total contradiction of the Epicurean system as would at first appear, and that Epicurus himself made a definite attempt to mitigate its difficulties. And finally it has been pointed out by Dr Bailey that the principle of the "swerve" was of the highest importance in the Epicurean ethics. Mechanist as he was in physics, in ethics Epicurus was passionately concerned to maintain the principle of free-will. If the motions of the atoms are always fully caused and preordained, then the atoms which compose the mind of man must certainly move in predestined paths; the decisions of the mind too must be predetermined, and there can be no free-will, no choice of good and evil. But if the atoms can ever, even to the least extent, deviate from their paths in a causeless and accidental manner, then, Epicurus thought, the atoms of the mind would admit similar variation, and free-will was secured as the basis of his ethical system. We must remember that Epicurus was not primarily a physicist: his interest in the atoms was great, but he was not interested in them for their own sake. His theory of the world was philosophical, designed to recommend a certain way of living, a certain attitude towards life. As Lucretius insists, the chief interests of Epicurus were ethical, and the atoms are important to him only in so far as his ethical system can be based upon them. In the matter of the "swerve", then, where there was a conflict between the consistency of the physics and the requirements of the ethical theory, there could be no question as to which Epicurus would choose. The claims of the ethics were paramount, and the "swerve" had to be accepted. Dr Bailey says of it: "From the point of view of ultimate consistency, the 'swerve' is a flaw in Epicureanism, but it is not to be treated as a petty expedient to get over a temporary difficulty, or an unintelligent mistake which betrays the superficial thinker."

If the reader is able to adopt Dr Bailey's attitude rather than Macaulay's; if he is willing to regard the philosophy of Epicurus as an ancient philosophy, and judge it by its proper historical standards; if he can admit that, whatever its shortcomings, it was a great effort of the human mind made many centuries ago; then he should not be troubled, as Macaulay was, by a perpetual fretting, a sense of irritation which mars his aesthetic pleasure. He should be able to enjoy Lucretius. And I think that Macaulay would have been pleased enough to see others helped to that end, in any way whatever, even if some hard things had to be said about his own marginalia in the course of the lesson.

H. SYKES DAVIES

TEXTUAL NOTES

The translator is of necessity a commentator, indeed the fullest of all commentators, since he must give his interpretation of every word in his original. And in dealing with ancient authors the task of interpretation is inseparably bound up with the selection of a text. However unwilling therefore, and however lacking in scholarly equipment, the translator is inevitably drawn into textual criticism. He can reduce his textual work to a minimum by selecting the text of one editor, and abiding by all his decisions; but even so, he has the responsibility of choosing one editor among many, one text among many. And after all, is this choice more easily made than a choice among different readings in one line? The choice of a whole text must be based on a consideration of each particular difficulty: that labour appears to be inescapable. And since that is so, it has seemed better to retain all the rights and privileges of a translator in my own hands; to take the interpretation which I myself prefer in each case, and the reading which goes with it; to attempt, in fact, a composite text, based on what seems to me the best in all the editors.

It would have been desirable perhaps to print this text with the translation, but as this was not possible, a shorter way of indicating my readings had to be found. The edition most likely to be in the hands of my readers is the admirable one of Mr Bailey, in the Oxford Classical Texts (1921). I have taken this as a standard, and the following notes are intended to indicate all departures from this text, with the authority for making them.

BOOK ONE

122. *permanent.* Politian.
205–207. Transposed to follow 214. Sturenberg.
404. *ferai.* MS. correction.
469. *Teucris.* Munro. But the reading is obviously uncertain.
491. *fere.* Wakefield. *ferventi.* MSS.

555. *conceptum summum aetatis pervadere ad auctum.* Munro.
557. *dies et.* Faber.
599. Not accepting possible lacuna.
657. *nasci.* Munro.
703. *quidvis.* Lachmann.
744. *rorem.* Christ.
752. *et illis.* Postgate.
860a. *et nervos alienigenis ex partibus esse.* Lambinus.
873. Omitted, with Giussani, Susemihl, Brieger, etc. No lacuna.
884. Following the punctuation of Merrill's text (1917); but rejecting Giussani's interpretation with respect.
998–1001. Order of MSS.
1013–1014. Not accepting possible lacuna. See Merrill (1916).
1068–1075. Munro's reconstruction.
1093. Using a shortened version of the lines supplied by Munro.

BOOK TWO

18. *mensque.* Marullus.
21. Punctuating with Munro.
42. *et ecum vi.* Munro.
43. *pariter.* Bernays.
43a. Transposed to follow 46. Munro.
193. *subigente.* Lambinus.
250. *sensu.* Giussani.
356. *noscit.* Lachmann.
453–455. In this order: 454, 453, 455. Giussani. *Perculsus* is taken as a participle.
460. *sensus.* Albert. But the whole passage is in great confusion and *saxa* of the MSS. may be right.
462. *sensibus esse datum.* Brieger.
515. *iter usque.* Lachmann.
529. *ostendens.* Munro.
601. *sublimem.* Lambinus. No lacuna.
652–654. Transposed to follow 660. Munro.
681a. *quis accensa solent fumare altaria divom.* Munro.
719. *disterminat.* MS.
748a. *corpora quae constant nullo conjuncta colore.* Munro.
805. *caeruleum.* MSS.
854. *propter eandem rem.* Lachmann.
859. *ceteraque; haec cum.* Greenwood.
903a. *ipsi sensilibus, mortalia semina reddunt.* Munro.
911. *alios.* MS. *respuit.* MSS. See Merrill (1916).
933. *quod.* MSS.

961. *possit.* Lachmann.
1005. *ut.* Marullus.
1072. *sique.* Brieger.
1146–1149. Transposed to follow 1138. Goebel, Munro.
1170–1172. Transposed to follow 1167. Bergk.
1174. *capulum.* Vossius.

BOOK THREE

43. *animae.* Lachmann.
84. *suesse.* Merrill.
97–98. The lacuna is patched up.
146. *ulla.* Havercamp.
240. *nedum quae mente volutat.* Polle, Giussani.
304. *umbram.* MS.
361. *dicat.* Lambinus.
428. *iam.* Lachmann.
433. *hinc.* Bentley. *genuntur.* Lambinus.
444. *is cohibessit?* Lachmann.
493. *animam spumat, quasi.* Lachmann.
574. *eo.* Faber.
617. *regionibu' corporis.* Merrill.
646–647. Punctuating with Munro, but retaining *simul* with Merrill.
657. *micanti.* Lachmann.
658. *truncum.* Giussani.
663. *dolorem.* Lachmann.
676. *longiter.* Lachmann.
690–694. Transposed to follow 685. Lachmann.
694. *subitis e.* MSS.
747. *toto.* MS.
789. *longiter.* Lambinus.
823–824. Supplying a probable sense for the lacuna. Lachmann.
843–861. Apparently an interpellation, but one made by Lucretius himself. It is bracketed for the sake of the continuity of the argument.
912–918. Transposed to follow 930. Susemihl.
962. *iam aliis.* Marullus.
1011–1012. There is obviously a lacuna here, and the translation is simply patched up.

BOOK FOUR

79. *patrum coetumque decorum.* Munro.
81. *his clausa.* Giussani.
126–127. Supplying Munro's probable end for the sentence. But it is followed by a considerable lacuna.
144. The lacuna is patched up.

289a. *hoc illis fieri, quae transpiciuntur, idemque.* Bailey (1910).
418. *caeli.* Bergk.
419. *mirande.* MSS.
532. *expleti.* Purmann.
546. *Berecyntia.* Vossius.
548. *validis cycni torrentibus.* Vossius.
567. *verbi.* Lachmann.
579. *dicta.* MSS.
633. *ut videamus.* MSS.
638. *est itaque et.* Howard and Greenwood.
706–721. Transposed to follow 696. Susemihl.
704. *decurrit.* Giussani.
818–822. Transposed to follow 776. Giussani.
990. *velle volare.* Munro.
1123–1124. Reversed. Giussani.
1125. *tegmenta.* Diels.

BOOK FIVE

28a. *quid volucres pennis aeratis invia stagna.* Munro.
133. *longiter.* Lachmann.
175–176. Transposed to follow 173. Lambinus.
201. *avidam.* MSS.
312. *aeraque proporro silicumque senescere petras?* Ellis.
571. *fulgent.* MSS.
613. *aestiferum ut.* Woltjen.
614. *certa.* Lambinus.
632. *etenim.* Lachmann.
704a. Supplied from Munro.
747. *algu.* Wakefield. Punctuating with Giussani.
809. *auctus.* Merrill.
833. *clarescit.* Lachmann.
881. *visque ut non sat par.* Munro.
979. *possent.* Brieger.
1012. Not accepting possible lacuna.
1013. *conubium.* Lachmann.
1076. *ubi.* Lachmann.
1082. *praedaeque.* Avancius.
1094. *insita.* MSS.
1225. *adauctum.* MSS.
1368. *terram.* Lachmann.
1386. *repertas.* Bockemüller.
1391. *haec.* Lambinus.
1442. *iam.* Lachmann. *puppibus; urbes.* Munro.
1456. *et ordine debet.* Munro.

BOOK SIX

11. *posset.* Lachmann.

47–48. A very corrupt passage. The translation merely patches up the lacuna, without claiming to be a reconstruction.

131. *magnum.* Vossius.

349. *transviat.* MSS.

490. *nimbis.* Lachmann.

550. *ut scrupus cumque.* Munro.

607. It seems likely that Giussani is right in suspecting a considerable lacuna after this line. 608–638 are bracketed because, though written by Lucretius, they are not connected with their context.

663. *nobis.* Lambinus.

674. *qui visu est.* Merrill.

697–698. Supplying from Munro.

698. *aperta.* Creech.

762. *posse his.* Translator.

804. *domans.* Marullus. *fervida febris.* Lambinus.

862. *tenet.* MS.

870. *miscente.* MSS.

927. *auras.* MSS.

954–955. Supplying from Giussani.

1012. *quod dico, ibus.* Munro.

1023. *motuque.* MSS.

1069. *uno.* Lachmann.

1074. *uno.* Lachmann.

1135. *coruptum.* Codex Laurentianus 31.

1204. *hac.* Faber.

1225. Transposing to follow 1246 with Lachmann, but keeping *certabant* with Giussani.

1262. *astu.* Lachmann.

1281. *praesenti.* Munro.

For EU product safety concerns, contact us at Calle de José Abascal, 56–1°,
28003 Madrid, Spain or eugpsr@cambridge.org.

www.ingramcontent.com/pod-product-compliance
Ingram Content Group UK Ltd.
Pitfield, Milton Keynes, MK11 3LW, UK
UKHW020320140625
459647UK00018B/1948
* 9 7 8 1 1 0 7 4 3 7 5 6 2 *